Rough Copy
Personal Terms 2

FREDERIC RAPHAEL was born in Chicago in 1931 and educated at Charterhouse and St John's College, Cambridge. His novels include *The Glittering Prizes* (1976) and *Coast to Coast* (1998); he has also written short stories and biographies of Somerset Maugham and Byron. Frederic Raphael is a leading screenwriter, whose work includes the Academy Award-winning *Darling* (1965) and *Far from the Madding Crowd* (1967), and the screenplay for Stanley Kubrick's last film, *Eyes Wide Shut*. The first volume of *Personal Terms* was published by Carcanet in 2001.

Also by Frederic Raphael from Carcanet

The Benefits of Doubt
The Necessity of Anti-Semitism
Personal Terms

Frederic Raphael

Rough Copy

Personal Terms 2

CARCANET

First published in Great Britain in 2004 by
Carcanet Press Limited
Alliance House
Cross Street
Manchester M2 7AQ

A CIP catalogue record for this book is available from the British Library
ISBN 1 85754 657 1

The publisher acknowledges financial assistance from Arts Council England

Set in Monotype Bembo by XL Publishing Services, Tiverton
Printed and bound in England by SRP Ltd, Exeter

*For Beetle, and our children
and grandchildren, always.*

Contents

Introduction

My notebooks are neither journals nor diaries: they are insufficiently sententious to be the former and lack the regularity of the latter. They are, quite literally, *cahiers*, of the same kind that *Lycéens* use. They provide privacy for mental as opposed to physical jerks: where better than an exercise-book to work out, to bend and to stretch and even to fall flat on your face? Their always handwritten contents were never designed for publication. Then why should anyone wish to write for his own eyes in a style sometimes formal and even convoluted? Well, a notebook is a place in which to see what one thinks when there is neither market nor public: they contain a writer's letters to himself.

In theory, I was amassing material which, as they used to say, I might later 'work up' into books or stories, but in fact I have seldom gone prospecting for recyclable gold. Although even dead wood can have its uses, part of the fun of being a writer is to tell oneself new stories. Sometimes, however, you can have had a good idea at a bad moment, or a difficult one when you want to take it easy. For instance, I am still planning to write a novel about Catullus which I began, and aborted, rightly, at Cambridge. There are fragments of a renewed attempt at it here.

The first volume of *Personal Terms* covered the years between 1950 and 1969. I assumed that the second would cover roughly the same span. In fact, I am slightly embarrassed to see, it covers scarcely three years. How should I defend what may read like vain prolixity? The truth is that, during the early 1970s, handwriting was a regular escape from the taints and temptations of the movies and public print. In private (if never in a private language), I could sketch people and things and ideas with no concern for what anyone else might think or say.

When looking through the sketchbooks of our beloved daughter Sarah, Beetle and I have been struck by the meticulous merciless-ness with which she observed even the people whom she loved. Her unbounded tenderness and generosity towards others never mitigated Sarah's urge to depict the truth. If these notebooks lack her genius, they echo that same will to accuracy. An artist's piti-lessness has nothing to do with malice, even though his or her vocation is, literally, to put things down.

As much as possible I have refrained from (or curtailed) intro-spective entries, but of course my most accessible target is myself. If in the course of depicting others I have supplied a join-up-the-dots portrait of myself, I am willing that it should be as revealing, and as merciless, as any sketch of anyone else. The self-portrait is least inter-esting when it is a form of self-advertisement. Michael Ayrton once taught Sarah a lesson she never forgot: your best model is your own anatomy. By looking at your own arm, he told her, you have a model for as many arms as Shiva's.

I have changed a number of names, both from prudence and to avoid causing what would seem unprovoked distress. In other cases, in particular when fame has affected the subjects' features, I have not concealed their identities. What I say about such people is not meant to be wounding, nor yet to raise me to some judicial role. When I pick up my pen, it is as it was when Sarah picked up her pencil or her brush: I write what I see and the pen becomes deter-minant in how I do it. I am *not* a camera: the medium affects the message. If what I say about friends, or even enemies, seems unfeeling, I neither apologise nor regret it, though I have no wish to give them pain. That is how they looked and sounded to me. *As a writer*, that is all I care about.

I began, and continue, with the illusion that my purpose is to tell what truth I can perceive, to pander neither to received ideas nor to editorial or public appetite. My notebooks are my conscience. Where they are callow, I wince; where they are pompous, I groan; where they are painful, I smile; and where they are joyful, I am tempted to cry. The effect of one's work is not part of *why* one does it.

My editorial principle has been to avoid self-humiliation by correcting spelling and by abating long-windedness and tedium. I have trimmed, but not falsified, and I have avoided smart after-thoughts (except in the rarish form of notes). While I have cut a great deal, I have kept some things in the text despite the sane advice of my wife, my friends (notably George Walden) and my peerless publisher Michael Schmidt. If anything infuriates the reader, that is fine; if it bores him or her, it can be skipped without losing the plot. Like it or not, *j'y suis, j'y reste*.

FREDERIC RAPHAEL
Lagardelle, 2004

1970

I trained to London and took the underground to Sloane Square for lunch with Jo Janni and Jonathan Miller. A clear, chilly Chelsea day when my out-of-towner's briefcase was a badge of shame. The kids, with their aloof glasses and pale faces, shaggy, long waistcoats, fun furs and unkempt wool, pace about carrying parcels or caressing their loose hair. Urgent loiterers, some of them lounge in the doorways of boutiques where, with a pinch of banality, you realise that they are, in fact, *employed*.

Despite a dawdle at Ward's bookshop, I was first at *Au Père de Nico*. Must those who travel furthest always arrive first? I sat in a corner of the no longer popular, no longer cheap restaurant sniffing at *Encounter*, now a pressed, unseasonable flower. An article on Oswald Mosley had snared me. Jo arrived in a neat, dark grey suit; white flesh bulbous under Huntsman's cloth; self-conscious with his first, black-rimmed, glasses. Had I ever had to wear them? My denial aged him. He had gone to Wales the previous day, but it was too fine for sport: the fish could see the cast and the shadows.

Dr Miller, rusty rather than red, bulked out in unfashionable gear, loomed over us with important shyness. He asked at once for cigarettes. I remembered him too barefooted and boyish for such urbanities. We practised a few philosophical falls and found we could still slap the mat with the old huggerhah. So: why had he in mind to do *The Portrait of a Lady*?

Vanity had brought him unprepared to discuss his own idea. I covered for him by asserting the essential cohesion of James's novel, saying – as if it were well-known – that it was a mistake to suppose that the suitors whom Isabel Archer rejected would have been any more suitable than Gilbert Osman. All were impersonations of her various delusions: the theme was not – as Jonathan had proclaimed – the corruption of American virtue by European guile, but misconceptions born of the proud humility with which Isabel herself approached the experience of Europe.

When Jo looked dubious about the project, Jonathan paraded

other ideas. He had the eagerness of a variety artist who, finding you don't want a comic, confesses that he has always preferred juggling. How about *The Golden Bowl* (which I doubted that he had read) and/or Kafka's *Amerika*? Set in England, of course.

Bragging of his victimisation by Hal Chester, who produced *Take a Girl Like You*, his sole 'commercial' credit, Jonathan disclosed that the picture had been taken away from him entirely, and re-cut. Hearing that Chester had even re-*shot* behind his back, I saw a director neither trusted by his associates nor sure of himself. He revealed self-doubt which doctorate, curly-headed fame and cosmopolitan connections were usually patched together to obscure: having failed to make a fool of Hal C., he remained too raw for reticence. Were it not for the big play he is able to make with 'Larry', whom he is soon to direct at the National, Dr Miller would now be threatening to return to medicine.

What he and I have in common creates a bond that both links and separates us: like one of those iron tow-bars used by heavy lorries. We proceed together, at a fixed distance. 'Weak like hell, I must say,' said Jo on the telephone later.

The Vice-Chancellor: 'I made allowances for everything except a desire for frivolity. I assumed that anything might be asked of me except that I should find myself ridiculous. I accepted that my office be accessible to all; I did *not* entertain the possibility that it might be used to piss in. The students actually pissed in my desk drawers. They may claim a serious purpose, but their vandalism cannot be validated: the piece was an antique. Should Vice-Chancellors accept such expensive furnishings? It is open to question. But the ruin of something of quality is vandalism.' Who could deny it? Right about almost everything, he did leave one with a faint, unworthy desire to piss in his drawers.

See a man as a victim and you can begin to imagine him a friend.

A screenwriter finds himself dreaming in print. Even in his subconscious he sees only the scripts of his fantasies. He cannot get his dreams produced.

Edward Hyams' *Killing no Murder* inspires a callous look at the death of Mrs McKay. She was murdered when her kidnappers' plan for extortion failed. Yet there are features of a mythic order in the case.

The poor lady was mistaken for the glamorous wife of Rupert Murdoch. The kidnappers were a pair of immigrant brothers (West Indians?) who assumed the wealth of the British upper bourgeoisie to be boundless. They demanded the 'unrealistic' – but appropriately legendary – ransom of a million pounds. At one stroke they would both do down the privileged and acquire the entrance fee to be counted among them.

The shattered family of the stolen lady – who, like all the female members of the pampered classes, was said to have not an enemy in the world – claimed that the sum demanded of them was absurd. Yet poor Mrs M. had been mistaken for rich Mrs M. because she was running round in the office Rolls (on business?). The McKays, no less than the Murdochs, made their money by invading other people's privacy; the business (and pleasure) of the Press is to break and enter. If ever there was a proper scapegoat – its innocence being of the essence – it was this nice lady who lived blamelessly on immoral earnings.

The police announced the crime to be one for which there was 'no British precedent'. Their amateurish investigation almost certainly ensured the death of the victim. The no less naïve kidnappers seem to have imagined that, as accepted immigrants, they were socially (and accentually) homogenised. Had not the local Master of Foxhounds called on them? They spoke undisguisedly on the telephone and showed themselves, with no fear of being markedly alien, near where the ransom collections were to be made. Their later conviction that they should be acquitted sprang from callow faith in British justice: they expected it to find them innocent even after they had been proved guilty, the form of justice which every patriotic criminal would choose.

It was always tempting to call him a phoney; his fame has made it a duty.

I shall die on a day when the undertakers are in a hurry to get away.

For *The Triangle ABC*: It is only when we are betrayed that we have a full sense of being alive, unless it is when we betray others. Or both; or both.

The rival professors were like the last two men to speak an esoteric language. If the other did not exist, the survivor would be unique; but then who would understand him?

Dinner with Don and Kay L. in Capener's Close, an enclave on the fat knuckle of land between Belgrave Square and Knightsbridge. Kinnerton St glows with tight charm; it contains the smallest pub in London: a counter in the window of a small shop chin-high to the pavement. The incessant moan of large cars being chivvied into small spaces. After Frederic Mews comes Capener's Close: metal gates into a narrow yard: doors on each side, a wooden barricade ahead. High above and beyond, a framed glimpse of navy-blue walls and white candle-brackets, glowing lights; the expectant luxury of a chic restaurant before the clients arrive. A man in a white shirt – a waiter who had not assumed his coat, maybe, or the *patron* checking the flowers – moved back and forth. We rang and the window went up: the *maître d'* was Don. 'You found it then. At absolutely the right time.'

I had bought a tight bunch of Belgrave Square pink roses for Kay, who came down in a long floral dress: pixie grandma. The first impression was of walls covered with pictures, mostly primitive, Victorian silhouettes, rag portraits, posters, lithographs; bric-à-brac everywhere, clocks, *pot pourri* under a glass dome, brass lamps: the cave of Ali Baba, *brocantier*.

A grand main room enlarged by the sumptuous paucity of furniture: big, elbowed sofa along the side wall under new pine panelling, faced by a pair of orange Conran chairs, a bench behind, on which our roses appeared in a majolica jug. Ice-blue rug on the floor, shaggy and lank; drapes *almost* to tone. Zena Marshall, the actress, had sold the place in order to appear homeless by the time her divorce petition was heard. A Welsh dresser at the far end of the room, hung with glazed pottery and china; white, hip-high cupboards along the wall facing the broad windows, designed (D. said) to cover the central heating pipes. You felt the place must be costing them a fortune. The rent is three pounds a week. They have a Westminster Estate lease with four years left. The two daughters go to a state school.

Odd to meet this socially ill-defined couple – whom we had only ever seen when they sold us Lagardelle – in the West End of London. They now revealed themselves once to have been the rivals of the Samuelsons, my distant cousins, who have become millionaires by renting out cinematic equipment. The Longs' first flat was near the old cut-through from Shepherd's Bush to Hammersmith: fourteen shillings a week.

After they had been there a fortnight, their landlord, who was a PO sorter, said that he had some bad news: a new rate demand meant the rent would have to rise to fourteen shillings and threepence a week. Every Christmas he came up the stairs with a bottle of port; the last Christmas they were there, he tripped and dropped the bottle.

Since the place had neither garden nor bathroom, they advertised for a swap. They came to terms with Tilly, a half-German blonde with a large bull-terrier and a garden flat in Maida Vale. When they told the sorter they were leaving, he was distressed. They promised to find him someone else. Tilly was presented as a friend, and accepted, provided there were no animals. They persuaded the old man that the bull-terrier had been given to her as a birthday present after the bargain had been struck.

Before moving out, they realised that the sorter no longer went off at six each morning; he had retired. After a lifetime at the Post Office, where he could get all his meals at the canteen, the old bachelor was unable to look after himself. Tilly – 'The kindest person you could ever hope to meet' – took care of him. Eventually, after she had left perhaps, the old boy died; of malnutrition, the inquest showed.

Don told us that someone had explained that the reason for all these new amusement arcades was that the owners were hoarding all the pennies. They were expected to increase sharply in value when the new decimal coinage comes in. A penny piece had only to be worth tuppence for people to make a 100 per cent profit. 'It makes you think, that.'

It was difficult to turn in at the gate of the *Auberge de la Montespan* in the evening of a brilliant day. The windscreen was poxed with the hard smudges of dead insects. Their pimpled traces flared in the jaundiced lights of oncoming *poids lourds*. The *routiers* had the *hauteur* of men who must continue work when others have finished. I had to turn across them to reach the gate of this untried hotel. At the edge of the wide and dusty pavement, a motorcyclist had been knocked from his machine. He lay on that dark, recently warm roadside, surrounded by silhouettes of attention, his *moto* twisted in the gutter. He supported himself, like his own most solicitous helper, on a thin ex-dare-devil's elbow; crash-helmet clamped red and white over a small, wan face. An ambulance drifted up through the traffic, yellow light rotating, like a relative looking for someone in a crowd. We wheeled under the lee of a panting lorry and through welcome gates and down to the riverside front of the prim hotel. Red flowers in concrete window-boxes dressed its *déclassé* nobility.

A., in Coventry at school, climbs a steeple on the old chapel, a traditional challenge: if he can do it, he will no longer be in Coventry. He is terrified but succeeds. And then, at the top, he realises that he has not had the foresight to bring with him the traditional po which would testify to his achievement. When he comes down and announces what he has done, no one believes him. Having failed to procure public redemption, he has – by witnessing his own fear – succeeded only in humiliating himself.

A.'s desire, which endures, to be punished – to be *recognised* – by someone more beautiful than himself. (Cf. the Ghetto child, quoted by Steiner, who wanted to grow up to be a German.) A. always remembers the handsome, naked young monitor taking roll-call in the showers. A later meets him, bespectacled and fat, at a bridge match where the other makes a buffoon of himself.

Robin Midgley called shortly before I finished my novel. Would I come to Leicester to do a production of *Cat on a Hot Tin Roof*? Fear of being afraid made me say yes. The pay was a hundred pounds for three weeks. Beetle was touchingly willing to make the best of three weeks of hotel life. After a few frantic days finishing *Who Were You With Last Night?*, we set off.

It was fifteen years since my previous, and only, contact with the professional stage. Theatricals are different from film and TV actors; even when the same people work in both, they adopt different personae for the camera. Fresh from Cambridge, I recall reading the cast of *Jubilee Girl* brisk lectures on their craft. They heard me out with doomed indifference: condemned men sentenced first to listen to the padre. Marie Löhr who, if she is still alive, must be in her nineties, nodded sternly when I chided them for their lack of discipline; she set an example by always arriving first for rehearsals.

Marie had been a *jeune première* on the Edwardian stage. She remembered watching the Grand Fleet sail out of Portsmouth harbour in 1914. While on tour, we were in Southsea when Bulganin and Khruschev sailed home from their less than triumphal tour of Britain. We asked Marie whether we should wave or not. She thought that, on balance, we should: they had been our guests.

Leslie Bricusse and I had been hired to save *Jubilee Girl*, which was already on the road, by Al Kaplan, who had written the music. Leslie and I had written a musical at Cambridge. *Lady At The Wheel*, though derided by the intellectuals, had a remarkable public success. Later, Leslie, as President of the Footlights, brought our May Week show, *Out of the Blue*, to London, where we had had a triumphant season (thanks, not least, to Jonathan Miller). *Lady At The Wheel* was revived, and revised, and was about to be put on (and soon taken off) in the West End when Al Kaplan acquired our services.

Jubilee Girl was probably beyond saving. The knowledge that Al had put something over £25,000 of 'his own money' into the production gave us no sort of an anxious conscience: those who disposed of such sums could expect no sympathy. In fact, though Al had inherited Canadian millions, the money was almost certainly his wife's (she was a grand-daughter of one of the founders of Marks and Spencer's).

My memories of *Jubilee Girl* are occluded by shame. How did I have the effrontery to claim that I could rewrite, and direct, a failing musical on the hoof? I did not shirk the work, but I lacked the muscle for it. Al Kaplan did not blame me; he blamed Leslie, whom he had first greeted as 'my boy'. I was the sidekick who had played the honest donkey; Leslie was, in Al's disenchanted eyes, the unproductive lion. Many years later (it must have been in 1969 or 1970) Al Kaplan telephoned The Wick. I was not there. He told Beetle that he had read the then unproduced script of *A Severed Head*, which I originally wrote for John Schlesinger in 1965, and wanted to make the film. Al was both flattering ('The best script ever written') and menacing: if I didn't help him get the rights, the film would never be made; he would see to that. When he called back, I told him, sorry, but I had no control over the script: Columbia owned it. I had learned in the meanwhile that he had been associated with Woodfall (John Osborne and Tony Richardson's company). He had phoned from Italy, and it was there that he committed suicide shortly afterwards. Unfortunately, he did not prevent *A Severed Head* from being produced a few years later.

Robin Midgley. At Cambridge, I heard that he agonised over the Catholic faith he was about to lose (i.e. had already lost). He then grew a beard and has stayed behind it ever since, rather like the mayor of Mijas who went into hiding when he was a young man and dared not emerge until old. Robin has an unfrocked air, as if emancipated from shackles he now misses.

We left Langham for Leicester in the dark, Stee's cot on the roof, chilly regret in our hearts. Mrs Southgate, our regular help, had left us ten days earlier in abrupt, melodramatic style. She once broke the foot off an eighth-century BC Persian pot which I liked very much. Without apology, she walked out, but – like the pot – consented to be glued back in place after a spot of *proskynesis* (on my part). This time, she was aggrieved by our having asked her neighbour to wash up one Saturday *and* Sunday when our intention had been to spare *her*.

Mabel is embittered by what she still craves: the demands of a real 'madam'. She is nostalgic for the youthful subjection she enjoyed when the mistress thought to buy her with a cheap Christmas gift, and expected to be served night and day. The old toffs had their world; she had hers. We tried to pass a plank across the social divide, and then fell into it.

I parked the Mercedes in a puddled yard, whose guardian would call me 'Squire' for the next twenty days, and walked down a wide, one-way road to the theatre. It was a greyish-black concrete cultural pillbox that might have been made of roasted Weetabix. Bill Naughton's *Alfie* was the current production.

The actors were sitting in the café up some steps to the right of the Box Office. They had the resigned air of those who are often called but from whom few are chosen. 'Anyone working?' There was a sighing murmur: I had cheated them by arriving on time. I threw over them that hurried gulp of the eyes which tries to look at a group all at once. I remember Donald Burton with his Dunhill cigarette-holder, his black and white nylon zip-jacket, his torpid alertness.

In the auditorium, Midgley showed us the model of the set. The reading began, everyone *très compétent*, a question mark against only Gordon Tanner, Robin's late 'choice' for Big Daddy and the only 'American' in the company (he was actually Canadian). Tanner wore a mackintosh and a little felt hat and walked with a jaunty shuffle. His face was brick-coloured, eyes anxious and guiltily hung with droops of turkey-red skin like the bobbles that run down when an amateur paints his own window-sills. His reading had the right truculence, but he was unable to follow the lines in the text. If he raised his eyes from the page, he couldn't find his place again.

In the afternoon, I asked what they thought the play was about, how true, and how melodramatic. Tanner emerged from his isolation – he had gone off by himself for lunch – and said that Big Momma was like his own mother, still hauling herself around sustained by memories of being Belle of the Ball in the deep South. It was disturbing, the contempt he revealed, like a goitre, for the old, indomitable woman who still haunted him with her European trips and her repulsive vitality.

Later he asked – with that attention to detail which often indicates, in actors and others, an incapacity to face the central issue – whether he should allow his whiskers to grow. Big Daddy was supposed to be sixty-five, which Gordon himself was not, 'even though I may look it'. Big Daddy did not come in till Act II; I need not yet worry about him.

Midgley had booked us into the Carlton Hotel on the Loughborough Road. Thinly painted, as if the undercoat had had to serve as overcoat as well, it stood behind a broad, suburban pavement. A sign 'OPEN' dangled lopsidedly in the glassed, curtained doorway.

The new Mercedes stood out in front of the drab digs. The owner said, 'I like your car.' It probably cost more than his hotel. Our room was at the top of the building. Beads of water actually ran down the walls. I left Beetle and Stee guiltily. By the time I returned, she had booked us into the 'Abbey Motor Lodge Hotel', to which we removed the next morning.

The owner of the Carlton was about fifty; dyed black hair and a pale, subterranean face. Midway between an undertaker and his corpse, his withered smile was both pitiful and pitying; the dark suit would have looked better on a dummy. He asked at lunch-time whether we would like a 'three-course meal' at six p.m. In for a penny, in for five and sixpence. Thin, glutinous soup with lumps of plastic vegetable in it; cremated chops, mixed veg.; rather good sponge pudding. The other guests – commercial gentlemen or mechanicals in Leicester on some assignment – ate gladly.

The owner, with his wizened Celtic smile, told me that he worked for many years for Mecca. Then he had a chance to buy this place and had to make the big decision. He had a young family, but he had been married before. His first wife, and their grown-up son, was in Australia; just as well because imagine if they kept bumping into each other.

The owner's new children's seaside holiday the previous summer lasted half an hour, on a Tuesday. They drove from nine in the morning to somewhere on the East Coast, played on the sand for thirty minutes and then – 'Oy, back in the car' – were home by five, when the help left.

'You should've seen this place when I got it,' he said. The previous owners had been Poles (not that he had anything against Poles), but it was in a disgusting state. Husband and wife had had terrible rows, terrific. No carpets anywhere; people came and found nothing ready, dreadful. The wife had had her 'brother' living in the house. When her husband died, she upped and married the 'brother' within forty-eight hours. By the by, he wasn't complaining but he had expected us the previous night. Rightly: we should have been there to see *Alfie*, but I wanted to give myself another day to get over the flu. He had turned away thirty or forty people, he said, who wanted our room. Yet the whole of our floor was deserted on the one night we stayed. The bed was narrow and the springs so domed we could not stay in it together. I slept in a narrow cot under the window.

The Abbey Motor Lodge Hotel (which cost us more in a week than I was paid in three) was a soft pleasure. At dinner with us on the Friday night, Midgley said that he did not believe in giving actors direct instructions. The trick was to make them believe that they had had all the ideas themselves. I consoled myself by thinking that a dull man hardly needed much self-control to prevent himself from bursting out with inventive intelligence.

On Monday, when we resumed, Sonia (the Cat) 'dropped the book' without any great show. The others – always excepting Gordon Tanner – were all appearing in *Alfie*, as well as rehearsing an Old Tyme Music Hall. G.T. had been little called until Wednesday, when we reached Act II again. He had, however, been visited in the Midland Hotel by Denise D., the 'consummate artiste', as she described herself, who played a minor role and told Midgley that I was 'lovely to work with'. Having gone to help Gordon with his lines, she found him in the lavatory; she made this sound somewhat sinister.

When she proposed a cup of tea, he said, 'I don't drink tea'. She said she was just passing and again suggested a cup of tea together.

'I don't drink tea. Did Mr Raphael ask you to come here?' 'No.'
But would he like her to hear his lines? 'Did Mr Raphael ask you
to come here?'

On Wednesday, he managed the ensemble opening not too
badly. He dried when it came to longer passages. At lunch, Carmen
Silveira said to me, 'I think we've seen it, darling. This is how it's
going to be when we open.' When I reported this to Robin, he was
between penitence and irritation. He confessed that he had never
seen G.T. work, nor spoken to anyone with experience of him.
Would I give it twenty-four hours? That afternoon, I worked alone
with G.T. We were in the Mission to the Deaf (cold and appropriate). I fed G.T. the lines one at a time. The colder it grew, the
darker the omens. Sonia came in; I let G.T. go, telling him that the
words had to be licked, very soon.

S. and I worked well together; I did not find her attractive, she
may not have found me so; but we were both attracted by the ease
of our rapport. Robin arrived to tell me that G.T.'s last reputable
credit was fifteen years ago. A replacement could not be found
before Monday. Robin assured me that he would take care of the
'unpleasantness'.

When B. and I were having our Bloody Marys before dinner,
Gordon Tanner walked into the bar. He wore his mackintosh and
his aged felt hat. 'Hullo, pal.' Beetle made herself tactfully scarce.
Tanner said no, he had not seen Robin. He had just come to say
that he just didn't seem to be able to 'get the hang of this guy'.
However hard he tried, he just couldn't 'seem to get the words into
the old noggin'. The timing of his resignation – I pressed him to a
drink to celebrate the gentlemanly course of things – was so oppor-
tune that I feared an explosion if he went back to the Midland Hotel
and found Midgley waiting to sack him.

I went to call Robin. As I entered the booth, I noticed a man
with a rigid jaw, in a lank overcoat, push through the unmanned
entrance to the hotel. R. said he would be right round. I came back
to where Tanner was sitting. Beetle was on the other side of the
lounge, annotating the MS of my novel. The rigid-jawed stranger
came up from the lower level of bedrooms, among which was ours.
Pursued by the haggard Buttons who was usually at Reception, he
went straight up to Beetle and began speaking in a low voice. I was
with Gordon and hardly noticed until I heard an aggressive note. I
went and, Lytton Strachey-like, interposed my person.

B. told me later that the man had approached her as soon as he
came in. He asked whether she knew Leicester well. No. How

about Coventry, Birmingham or Northampton? Northampton she
was too honest to deny: she had spent happy wartime schooldays
there. So where was the restaurant, where could he get something
to eat? She pointed the way. He ducked down the stairs in the opposite direction. Fetched back by the brave boy, he guessed that B.
had given the word. 'You told them,' he flung at her. 'Why did you
have to do that?' When we pulled him away, he charged up the
stairs towards the bar. The headwaiter, Mario, a self-consciously
hard man, bundled the madman out of the place. You could imagine
the thud as he hit the pavement, and the dusting of Mario's hands.

Meanwhile Gordon Tanner sat sipping his half of bitter. Closet
alcoholics ask only for modest drinks. The most touching moment
in rehearsal had come when Brick asked, 'Have you known many
drinking men?' and G.T. had to reply, 'I have known a fair number
of that species.'

He reminisced about great actors he had worked with. He dwelt on
Wilfred Lawson and Trevor Howard. Gordon's wife, who was
supposed to join him for the weekend, was a successful business-
woman. She wrote 'courses' for businesses, how to do this or sell
that. She was often the only woman in a whole convention of men.
He had to go along as escort. His first marriage had been a wartime
affair. He had not been abroad a year before it ended. 'You've heard
of those Dear John letters. You hear about them but I can tell you,
it's quite something else to get one of 'em.'

Alone with Robin and me, he told us how Wilfred Lawson had
'pretended' to be a drinker in order to 'keep up his reputation'. They
had been in *The Wooden Dish*, directed by Joseph Losey. On the last
day of rehearsal, they had a run-through. Lawson was 'assing about'.
Losey came to the front of the stalls and said, 'Either do the thing
properly or go home.'

Lawson said, 'I think I'll go home,' and walked out of the theatre.

They all wondered whether he would make it for the train-call
next morning, 'But Wilfred was there.' What did G.T. think of
Losey? 'I don't know much about him, except that he's untalented.'
G.T.'s euphoria was marred only by fear of what his agent would
say: 'He's going to tear my head off.' He used to have Al Parker,
but now it was some nonentity called Harold.

Gordon had been in *The Devil's Disciple* with Trevor Howard.
They had a scene in which, every night, T.H. would flick out his
tie. One night, tired of this unrehearsed exaggeration, G.T. wore a
bow tie. T.H. caught hold of the ends and pulled. 'I went purple in

the face, y'know? Damn near strangled me.' You became an actor because if you didn't like yourself, it gave you the chance to be someone else. We parted with bogus declarations of regret. Robin had already found a substitute.

I had one magic, cold afternoon, in the Mission, with Donald and Sonia. She had been tight with him at first, bursting out when he said that he felt she was annoyed with him for 'not giving her enough'. She had heard that story before, she snorted; it always made her furious, that kind of mock-modesty. When she forgot a line, she would exclaim '*Fart!*', as if it were the crudest thing she could think of.

Donald. His father was on the Halls as Billy Burton. He has a certain idea of himself ('Me Gauloises, me cigarette holder') and constantly alludes to his sexual needs and successes. 'I told them if I don't get me SEX regular, I get bad-tempered, but I haven't had it yet.' After rehearsals in the Mission, we played snooker on its uneven table. He subscribed to Time/Life's *Wonderful World* series and was a Sci-Fi addict, very impressed by Arthur C. Clarke's *Profiles of the Future* (in which we are promised intelligent hybrid animals who will literally do the domestic donkey work). Every single prediction made by scientists had been, Donald assured us, 'fantastically conservative'. A Harley Street man had once announced that rail travel was impossible: anyone travelling at over forty miles an hour would be asphyxiated. The future would be here a lot sooner than we think. The crucial question was whether we would be able to fuck at eighty.

Since there is an infinity of galaxies, there must, he said, be other worlds. Given an infinity of instances, there must be an infinite range of living things, literally every possibility you can think of. Is there a fallacy here, I wondered, for instance the assumption that the universe, as it were, speaks English, that it is has a verbal, not a numerical, notation? No, not at all.

The vigour of Donald's opinions is endearing. He has written a play, about a moon station, which everyone likes and no one has offered to do. The speeches are too long. But that is how scientists speak. He knows a number, including one who has 'invented anti-gravity, the fucking man has actually *invented* anti-gravity, and nobody wants to know'.

'What does he want them to do?'

'Back him. The cunt wants money to go on with his experiments.'

Donald said of his cock, 'It's done everything except stab shit.'
  'Pleasures to come,' Bob Cartland said.

'Mac' is married and has a son, Simon, whom they sent to Frensham
Heights, a progressive school we turned down for Paul. Simon was
bright, but suddenly contracted his ambitions, then he gave up
school entirely and became a hippy. Communication with his father
broke down. The boy has been living rough, has had VD, is addicted
to the cult of experience. Recently he found a job: grave-digger, at
sixteen pounds a week.

As opening night approached, I told the cast that time was short.
'In future, therefore, you can continue to laugh at my jokes, but I
shall stop laughing at yours.' They took it well. The lighting
supremo was a fat Canadian with an unlit complexion. He was inde-
fatigably lethargic: it was impossible either to exhaust him or to bring
him to life. Only once did I venture to overrule him. I wanted very
little light at the end of Act II. 'That's the minimum really,' he said.
'Then take it all out,' I said.

Alone that week (Beetle had suffered enough hotel life with a two-
year-old, but would be coming to the opening), I went to see *He
and She* at Cinecenta. The atmosphere was rosy with salacious
expectation. Bolognini's titles were seen over images of bourgeois
life, at the turn of the century, sculpted in funereal marble. The stip-
pled stone reproduced exactly the forms of crinolines, shoes, bowler
hat, umbrellas: the hard ghosts of an inflexible society. It might have
been the Trieste of Svevo. Among the frozen shades, more solid
than reality, Larry Harvey and Sylva Koscina were less substantial
than the stones through which they walked. Clever! The provincial audience had little appetite for Italian ironies; a squad of Archie
Rices, they had come to see Sylva's tits.

The first D.R., a 'tech', had only a few glitches: no hanger for
Sonia's dress, not enough liquor in the bottles. On Tuesday we had
an audience. We held the curtain for a party of Russians from the
university; they were awaited with indulgent awe. The performance
went well. We seemed hardly to need Wednesday's D.R., but Bob
could do with another work-out. I spent the morning going over
my novel and ordering modest flowers for the female dressing room.
The D.R. – for which, unwisely, I allowed them to dispense with
make-up – began lumpishly and got worse; Carmen missed an

entrance entirely. Someone had been talking audibly, at length, on the telephone. After Act II, I called them all down and gave them my iciest tones. Carmen was so mortified she forgot a line in the third act. I embraced her forgivingly afterwards.

The only person to react badly was Denise, with whom I had had a spurious Jewish affinity since day one. On the Monday she had given me a fat paperback on The Theatre, 'something to dip into' during the tense days to come. Sweet! I failed to recognise a demand for attention (when an actress thinks of you, you are advised to think of her). Now suddenly she accused me of having my 'nose in the book all the time'. 'Denise...' 'No, I've been watching you,' she said, sounding more and more like Portnoy's mother. 'I don't like any kind of sneaking and spying,' I quoted at her from the play. She was irked that I had failed to appreciate some new 'interpretation' she had lent to her small part.

I should have remembered an early experience in rehearsal for a TV drama, in the days when I wrote three or four 'plays' a year for ATV. An actor came up to me and asked me whether I thought that the hydrogen bomb really represented a threat to the future of the human race. I answered with a lot of on the one hand, and then again on the other. I had given him, he said, a lot to think about. Another actor sidled up to me and said, 'May I say something? When an actor asks whether you think that the future of the human race is threatened by atomic weapons, the required answer is, "I think you're giving an absolutely *wonderful* performance."'

I bought the whole cast a Chinese dinner after the last, successful D.R. It cost all of a fiver. They were amazed by my generosity. It is a long time since I ate with people so glad to fill their stomachs.

55 BC. The crowd booed Pompey for murdering the elephants in his triumphal games. The elephants came to the pickets surrounding the arena and scanned the audience with baleful eyes, craving fellowship from the spectators.

The Producer. His frigidity is tempered by fervent left-wing convictions. Beneath the ice is a charge of violence and resentment. He cannot forgive his parents for his happy childhood. He thoroughly enjoyed his Public School; he had a wonderful time at Oxford. He was deprived of nothing. How can a man with such a history not be scarred for life?

'You'd think that woman would relent.' Mr Starling, the taxi driver who often takes us to and from Colchester station, bought a Ford Zephyr in partnership with his wife. Even under guarantee, it never went right. The days it spent off the road cost Mr S. money. He put the mileometer back in order to stay inside the guaranteed mileage, but even that has now been exceeded. Every breakdown costs the full amount *and* deprives him of income. It makes him hate his wife. 'I had a thousand pounds put by, but that's all gone now. I spent twenty-two pounds ten yesterday. I don't know where it's going to end.'

Mrs Southgate once told us that, during the 1930s, the Hunt Lunch used to take place on the village green at Stratford St Mary. One day, they had just sat down to a table laden with goodies when word came that the Jarrow hunger marchers had reached the outskirts of the parish. The hungry-as-hunters gentry were not shamed. As the marchers came within range, they pelted the ragged men with rolls.*

May 1970. A dinner given by Bill Frankel, of the *Jewish Chronicle* at the Athenaeum for Dr Nahum Goldmann, the president of the World Jewish Congress. I could not escape a certain feeling of taboo-breaking as I went up to the steps of what my father always regarded as the *penetralia* of the English establishment. Once inside, I might have been in a skimpily staffed South American hotel in a boom town that no longer boomed.

I sat next to Tom Wiseman, who looked haunted and exhausted, and Jack Gewirtz, the buttery Lit. Ed. of the *JC*. Brian Glanville, with whom I had kicked a football in the park that afternoon, winked at me. David Spanier was next to Tom. Arnold Wesker – in the centre of the table – looked like someone auditioning for the part of Jesus in an Arts Council production of the Last Supper. Long-haired, face messianic with gentle vanity, he made it seem that this whole occasion had been arranged in his honour.

---

* This story is, I have since been told, a rural legend. It is often said to have happened elsewhere along the march. However, Mrs Southgate claimed to have a clear memory of it.

Gewirtz – in his physical thirties, but his spiritual sixties – trotted out the old arguments about Judaism's seminal place in the 'Judaeo-Christian tradition' and about the need for a theological sanction for morality. Whether it was possible to be good without God was a question of which we wearied in first-year Moral Sciences.

Tom said he had no use for organised religion, but the sense of the mystery of existence, the spiritual longings of men, impressed him with the need for belief, not in God in the accepted sense but in some immaterial principle. No cue for a song there.

Goldmann was a shrivelled old man with a crippled nimbleness of mind and eye. Frankel was an ageless Anton Walbrook, slyly intoning '*Tournent, tournent mes personnages…*' The dinner was sublimated kosher: melon ('I hope it's from Israel,' Gewirtz said; I hoped it was ripe), sole *cardinal* (Judaeo-Christianity creeping in), broccoli *au gratin*, apple pie, coffee.

Arnold cannot but seek to make any association reflect his personality. He breathes upon it, buffs and polishes, and looks for his own image in it. He wore a blousy blue shirt with unbuttoned sleeves and a little jacket, like an undesirable midshipman. You feel ashamed not to love him; he does want it so. He is forever announcing the goodness to be found in us, if only we would swallow his pills. The charm he seeks to exercise is rendered ludicrous by an inability to gauge the effect of his embraces. He is a dwarf who insists on measuring himself against giants. You can imagine him murmuring, 'Nearly there!' (to encourage the giants).

Goldmann's after-dinner message was plain and pessimistic. If a settlement with the Arabs, and the Palestinians in particular, was ever to take place, then – logically – it must be closer, but that was the only sense in which hope could be expressed. The policy of the Israeli government was to have no policy. Its survival depended on a coalition of irreconcilables; at the first peaceful opportunity, it would disintegrate.

Goldmann is not popular in Israel; he is said to have opposed the formation of a state in the first place. He has quite easy access to Arab contacts; they do not hesitate, however cautiously, to get in touch with him. He told of nocturnal rendezvous and unofficial dialogues. The Egyptians are the main problem, and the main hope: they have no important common frontier with Israel and their main concentrations of population are remote from Gaza. As for the refugees, they are mostly a Jordanian issue, and it is easier to make contact with Amman than with anywhere else. How hopeful it all began to sound!

As Professor Bernard Lewis was to reveal, at length, the Arabs are more reasonable in secret than it is politic to appear in public. The Israelis fail to reckon with the political complexities of the Arab countries. They strike at them as if they had single heads and all they do is turn them into hydras. If they ever did have a single head, they have grown several under the sword.

Life is full of Gordian knots, and hacking Alexanders wanting in greatness.

David Spanier and I had had a silly spat in the hall of the Athenaeum after the dinner. I wrote and asked him to have tea. He said that would be 'naice' (he works for *The Times*) and invited us to dinner. Finally, he and I arranged to have lunch. He booked it; I paid. He wanted to explain to me the crucial importance of Israel, which I had failed to appreciate at the dinner. I expected some inside story of how Israel was a bastion of freedom and its defence the duty of all good men. David had had a we-insiders *tête-à-tête* with Professor Lewis; journalism had made him familiar with the famous. He was half an hour late. I had crossed to the Chelsea Bookshop and bought some Graham Greene short stories (very poor most of them) to pass the time.

At close quarters, I found that David's schoolboy pariahdom had metamorphosed into ponderous courtliness. So what *was* the importance of Israel? It was that since 1967 he had felt completely different about being a Jew. And? And when he considered the sneers and insults he had endured, he was filled with Zionist pugnacity. Let anyone say again the things that he had heard said in the officers' mess when he was in the army and he would pick up a bottle and break it over the slanderer's head. D.'s personal history (albeit not unusual, or unaffecting) supplied a thin reason for Israel's cause to be absolutely demanding.

What whispers from the diplomatic *coulisses* had I hoped for? What secret codicils to the General Will? D. offered only the genial fable of a once frightened rabbit now blessed with a snarl.

Ahasuerus, the Wandering Jew, who cannot find his rest until the Second Coming, finds a fixed abode, at last, in the concentration camp. It is there that Christ comes again, in a cattle truck. He gives another chance to all the Jews who were never converted to see the

Truth of His message. He is then gassed. This time, the *Nazis* kill God – without recognising him – and, involuntarily, liberate the Jews from their curse. The State of Israel follows. The Jews cease to wander, but their state is unsupported by notions of divinely-sanctioned sovereignty to which the Second Killing has put an end.

Jack Lambert told me of Willie Maugham lunching alone at a window table at the Garrick (a magazine open on one of those truncated music-stands which avoid your soiling the text). Young Jack watched fascinated as that jawbone, so notorious for cracking down on asses, masticated the club meal. Afterwards, by chance (as the ambitious always say), Jack was standing next to W.S.M. in line for the cashier. The Master turned to Jack and found only an unknown young man, who waited for some viperish *aperçu*. After a moment's rumination, Willie announced with mordant clarity, 'I'm p-paying my b-bill.'

Last summer I lunched at the Reform with Spencer Curtis-Brown, who had heard that I might be a suitable biographer for W.S.M. I had been told that he had a 'hold' over Liza Maugham, but this proved false. There were no 'papers' since Alan and Willie had spent wicked evenings destroying everything a publishing scoundrel might wish to find. There were no revelations, and without them there could only be a rehash. We let it go. Then, this June S.C.-B. called and asked if I should be interested in writing a film of *Cakes and Ale*. Would we come to dinner and discuss it? We met him at the Bull in Long Melford; he would guide us from there to Glemsford.

It was a Novemberish June evening, the bleached sky panelled with grey. He looked younger, in a sports jacket and blue ascot; he also looked more fly, without the gentlemanliness that the Reform had lent him, as they might someone who had no tie. We followed his Viva to Monks Hall. It is old, but glum; the cardboard setting for a ghost story: you cannot believe that it is genuine even though it is. Mrs Margaret MacLaren who, he said, 'entertains for me' greeted us with blanched correctness. We were offered drinks in front of an iron basket of logs and paper, but – after a tense debate – no fire was lit. My sherry was in a chipped glass. The 'joint' of lamb at dinner, scarcely bigger than a chop, was less broad than the knife that carved it. The boiled potatoes lacked butter; so did the greens.

As for *Cakes and Ale*, the transparent hope was that I should take an option (he thought it would help my tax arrangements, or was it his?) and then do the script as S.C.-B. thought it should be done. Through the draughty, underfurnished house, which sported a few pale prints for art, there blew the unlovely air of provincial world-liness, as if this man who lived on 10 per cent of his authors' earnings were himself only one tenth alive. Mrs Maclaren, pink eyes and white hair, like a shrewd old bunny, fancied herself sharp as a thorn. Stella Gibbons was a favourite visitor, she told us. Perhaps she was inspired by Monks Hall when she wrote *Cold Comfort Farm*. When S.C.-B. was talking of Rosie, in *Cakes and Ale*, he kept saying how, in his youth, the question one asked oneself about a woman was, 'Will she sleep?' Mrs Maclaren – it was clear, but not credible – slept.

Who will now say a good word for Maugham? His reputation as a storyteller has lost its gilt, and much of its ginger, in a world which has heard everything. Yet his novels were the bible of my adoles-cence, if only (only?) because no one could have been more systematically deprived of the truth than the privately educated 1940s schoolboy. One did not know where to begin, in life or in art, and had the same aching appetite for both.

Willie's apparent familiarity with sex was a medico-literary affec-tation: he was well enough read, in anatomy and in the French novel, to seem both experienced and unshocked. There are hints of incest in his stories, but little of homosexuality. Elliott Templeton, in *The Razor's Edge*, is more narcissist than manifest homosexual. Maugham's mockery recruits him to the bullies. He refused to subscribe to any revocation of the anti-homosexuality laws. Only once did he publicly show himself on the side of the queer minority: Vyvyan Holland records his presence at a testimonial dinner to Oscar Wilde, after his conviction.

Maugham was, in a sense, a master of parody; that he parodied only one style made him seem a stylist. Gosse often said how wise Willie had been, after *Liza of Lambeth*, never to write anything else. Liza was born of a sense of outrage at the treatment of the lower classes; his later work solicited readers from the fortunate.

Leslie Fiedler remarks how populism dwindles into sentimental simplicities and/or witch-hunting: the belief that Wall Street or the Jews (or both, or both) must be 'behind everything'. What begins, in Theodore Dreiser, with 'realism' becomes radical paranoia without any observed evidence. The author of *Of Human Bondage* was compared to Dreiser, but did not resemble him closely: he could not remain sufficiently unamused. His friends came from that stratum of English society which had great connections, and successes, but would not quite do: Beaverbrook and the pre-war Churchill, the Windsors and H.G., the grandest possible outsiders. Not wishing to commit himself wholly to art or to society, he ended up halfway to everything: not quite a man, not quite a great writer, not quite English.

The 'memory' of a chaste, moral Rome was hardly more remote from Catullus than is the Regency from us. The decision to enslave the world, and hence to lay the foundations for Caesar's hegemony, was urged by Cato the Censor. *Delenda est Carthago* precipitated the autocracy which his descendant would find intolerable.* The Third Punic War – a fancy name for a genocidal mission – was a squalid triumph. From the battle of Zama, in 146 BC, Rome ceased to be a city-state. A hundred years later, it was a tyranny. After Cannae, republican solidarity gave Rome the resilience to overcome disaster; it could not survive success. The inability of the Scipios, Africanus and Nasica, to impose intelligence on the Senate presaged the crassness which would lead to Marius and Sulla, Pompey and Caesar. Out of conservative apprehension, the *Optimates* created the conditions for their own eclipse. They contrived a state which gave absolute authority to the sword, but themselves remained unarmed.

Ios. The Lump was how I always thought of her. One evening, seen through an open window as we walked past the big house, she was standing naked under the shower with her hair full of suds, gleaming body turned half away, breasts swinging. She had the cowlike radiance of a pre-Raphaelite lady; naked and unself-conscious, she had not removed her clothes but was simply without them. Divested of her public, uncomely persona, she was an illustration of the age-old routine of washing, the condition in which Artemis herself was dangerously observed. Desire which ignores personality – the erotic dart that strikes without warning – hit home with fierce, if fugitive, force at the sight of a young, naked girl who, when dressed and doing her social best, was gauche and unlovely.

A few days later, I was sitting on the beach, in the evening, with Lois and talking of the indifference of 'the kids' towards children. An unattractive young girl seemed to refute the generalisation by

---

*The Younger Cato was furious when the Scipio family, whose policy his forebear had derided, refused to let him marry into it.

smiling at Paul and Sarah and at John Summerskill's son, John-Paul. Lois said, 'Do you think this one will say hullo to us?' I looked and saw a fat girl approaching in the fading light and said, 'She looks plain enough.' It was Lois's daughter, Magda, in jeans and a Mexican blouse. Get out of that! I was quick to pick out another girl in the landscape and claimed that I was referring to *her*, not to Magda. If Lois had not been an incurable snob, who imagines me worth knowing, she would have taken understandable offence. As it was, she absolved me by saying, with convenient complacency, 'I knew you couldn't mean Magda, because I know she's beautiful.' Ouf!

When you receive handwritten letters from those who usually dictate to secretaries, you get a glimpse of their uncertainty. It is like seeing a picture without its important frame, or the urgent blank face of someone reaching for his spectacles from the shower.

26.7.70. In the post from England, a cutting about Don L. He has been fined nine and a half thousand pounds for currency offences.★ I warned him, when we bought Lagardelle, of the folly of his temerity (no one is more timid than I in fiscal matters), but it was too late. He relied too confidently on being the last sort of person to be suspected of being sharp. His misfortune was to be just a little less unremarkable than he thought.

Solitary Confinement by Christopher Burney. Commended by Frank Kermode in *The Sense of an Ending*, I extracted it dutifully from the London Library. The cogitations of an upper-class Englishman under threat of torture and death are decently ordered, but of no marked originality. The accident of solitude creates an appetite for it. Loneliness has a purity which makes its rupture, though longed for, somehow discordant: the Stylite and his style have a chaste affinity.
   Burney tells nothing of his past: neither his sexual nor his social history. We accompany him to the verge of the torture chamber (the 'rooms downstairs') but we are the companions of his thought, not of his experience. It might be claimed that Burney shows decent reticence in denying us knowledge of whether or not he masturbated, though he does not conceal his prayers. He seems to reject the body at every stage, an imported Cartesian in a French prison. He was lucky, in a certain sense, that his ordeal – over five hundred

---

★ Everyone at this time seemed to be committing currency offences.

days of solitary – took place early in the war. Burney was undoubt-edly a British officer and entitled to certain civilities: he even received food parcels, though deliveries were capricious. The Gestapo's chief interrogator was put on his best behaviour by his captive. The coldness of Burney repressed his opponent. Although he failed to convince him (his parting words were, 'Goodbye, I don't believe a word you've told me'), he succeeded in inhibiting him. In denying the enemy access to his privacy, he displayed the same (apparently) unpremeditated reserve which he offers the reader.

As a writer, he has precision without curiosity; the mark of a clas-sical education. Never cracking his own code, he remains happily in control of himself. His practical salvation reveals (and required?) his literary limits. Kermode reads profundity into him, less because of any originality as thinker or artist than because Burney's experi-ences are so alien to a well-kept academic; by playing the exegete, Kermode takes a share of his credit.

I thought that Kermode had a chapter on Brian Glanville some-where, in which he praised B.G.'s 'self-justifying' fiction. When I mentioned K. to Brian in the latter's garden (25.9.70), B. denounced him as a pretentious fool who always got everything wrong. e.g. his review of Edna O'Brien's *Girls In Their Wedded Bliss* and of Malamud's stories. Either it was not K. who spoke so well of Brian or B. is capable of admirable detachment.

The beginning of Kermode's *The Sense of an Ending* is so arch it almost topples over. Somehow the fact that the lectures were given first at a ladies' college comes through in the preening precision of the prose. He excites the girls by being so very *dressed*; it challenged them to wonder what he is 'really like'; he proposes, without any obviously flirtatious gestures, that they come a little closer.

The pain he felt was at once so acute and so absurd that he could think of nowhere to go for its relief except in the company of those who had caused it.

The 1970 election proved that Ian Macleod was a vote-getter. Physically uncharming, publicly unengaging if privately authorita-tive, he was the only one on his side whose sneering did not cause *class* resentment; he might be a Tory, but at least he was not a toff. When he hounded the Socialists, he did so like a watchdog, not a thoroughbred. His bark seemed genuinely to denounce the Socialists as a Bad Thing. He supplied no reason to vote

Conservative, but made it irrational to support Labour. The voters were amazed to find that Edward Heath was suddenly Prime Minister. They never *intended* to vote Conservative, they merely did so. The electorate had been persuaded to ambush itself.

26.8.70. Catullus. The content may be scabrous, but the metrical resource promises refinement. His spontaneity is too artful not to be premeditated: jealousy is something one thinks about. The tender, early(?) poems mourning the death of Lesbia's sparrow have a flippant poignancy; they declare the vanity of love when it has to sympathise with a pampered woman lamenting a frail pet in a world of organised cruelty. If Catullus were not in love with Lesbia, what a fool he might have made of her! Fear sponsors indulgence; he will, since he must, supply her with whatever she wants. Servitude blinds and binds. Until he is finally disillusioned, the poet is degraded; he barters bondage for favours. The betrayed Catullus recovers his self-respect, and frees his tongue, and his Muse. Unless the wound had been re-opened, could his bow have been re-strung?

Lesbia enjoys variety; Catullus constancy. He tortures himself, and abuses her, by imagining the brazen succession, and foibles, of her lovers. He finds enduring pain in her transient pleasures. The final, suicidal climax comes when he realises that she does not even want – *mean* – to hurt him. It is difficult to ignore the Oedipal dimension here: Lesbia is a great, and married, older lady whose allure, at least to begin with, has to be that she is a *prize*, and one which has been won before, by others. The ensuing dream of a romantic *amicitia* – 'friendship' hardly translates the word (nor *amicitia* the Greek *philotes*?) – has an archetypal force; it is at once the fulfilment of a fantasy and a cautionary tale of its crucifying consequences.

The driver, a Scot, had been a factory manager until fired, after a quarrel with the owner, who wanted to advance his own son. The Scot had set up and run a factory in Cornwall for six years, during which he had seen little of the man who put up the money. He organised the factory floor and re-jigged the equipment as necessary. The business was 'Promotions and Offers'. A Promotion can never be thicker than three sixteenths of an inch and must not cost more than six pounds a hundred, max. An Offer can be more expensive. A Promotion is actually included in, say, a woman's magazine, the solid bait attached to the printed hook 'INSIDE!'. An Offer has to be sent for after filling in a coupon. The coupons are sent to the manufacturers, who insert them in the packages of goods. Promotions and Offers were always made of plastic. A Promotion might be a plastic bottle top; an Offer was a butter dish or a set of hangers. The Scot had done very well. You have to be 'absolutely straight' with the magazines because they held you to what you told them about your capacity. The boss's son had come back from America, where he had 'scraped through business school'. He was going to reorganise everything. The Scot accepted his relegation to mini-cab driver without evident rancour.

Queenie and Kenneth were once our closest, or at least most regular friends. 'If she had been able to sing,' a Russian translator once said to me, 'she might have been an English Piaf.' Piaf came from the gutter, Q. from provincial Quakerism. Yet they *are* alike, if only in their embattled smallness. Q. was flattered by success in Cambridge, and flattened by failure in London. Defeat deadened her face, but spiced her intellect. All her aptitude for analysis is now brought to bear on herself. Shot to pieces by her own mental fire-power, she announces herself a drinker, and refuses to laugh it off. She is too clever for illusions. Yet what a bore she is! Beetle never liked her; unlike me, B. was not disposed to deceive herself. Q. imagines herself important; that much of her Cambridge renown clings to her. I remember a party in King's, with Q. in a rather tight low dress, though it had little to tighten on. She swarmed up to '*Dadie!*' with the familiarity that glories in public intimacies.

Queenie has no idea that her life might not be of abiding interest to others. Even in despair, she is irretrievably self-centred. She cannot make one care for her. Never a girl, she is not now a woman. Having surrounded herself with children she *would* have, she now boasts of exhaustion. Yet she cannot bear the idea of half an hour off, because she doesn't know what she would do with it. She has not got round to putting up curtains in their new house.

Still obsessed with 'Sister A.' and 'Sister B.' and 'Little Sister C.', she assumes that their fortunes are of interest to us. Having got her own way in everything with Kenneth, she fails to notice that he is as indifferent as he is docile. Their children have been exacted from him. Queenie has got what she wanted, but she has not got him. 'Do you love me, Kenny, do you?' she used to say. A *nonne* question that has gone *num*.

We had not seen them for years before the day they drove over from Harlow. When I asked her whether she wanted wine or tea (for elevenses), she replied 'Wine.' Her eyes glittered in cavities which looked hexagonal, the corners sharply angled; no warmth or humour, only blazing frustration. I sat with her and a bottle of hock. She wished that they lived in France. They had a camp near Cahors they went to in their VW van. In the summer, they liked to take their clothes off. The aggressive suggestion was that we should be scandalised. In fact, the idea of going to a camp in order to remove one's clothes seemed so dated, and so dismal, that I should prefer a Bridge Congress. Nudism is the most timid form of exhibitionism; de-eroticised promiscuity. Later Queenie said, 'I don't know why we go camping really. I don't like it a *bit*.'

Kenneth said, 'I do.'

She lamented constantly, 'We don't know who we are.' How she did want us to be in similar case! Her misfortune is that she does not suffer; she merely has pains. She lives now in a partly unfurnished house: no curtains, no cushions on the sofa, and doesn't know what to do about it. Her imagination has given out, though her energy – she insists – is unimpaired. She resents the children ('I won't have anything to do with them after eight-thirty at night'), but won't have help in the house.

She has not lost her acuteness. Of Margaret Drabble's novels, she says curtly, 'Not very good.' Of Daniel Deronda: 'Half of it is very good and the other half is very bad.' When Beetle said, by way of flattering tact, that she had come round to Trollope (whom Queenie was always reading in the old days), she said, 'Now you'll be able to go on to Henry James.' She gives a strong impression of unimpaired intelligence. For the rest, 'We don't know who we are.' She looks round with the reproachful glare of someone who was promised a future which has never been delivered.

At the plastics factory. Roger came to collect me (I was reading Jack Marx's bridge column in the *Illustrated London News*) with a Scot, Hamish, with whom he continued to discuss the possibly *political* reasons for some manager's rejection of a new process which both of them thought acceptable. They interrupted each other quite angrily; though pursuing the same train of thought, they jostled impatiently in the common haste to be aboard. Hamish seemed to say 'Roger' very frequently; Roger merely increased his volume, till their joint 'worries' were being loudly announced to unsurprised and uninterested colleagues who descended the dull staircase (a cardboard crate wedged under it) from the upper offices.

Roger wore the trousers of a charcoal suit, shirt, maroon tie. He has been promoted for the classic reason: he has 'turned round' a losing operation by the usual means, cheapening the product. There was a 10 per cent tolerance, within which he has reduced the quality of the plastic to a point adjacent to the customer's minimum requirements. He has also found cheaper – no less efficient – plasticisers and other ingredients. The result is that while other heads rolled, his was enlarged. Since he has great charm, his advancement seems more a happy accident than the result of accurate intrigue.

The pleasure he takes in the casualties of reorganisation seems no more wicked, or callous, than that a young ensign might derive from surviving a bloody charge, especially if his own dash had contributed to the final victory. Yet he is practising a ruthlessness which will, sooner or later, cease to be boyish. He told me later that the Scot with whom he seemed so vociferously allied would probably be someone he would 'have to get rid of' in eighteen months or so.

The factory, much of it built over seventy years ago, is a collection of brick sheds, linked by steam pipes which leak beards of steam. We went round in the late afternoon when the female workers ('They think of nothing but cock') had already left. Their jobs are mostly in doubt; large numbers have already been declared redundant. They cover car components with plastic. In another shed, a slicing machine like a huge plane was shaving white plastic off a great nougatine slab. 'We make 40 per cent of all ping-pong balls here,' Roger shouted. The plastic comes away in tight shavings until, at last, the whole surface is engaged, polished by the scraper's lubricant. The two operatives went ahead almost casually as the huge oiled tool pared off pallid, papery petals. The workers upstairs – where large sheets were coming out of the oven – seemed under the lash of time. They performed with a naked haste which made it embarrassing to be a spectator. They were working, Roger told me, 'at about eighty to eight-five. When they really get going, that can rise to ninety.' They never spoke; each relied on the expertise of the others. Their attitude was one of fast boredom.

Roger treats the men loudly as equals, the only practical way to patronise people these days. His ruthlessness is very considerate; he delays and delays the moment when he must sever himself from mateyness. He still has the playful elasticity of youth, which must eventually harden into the loneliness of decision.

Clever women. Rachel asked me what I thought a typical female fantasy was. I replied, after thought, 'Attention.' She agreed; she dreams of being in deep conversation with someone very famous. How will she get the chance? She has been betrayed by fidelity.

Melanie (also a First, of course) vaunts herself as a 'meek wife'. Her Cambridge ambition was fervently intellectual. She believed in brains. She had a certain Burne-Jonesish beauty: pale face, huge, febrile eyes, a pout of unfulfilled appetite on the unrouged mouth, a flourish of black hair. The intensity of her calculations gave her an air of heedless passion. She chose Lomax first, since he was the *arbiter literarum*, but moved on to Simon whose achievements (President of the Union, etc.) promised a brighter future. She told people she wished she could cover him with raspberry jam in order to have the pleasure of licking it all off again. Her real appetite, however, was for the big world. Her tongue was out for something sweeter than jam.

Pamela. She was the prettiest and the least interesting of the Cambridge females. Shapely and ostentatiously sexy, she often sported leopardskin trousers. One day Mike and I met her walking down King's Parade as we returned from John Wisdom's nine o'clock lecture. Mike shrieked, and pointed at her with a long arm and drooping wrist. I can hear his shrill derision still; it was a sickening, cruel, jealous, cowardly assault in the name of some false notion of – what? – female propriety, perhaps, which gave him the right to such callous jeering. Pamela stood her ground, a glittering, effortful humour in her pale eyes, the mouth gathered in a characteristic bunching of the lips, a flattened O in which, just, there was a tincture of scorn. I stood by in cowardly neutrality.

Resentment of others' beauty, and grace, is never far from Mike's mind. His present alternations of melancholia and rage are the late consequences of an early disorder. The loveless, unlovely man avenged himself on a girl whose beauty made him think that she had to be strong enough to deserve – and perhaps be impervious to – his shrill resentment.

Lomax. When Melanie dropped him, he took up with Pamela, who was not first class, but was certainly pneumatic. Lomax is a left-wing right-winger: radical views, conventional ambitions, an iconoclast who observes the proprieties. When in the Treasury, he was a bowler-hatted Marxist.

Bob Kee said that Lomax was surprised, after getting married, to discover that one could continue to find other women attractive. He then questioned the virtue of official pairing. It is to such unimaginative prigs that intellectual London bows its knee (*and* furtively thumbs its nose). But there is a brain at work there! Yes, and it is busy cramming life into the compartments which scowling premeditation has decreed for it. Lomax is such a prig that he recruited Mike – because he is now *Professor* Mike – as a reviewer for *The Back of the Book*. The man who had insulted his wife had the credentials to trump her grievance. Or was she so ashamed of the incident that she never told Lomax about it?

Meanwhile, Pamela has become a reviewer for one of the Sundays. These people will sit in judgement on my new novel in a month's time. Prepare for English justice.

The Plebeians Rehearse the Uprising. We saw it last night (8.9.70) after taking Pau and Sarah back to Bedales. We expected an agonising parting from Sarah. She had dreaded returning since the very start of the holidays. Yet when we actually arrived, to find the new boarding house clean and light and charged with familiar faces, Sarah became so excited that she scarcely paused to say goodbye. P. was tearful at the discovery that he was back on 'top landing'; he was afraid that he would be kept awake all night by Olly Rye, who 'likes to talk'. The tears which accused us of devoting too much time to Sarah's problems were dried by the red fear of being observed. P. concluded that he had very agreeable company and all would be well.

On the way down to Petersfield, I happened to say to Paul and Sarah, 'You know Beetle and I aren't related.' They were mildly shocked, and amused. On the way back to London, its truth was evident: we were alone with each other. Separation from the children separated us.

So did the Brecht. Agreed on its demerits, we were divided by its content. I recognised in the slogans the sort of second-order humour which made the old 'Intimate Revue' so delicious for insiders and so baffling to provincials. References to Lenin's letter to the Kronstadt workers were as flattering as jests about Binkie were to the queens of yesteryear. The audience was sparse, its lack of sympathy unconcealed. German ironies were lost on the English; the show had had good reviews and they expected a work of genius. Instead, the play had a disturbing, acrid flavour; its spite was always directed at some oblique enemy, not *quite* the audience, who were both judges (hence their laughter) and irrelevant (hence their shifty boredom). The English cannot get away from the idea of theatre as entertainment. Having seen an outrageous, if apt, display of mugging at the Globe the night before, when we took P. and S. to *Blithe Spirit*, we were unprepared for intellectual nuances. Beetle was immune to the snobbish involvement which made me feel that the play *had to be*, as they say, for me. We are *intimately* not related.

A paper sack labelled 'Jonathan Langley'. Literally, remains. Should the story start with the wife visiting the dying man? She begins, in spite of herself, to feel a desire for his death. She explains this to the family solicitor, to his embarrassment. He is a young contemporary who has always admired J. and at times been on the verge of making a pass at her. She hates the period of nullness, protracted and yet with only one possible ending. She feel that J.'s disease is killing her too. The world recedes; she has no use for it. The husband seems to understand this; he does not press her to stay long when she visits him. When he dies, she invites the solicitor to spend the night with her. Since it is what he has always wanted, he is very shocked. He is not sure that he can continue to represent her.

Morry's brother Harry told him, 'You're entitled to once a fortnight. You've got a right to once a fortnight.' Harry was actually having an affair with his brother's wife at the time.

The only state which saddled the electorate with *daily* responsibility was democratic Athens. The *demos* refused to show patience or to accept failure as being, possibly, their fault. They voted less for good policies than for good news. In *Armada from Athens*, Peter Green admires Athenian resilience after the Sicilian disaster. True, the people rallied, and united, against the prospect of annihilation, but their measures were limited, by necessity, to doing only everything that they could. Having no choice, they cannot be accused of having been in error. They never again had the resources for disastrous initiatives. Similarly, 'Socialism', however virtuous, has destroyed the confidence which the British derived from imperialism, however iniquitous.

We drove all day, from 7 a.m. to 8.30 p.m. to reach Lagardelle after spending the weekend in London with P. and S. How complicated everything seems till we get to France. And then there are other complications: hornets, for instance. We left the kitchen door open while we unloaded the car and prepared things for the sleeping Stee.

The hornets were like huge wasps, almost two inches long. I swatted and squirted and eliminated all that had entered the house. They could have killed us, but meant us no harm.

Next day I drove into Belvès. It was the last of an unbroken chain of autumn days. Monsieur Marty was no longer the *chef* of the *sapeurs-pompiers*, who would, I hoped, take care of the hornets' nest which Norbert had pointed out to me in the ruined house next to the *grange*. M. Marty took me to the new *chef*. He was working in blue overalls in his *atelier* and offered me his wrist to shake. '*Demain soir*,' he said. I was nervous of so long a wait. M. Marty pressed his successor, offering to come along himself. '*Vingt heures trente*?'

Yellow lights flared as the first truck snorted up the hill. Heavy figures in helmets and waterproofs jumped from the ponderous jeep. Then came a heavier machine, more men, with torches. Where was the hole? In the darkness, the masses of bramble were wilder and higher than daylight made them. The ladder was unloaded. The helmets owed their gleam to the torches and the flashes of lightning which began, like an excess of effects in a drama, to explode all around us (Elia Kazan had wished such a storm onto the third act of *Cat*).

The *ancien chef* could be seen wearing a yellow straw hat hooped with black veiling. He asked for a jam jar or glass. I brought a selection. He chose one, and filled it with a reeking cocktail; bare-handed, he climbed the ladder, like blind Dandalo at the walls of Constantinople, and flung the liquid at the hole. A trail darkened the wall. Now matches. Heavy drops were falling from the constipated storm; the wind bent the darkness. The trail was awkward to ignite; match after match went out. Marty leaned towards the wicked hole, the old campaigner, and suddenly whoof!, up she went. Vertical flames clung to the wall and burned and burned; one jarful scorched the night. No sortie, no buzzing of trapped victims. We stared at the flames.

'*Plâtre? Vous avez du plâtre?*' We did; in the *cave*. They had a *plâtrier/pompier* with them. He mixed the stuff while the pumps were activated. At full velocity, the hoses drenched the scorched nest, whether to extinguish the sparks or the hornets, I could not say. Hoiked out with a stick, the nest fell in two lumps into the brambles. The *plâtrier* climbed and flung a wet handful; it badged the wall, but he had to stick a stone into the aperture before he could caulk it. The *plâtrier* offered his limed hands to the hose all the way up to his waterproof elbows.

I asked them all in for *un verre*: *ça s'arrose*! '*Vous croyez?*' M. Marty brought in a round of nest to show us, like a slice of special cake. It was packed with hexagonal cells, each loaded with a fat, cycloptic grub, white as lard and turning with sluggish agitation in the premature light. Marty shelled a chrysalis (its cell door already cataracted for the final transformation) and out popped a packed hornet, bullet-shaped but without wings or fuselage. Another cell produced a living inmate. It floundered on its back under the penknife of the destroyer who squeezed the double sting into prominence with the callousness of a guard displaying the futile virility of a condemned man.

The relief is considerable, but – like D.H.L. with the snake – I have a pettiness to expiate. Today Norbert brought another section of the nest into the kitchen. The grubs were still alive, fat and imminent. I understood, to my shame, the hateful revulsion the guards felt from the inmates of the camps. The more helpless one's victims become, the more implacable one's hatred, because the more irreversible the wrong one has done them.

Annihilation becomes a mania, a frantic compulsion; all trace of the damage must be eliminated. When the strong attack the weak, there is no limit to their vindictive self-righteousness. The happiest conquerors massacre their enemies to the last man and manure their crops with the corpses. Today I gave the *sapeurs-pompiers* twenty-five francs for their trouble. Hush money.

5.11.70. After three years, another Publication Day. It began with a cold wind from the *Daily Telegraph*. England's unresponsiveness is like a boycott. Tired from the drive home from Montreux, I re-enter a country I can neither love nor renounce. If I amputate myself forever from the audience, I shall be doomed, like Nabokov, to spend a lifetime preening myself.

I had left Lagardelle on the way to see him, looking forward to my own company on the way. It proved more dull than invigorating. Vain of great thoughts, I felt only an anxious, nannying concern for myself. Solitude had small dignity. The first night, I could not bring myself to stop for dinner. Finally, I munched an apple in the last hotel before Lyon, in a place called L'Arbestre. Fog had come down, like the final chapter in a tedious thriller, too late for mystery. Relieved to find a bed (I had the feeling that the woman who showed me my room would willingly have shared it with me), I failed to remark that the hotel was alongside the main road as it approached a narrow bridge. The night was full of charging lorries, boosting themselves to take the bridge.

I spent the Sunday morning in the sun under a tree by the Saône. The whole landscape seemed over-exposed, fumed and brilliant. Racing fours creased the silver-plated stream. Built in the style of an inflated suburban villa, Paul Bocuse's three-star restaurant offered a whore's welcome. Why ever did I fall for it? Eating grandly alone in public proved a joyless ostentation.

The *friture gratuite* was the most delicious dish. The *écrivisses* were steeped in brown salt water, for which a soup spoon was provided. An habitué sat with his friend, and their newspaper, in the window ahead of me, at right angles to me. He ordered with peremptory weariness, stipulating the *pain grillé* which he regarded as his privilege. He stared fish-eyed at me. Towards the end of my *écrivisses*, I dipped my fingers – nervously? absentmindedly? – in my soup, instead of into the fingerbowl. *'Tu as vu ce type-là, tu as vu ce qu'il vient de faire?'* I met his gaze with hatred. He withdrew his attention to the ugly beams on the sloping ceiling, quite as if they had three stars in the Michelin. *'Je peux repartir à zero,'* he kept saying to his companion. *'A n'importe quel moment, je peux repartir à zero.'*

Geneva. The unruffled lake reflected a city founded on money. In preparation for an underground carpark, they have built a coffer dam on the left bank; a wide belt of concrete sheathed between lengths of corrugated steel. Even in November, the streets have an indoor air; one might be walking along a corridor in a clinic.

The Montreux Palace, where the Nabokovs have settled, is full of echoes, yet void of sound. I drove from Geneva along the autoroute to Lausanne, then through Vevey to narrow Montreux. The stepped vineyards were green and gold, leaves like foil in the November sunshine. Terrace above stone-grey terrace, the angles of the rows shifted like second-hands on the faces of wide, simultaneous clocks.

I had not finished re-reading *Ada*. I felt like some doomed examinee who has started too late on Metaphysics Lamda. I sat on a red bench facing a lake as placid as soup. Was it hereabouts that Shelley folded his arms in the stormy sight of death? German-Swiss strolled in the sun; their intimate conversation as denunciatory as a People's Court. Behind me, the over-terraced façade of the Montreux Palace was corseted in green scaffolding.

Headlines in the local paper told me that the *sapeurs-pompiers* of Montreux had been so little troubled by the fire-proofed inhabitants that it had been necessary to fabricate a false alarm in order to test their rusting reflexes. I checked into the Montreux Palace and sat tightly on my narrow single terrace: room for one upright wooden folding chair, feet on a grating. Madame Nabokov phoned. She sounded courteous, and hungry; we agreed to meet in the 'Green Room' between the bar and the dining room.

The Coca-Cola machine next to the automatic lift doors was a rectilinear contrast to the rounded *Art Nouveau* grandeur of the public rooms. English, American and Swiss newspapers were pinched in holders. The Nabokovs were moving about in the sunlit room. Not tall, he has a slightly hunched, woollen appearance, more ageing than elderly; rather narrow, domed head covered with the decorous equivalent of a crew cut, spiky hair that might just have been washed. He wore a beige sweater and a tweed coat, a broad, not-quite-kipper tie, pale yellow and orange. The un-English, un-American accent had no precise source. He was polite, but not formidable; I felt I was visiting the sick. Véra was slim and alert, a curved nose in a much-powdered face; she might not bite, but she could well peck.

Glad to begin without John Van Eyssen, Columbia's legate, I hoped for some literary chat before the movie business began. The Nabokovs had lived in Montreux for ten years, ever since the *Lolita* affair made America uncomfortable. Véra seemed less hostess than agent: she ticked off his triumphs and proclaimed his fame with an insistence which almost put them in doubt. He said that he was reviewing a new book on European butterflies for *The Times Educational Supplement*. He was halfway through when *The Sunday Times* asked him to do the same book; he was already committed and had to refuse. I remarked that it was as well, since he would be able to spread himself in the *TES*.

'He could write as much as he liked for any newspaper and they would print every word,' Véra said.

I tried to address myself as much to her as to him; a wise man flatters the consort no less than the king. Her attention, however, was all for him and for the reputation of which she was the curator. She was expert in the chronology of his campaigns: he demolished Freud, in 1937, and Edmund Wilson more recently.

They assured me that the Tsarist regime was less oppressive than the Soviet. In statistical terms, they may be right, but the uncounted crimes committed by the old regime against the defenceless or the powerless are ignored by the slap of whitewash. There is about N. a sort of refined coarseness; he could be a lot nastier, and cheaper, than he has chosen to appear. Kingsley Amis is now of his party. As if to emphasise the distance K.A. had travelled to join their company, Véra says that he was once 'very far to the Left, very far'. She lends an extremist air to mild Fabianism.

V.N. does not go so far as to endorse Kingsley's novels. He thinks them third-rate, but he makes his judgement indulgently. A friend confessed to him that he had passed on his views to Kingsley. 'You *didn't*!' V.N. said.

'Well,' said the friend, 'I softened it a little: I said you thought him *second*-rate.'

He admires Updike with a politely reciprocal smile: U. admires him.

The exile is an expert in protocol; he conducts an elaborately formal palace life in the hermetic private apartment of his head. V.N. is, he says, a liberal, as his father was half a century ago (I mentioned how well Trotsky spoke of Nabokov senior in his *History of the Russian Revolution*, but V.N. was not markedly gratified). Edmund Wilson had denied that liberals existed in Russia. Nabokov suggests, rightly I daresay, that E.W. knew little about Russia except what ideology supplied. Recently – last Christmas? – he received an envelope with a black butterfly in it ('It flopped out,' he said, making it sound vaguely jellified) and a note from E.W. re the *Eugene Onegin* controversy, saying that he had 'never enjoyed any literary dispute so much'. I guessed that V.N., whose victory was apparently complete, had found little pleasure in it. Was the famous clash of erudition actually a political conflict? E.W. launched himself with astonishing self-confidence on a Pushkin scholar disputing in his own native language. The fact that Mary McCarthy wrote an effusive eulogy of *Pale Fire* is unlikely to have kept E.W. an unqualified fan. The closer one gets to the famous, the pettier their motives seem.

At lunch, Nabokov asked, coyly challenging, could I identify the origin of the little poem, in *Ada*, about Peter and the Princess? I imagined a literary tease; in fact it was social: 'Margaret and Townsend' was the naughty-boyish answer. Homage and voyeurism, the oldest of courtiers.

Later, V.N. said suddenly,

'You like anagrams, don't you?'

'Not really,' I said.

He passed across the name of what looked like a forgotten Russian writer, ending in -ski, and asked me which English novelist it anagrammatised. I looked at it for half a second and replied, 'Oh, it's Kingsley Amis.'

Nabokov said, 'You're good at these things.'
'No,' I said. 'Just well-prepared. I saw it in the *Tri-Quarterly*.'

After lunch, V.N. said that he was going upstairs to have a rest and take another look at my review of *Ada*. He came down in amiable mood and we talked about ways of filming *Ada*. My only practical suggestion was that we begin with a shot of the White House with the Union Jack still flying over it, busbied sentries boxed at the gate: in the alternative world of V.N.'s fiction, the Revolution could be taken to have failed and the British would still rule America. As other problems were raised, I fell into the habit of saying that they could be dealt with quite easily. V.N. said, 'This man is like a good doctor. Whatever you say is worrying you, he says he can take care of.'

Nabokov had recently had as a visitor a now old woman who had known him in Berlin in the 1930s. She recalled that they had once discussed where they would like to live. V.N. had said, 'In a really good hotel.' He had no notion of ever having wanted such a thing.

In spite of his own ravenous memory, he seemed impressed by my recollection of an article he had written. John Fowles was equally amazed when I remembered that he collected New Hall china. If you want to impress people with the distinction of your mind, you need only treasure some small detail of their personal emotional wardrobe, take it out and brush it.

John Van Eyssen. His six-year-old played with V.N. when John was there to make the deal on *Ada*; V.N. was his elephant. He dresses very snappily: double-buttoned cuffs, striped shirts with long points, generously looped floral ties. He buys clothes 'everywhere except in London'; he has a feud with Douggie Hayward.

He spent a lot of time in Montreux in his youth. You could fiddle currency to such good effect that he had free holidays every year. He used to take cash down to Nice and change it. On one occasion, in the train, when he had a back pocket stuffed with notes, he was hauled out to be searched. He managed to extract the cash and slide it between the cushions in the compartment. He said to an English girl – 'with whom I'd got very friendly' – 'Sit on the crack'. He recovered the cash later. He was searched in the next cubicle to Sonya Henjie, who was caught with $5,000 on her. You could hear her screams for miles.

I left Nabokov a copy of my new novel, *Like Men Betrayed*, and we parted with expressions of mutual esteem. Despite the enthusiasm of our huddles, Columbia declined to commission a script from me or, I believe, from anyone else. Nabokov kept the money for the rights, of course, but no film was ever made. Nor did he write to me about my book.

A few years later, we passed through Montreux. I considered calling on V.N., but feared that he would not even remember who I was.

Some years after that, I was on the tennis court at our house in France when I was called to the telephone. It was The Canadian Broadcasting Company from Ottawa: did I know that Vladimir Nabokov had died earlier that day? I said that I did not, and was grateful for the sad news, but why had they bothered to call from Canada to deliver it? 'His family say that he had a particularly close rapport with you. We wondered if you would say something to us about him.'

I said, 'I met him once. He was, I suppose, the greatest writer of his time not to receive the Nobel Prize. Will that do?'

'Thank you, sir.'

I thought to myself: damn.

John van E. spoke with casual emphasis about his great-uncle: Jan-Christian Smuts. His vanity is based on happy alliances. On the Monday night, he took me into Lausanne for dinner. Since we had not booked, the chauffeur was sent in to blow our trumpet. Caviare, pheasant, fruit salad: thirty quid, including a bottle of Haut Brion 1960. John fears that the successful doubt his credentials. Carl Foreman told him that he didn't owe anybody anything. He ticks off the names of the famous like a cabbie telling you of the celebrities he has driven. He is touched by the trust which old Columbians place in him, 'men who've been with the company thirty and forty years', and have seen their stock dwindle from $30 to $9.

When their son David was born, John's wife was told that she should have no more children. They have peopled the boy's world with imaginary, unthreatening siblings, including a family of *esquimaux*. J. bought a huge postcard of reindeer which he flourished at lunch on Tuesday, telling N. and Véra that he had to concoct a story for David and again explaining the genesis of the fantasy family. He twice forgot the card in the next twenty minutes. Only my reminder saved the boy from a reindeer-free day.

Promised that Columbia had bought the rights to *Ada* outright, I was not aware that the visit was anything but a courtesy. Now I realise that I was there to win V.N.'s agreement to a free extension of the option.

Like Men Betrayed. *The Times* accuses me of being without humour. It is at least a new accusation, not that I agree: the characters of the minister's wife and some of the rank and file are funny enough, if you know anything about Greece, or human nature.

Two years later, I published *April, June and November*, also set in Greece. The critics said it was *too* funny. The *TLS*'s anonymous reviewer couldn't even begin, he or she said, to believe in the characters; so much time had obviously been spent in the elaboration of their jokes. I typed most of them out as quickly as I could write them down. (Note of 8.12.72)

20.11.70. Lunch with Clive Donner; he ate oysters; I had consommé; we both had poached sea bass. He has taken the Advanced Driving Test. 'It's the other fool you have to be afraid of.' Like the movies.

After a guilty session at the Hamilton, I went back to see Beetle in the nursing home where she had had her varicose veins done. She felt lousy; she cried; it was wretched. Soon after 9.15, a nurse came in to say that there had been a phone call, an important one, but the lady had rung off, very agitated. I couldn't believe it was the children; it was too late. I went back to Seymour Walk and called The Wick, then Beetle's sister; Putney then. Yes, there had been an accident. Gertie Guest was with my grandmother. My father had been seriously injured. Did she know the name of the hospital? Chertsey.

It was a fine, dark night. I was trembling, but excited by the purpose with which I drove; purposeful, but not pleased: in a thriller. I got lost and found myself on the towpath, amid the fatuous lights of pubs. Cars along the verge, couples lost in each other. A man in a filling station directed me: left at the statue of a soldier. I found it, drove along another dark road. The hospital seemed like a town; I charged into two cul-de-sacs before reaching the Accident Unit.

A dance was going on in the hall across from the Intensive Care Unit. Medical staff in dinner jackets were visible through the glass walls. There is a ribbed ramp across the kerb of the Accident Unit, sliding doors; ambulances can back straight in. The doors roar as they are opened.

My mother was in a waiting room next to the Sister's office; a modern box with a strip-light, tweed sofa, coffee table, desk, chairs. A big paper sack contained my father's things. He too had been in a dinner jacket.

Irene was lying on the couch, covered with white cotton blankets. She was bruised on the forehead, cut and stitched over a blackened left eye. They had crashed at an intersection. Brigadier Long, the driver of the VW they were in, was dead. My father had been flung through the windscreen; he was terribly injured. It had taken so long for the ambulance to come; and all the time he lay moaning in the road. There was much blood. The accident had happened not three hours earlier, but it seemed that an ancient tale was being told. My mother did not cry; she refused to lie down again until I insisted.

We went into the ward. He lay almost naked on the table; great chest, thin legs, belly and genitals exposed; they must have been inserting the catheter he so dreaded. His nose, clotted with blood, rose in a sharp curve from his sunken, unpillowed head. There was 'extensive brain damage' and 'serious chest injuries'. His prospects, said Dr Little, were 'very poor'. We lay there all night, my mother on the couch, myself on the back-rest which I detached and put on the floor. The dated modern furniture of the little room, with its louvred window on a manual bracket and its inquisitorial lighting, offered a mixture of the institutional and the solicitous. What did it matter? One would have accepted anything, as we did the footsteps in the passage which might at any minute bring us the news of my father's death. I faced it simply as a fact, without secret hope or dramatic dread. It seemed that he would die.

After a while, Little came and gave us the news. He was young and carried half a cigarette in a nervous V of fingers. His brown eyes were slightly bulbous, the long straight nose was at strictly an artisan's angle; the curate's understudy. It seemed a courtesy to treat him as a full-blown medical authority. I felt beyond motive when I asked him, knowingly, not to perform any miracles of rescue – this in the corridor beyond my mother's hearing – and not to bring my father back to clever suffering. I hardly thought in terms of recovery. I touched the young doctor's arm; he did not flinch, but he was not warmed. They had certain procedures, I realise, and neither intelligent anxiety nor special pleading would interrupt their course.

I have never known my mother so straight. She seemed sprung from the coccoon of suburban falseness. She admitted, without shame or fear of callous accusation, that as she got out of the smashed car she heard her earring fall. It was all she could do not to scrabble for it in the dark interior; even now she was concerned about it. The unquestionable primacy of her love – what else can you call it? – for my father permitted these petty confessions. We assumed he was dying. She regretted the end of their 'happiness' when so many unhappy couples survived. Again and again we yielded to banal lamentations about seat belts and unwanted invitations. Had Lucy Long had a blackout possibly? Why else should a disciplined man have crossed a white line on a road he had driven a hundred times before?

My mother had been temporarily knocked out; she had no memory of the accident. She came to with the two front seats empty. For a moment, she thought the two men had simply got out. But the windscreen was missing too. Lucy was lying inert; my father was groaning, in a pool of blood. Kind people stopped. Lady Gracie asked my mother not to move her. 'I'm in pain.' She is the widow of the General Sir whatever he was Gracie, 'the mightiest of the Gurkhas'. Long served under him in the Far East; on the general's death, he became the widow's devoted escort. 'I've lost the best friend I ever had,' she said later.

I met Long when, for a short time, I was on the Appeals Committee of the Hospital for Incurables. Tom Parrington, the vice-president, referred to him as a 'jumped-up ranker'; he was never a leader, or if he was, he always needed a C-in-C above him. He liked responsibility, I was told, but so that he might gain praise by taking it, not for its own sake. He had a sense of social inferiority which Parrington, with his vulgar refinement, was quick to notice. Now, after surviving a dreadful Japanese POW camp, where they played bridge with the rice ration as stakes, and where cannibalism was widely suspected, he was killed by his own steering wheel in a lane near Woking: ruptured aorta.

The ambulance took a long time to come. All the while my father lay groaning terribly. 'Isn't there something you can do?' The policeman was sorry; no. You cannot move serious injuries. One speaks always of the victims of 'tragedy', but perhaps they are being returned to the state of exposure to nature which is our common condition. The illusion of security is broken; peasant dismay, and endurance, take over. The pillow-fight of civilisation is shown up for what it is; we face the abyss with the naked fatalism of those with no more to lose. The illusion that death is a long way away (and will approach slowly) is lost. Death is not a complicated process, a legal action brought against us by eternity; it can be served without notice and executed without appeal. It is an ever-present and suppressed alternative to every action, every moment. It is no distance away. It has no separate realm; it is the one we live in.

Early on the Saturday morning I drove into London. It was still dark. The landscape of the accident persisted: the narrow Surrey roads; the little towns with their public conveniences; the bends, arrows, prudent commands, all too late. A feeling of dull importance gave my driving a certain swagger. In the event of a petty dispute, I had an unanswerable defence, like the schoolboy who claims immunity because it's his birthday.

I had slept little and burst into tears when I reached Beetle and told her, 'There's been a terrible accident and he's going to die.' She was kind, and comforting; she was everything I could have wanted. I felt no purpose in my declaration; I was too tired for strat-agems. If there was accusation or self-pity in my delivery, it was not intended. I was exhausted and confused.

I was due to go to Bedales to see Paul and Sarah. I decided to go, and come back via Chertsey. I hired a car and a driver and slept on the way down to Petersfield. Paul and Sarah were very under-standing; P. sensed a promotion, and claimed it, with tact. In the afternoon, we delivered a plant to the house of Paul's friend, Saul Hyman, whose mother had allowed P. to use her phone earlier in the week. The Hymans moved to Petersfield because they did not want Saul to go to boarding school; now he wants to be a boarder. I was touched and comforted by their hospitality.

There was no reason to stay at the hospital. Towards eight, I drove my mother home. For a week, nothing changed. C.M.R. was in a deep coma; he might well never come out of it. Last Monday, I went up to see Gareth about the script of *How About Us?* and drove on to the hospital. C.M.R. opened his eyes a few weary times. He was still badly bruised, the eyelids especially tender-looking, but the wounds were healing; he was recognisable. The huge bunion of an eye had lessened; the thick lips were less punished. On Friday I went again, and he was prompt to open his eyes, the right one at least; the other was reluctant. I said, 'Aren't you terrific? You really are a terrific fellow.' And he smiled, a full smile that filled his face with wrinkles. 'You really are fabulous.' And he did it again. Had I ever praised him so comprehensively before? The warmth and gratitude of his smile seemed to reproach caution. Fathers are sometimes admired, but rarely praised.

Dr Little, saying that he had no right to be any more optimistic, told me that the brain damage *may* not be irreparable. At the peak of despair, my mother was ready to accept a 'vegetable' rather than have him die. Now he can be seen to understand; he indicates assent or its opposite. He would speak, the Chinese male nurse says, if it were not for the gagging tube in his throat. The risk of pneumonia remains; there is a patch on his lung; it gets sucked out regularly. The antibiotic drip should control it. His temperature is down. At one time, when it went up to 103, they had a fan on him. Now he lies below an open louvre, naked under a white sheet, fluids draining into packets and jars, but no blood or plasma is plugged into him. 'We nurse them naked.'

On the night of the accident, they had to cut his clothes off him. They put his dinner jacket, which he had had for thirty years, and his other clothes in a paper sack. It spent several days in the little waiting room. Then one of the Sisters arranged for it to be incinerated. The contents of his pockets had been put in a separate envelope. That Saturday night when I broke it open, in Putney, to find money for Irene, I felt as though my father were certainly dead and my authority over his things established. I felt no pleasure or relief, but perhaps a sense of growth. My father's reign was over. His survival is almost incredible, clinically: Little still says his chances are poor. But it brings tears to my eyes. 'You poor little old chap,' I said.

On the other hand, it is a sort of embarrassment, this recovery: the fourth act of a three-act play. If he recovers, the accident will become an episode, a mere interruption. But last Friday, his baleful, resentful glare, the heavy painful lines on his face, the dazed suspicion of a swindle which covered his silent, shackled person suggested a future fixed in the cavity of the accident. He will, I fear, make his home in the pit, the shell-hole of the explosion which ruined him. He is very thin; he trembles. How much do I wish incurable senility on him? I pity him and I do not fear him; in the last years, he has conceded power to me. Yet I understand the emperors and tyrants who cannot endure the physical existence of those who once dominated them: Nero, his mother; Stalin, Trotsky. What feeling is primary here? Need any be? Am I a hypocrite when I wish him well? Is it only guilt that longs to hear him speak? Or do all these logics exist, immune from contamination by each other, simultaneously valid? My responses have been commonplace, and decent: concern for my mother – whom I have liked more than I have for years – and pity for the old man. I have been scrupulously considerate to my mother. If she has seemed false in the past, it is likely that he has falsified her. Now that the landlord is laid low, the weeds sap the concrete.

While we were standing by the bed, when my father's greatest physical achievement was to open an eyelid, my mother said, 'Of course if he recovers he'll never want to go in a motor car again. Oh well, we shall just have to walk.'

If she maintains that she would sooner have him a vegetable than not have him at all, she spoke at once of the need to get a job if he dies; there was a quickness in her decision that suggested repressed ambition. She has spent so many years in that damned flat. She has become very impatient with her mother, whom she quickly accused of indifference. The old lady, on the phone to Beetle, proved far from that. My mother needed an enemy; the dead Brigadier was one – his Memorial Service was one thing she would *not* be going to – and now her wonderful mother is another.

Loneliness has compelled her to conformity; American in England at a time when it was rare, she was recruited to snobbery, if only by apprehension. Now she was disturbed that she had written back to one of the RHHI governors, General Sir Somebody Something, as 'Mr Something'. 'Robbie' has promised to retrieve the delinquent letter. What does it matter? It matters to her, even though the RHHI people have, on the whole, given her no support or comfort.

The head that Irene sculpted of my father was the centrepiece of the Wandsworth Art School exhibition. A friend saw it in the spotlight and burst into tears. The accident was the lead story in the *Wandsworth Borough News* (in which, years ago, I used to check the local movies). Irene took the paper to the hospital, when the old man was still comatose, to show the nurses. Sister Reeves, the 'well set up' blonde who said, 'tears in her eyes', that she knew what it was to lose a husband, is the main target of my mother's urgent affection. Irene is a mistress of ingratiation, especially among women; she is immediately alert to the politics of a group. The 'little Indian nurse' confessed being dumped by her lover (no surprises there) and

Reeves's rivalry with Thomas, theoretically her superior, has not been unremarked. Peggy, the receptionist, brings lemon for Irene's tea and is rewarded with cookies (Fanny is restored to being wonderful in order to gild the gift). I am an intruder in these feminine circles, though the flattery of a South African nurse – 'I didn't know you had fellers like that in England' – enhances my mother's vanity. She shows no self-pity. Reeves says that she should have been admitted to hospital that first night. Dr Sutton (whom she calls her '*bête noire*', always) must feel some guilt over this, hence his defensive aggression.

Irene will not drive to the hospital. (I can't blame her. My mouth still grows dry, my hands prick, my voice tightens.) Friends sometimes take her. Pat Cotter prays daily. Last Friday (11.12.70), I went back to the Hamilton for the first time. The staff seemed more genuinely concerned than the members. When Kenneth Konstam died, those who had played with him almost daily were irritated by the hiatus the announcement caused in their game. Emotionally, they are counterfeiters who do not know what to do with the real thing.

Dr Little said, 'You're going to get to know the road to Chertsey very well in the next few months.' One goes up Kingston Hill, over Kingston Bridge, past the waterworks, Hampton Court, Molesey, Shepperton, Chertsey Bridge, the level crossing, and there you are, a drive through narrow lanes, and busy villages in the Thames valley, an area full of moored boats and, in these December days, often creped with fog.

16.12.70. C.M.R. is due to be taken down to the Ward. My mother will be able to visit only one hour a day. No longer queen of the Emergency Unit, she will be forcibly absolved from constant attendance. She will drive herself through those narrow lanes and tight villages, past Benthall's and David Garrick's house, Molesey, the waterworks, Shepperton and the bridge at Chertsey.

The baleful look, to what extent is it 'only physical'? Was it not always a component of his character, an aspect of that repressed intelligence which once read Greats and latterly found culture in the *Black and White Minstrel Show*? Were all the distractions – golf, bridge, the committees, even family duties – mere camouflage? Sealed in his silent body, coffined in inert flesh, he looks out with suspicion at the strangers by the bed. My mother offers tepid kisses to his hands. She calls him 'Ceddy', which is what he liked when they were first married. She hated the name; only subservient despair leads her back to it. She kisses the cold fingers with distinct sound and – true to the tradition of loving what is lost – calls him 'My love'.

The nurses go almost skittishly about their offices. They came back one day with an unconscious woman on a trolley. One of them was holding up a bottle of colourless plasma. In order to get the trolley into place, they had to winkle another out of the cubicle. Though there were several of them, the manoeuvre proved awkward. The nurse holding the bottle got the giggles. She pressed her forefinger under her nose, a pretty blonde girl, hair pulled round and pinned. The others laughed too, four women including a Sister, seeming larky and unsupervised in the absence of a stern man. The plasma remained high; humourless gravity continued to work.

A girl called Anna had taken an overdose. They called to her sharply, 'Anna, wake up now.' My mother was prudish: 'How dare she?' How dare she distract attention from C.M.R. or how dare she be so dramatically unhappy? She lay inert. When I walked past, the bedclothes were pulled back. Her young, handsome, unsupported breasts, nipples like brown plums, lolled either side of her chest. Facts, not charms; no one troubled to hide them.

Death is not something that concerns the staff. It is the one thing they cannot worry about. Respect is for the living. Why should medicine show false concern? Let religion do that, whose domain is falseness. Death is the last of a doctor's worries. The oppressive sanctity of the sickroom has been exorcised; attentive briskness has replaced it. The patient is a repair job, to be returned to his function. He is not lingering on the verge of some great metaphysical adventure. The doctor may mystify and pontificate, but he is the garageman who sighs and purses his lips in order to enhance his expertise and justify his bill. Yet we still hope for salvation from wise white fathers who will comfort and exalt. We meet genial African doctors (admired by South African nurses), men younger than ourselves, and probably less bright. Why expect them to produce a cure for dying? We take refuge in titles; Registrars and Consultants, how can they not be superhuman? In fact, they offer odds, shrug amiably, make no claims to certain knowledge. Is there anything money can do? Not much; very little; virtually nothing. How small these things make us! We are glad to have the right accents and education to ask appropriate questions, but these are social consolations; they do nothing for a broken man's chances.

The splintered ribs must do their own mending; the lungs reflate their own economies. Medicine builds a tenuous coffer dam against death, against the greedy tide that would reclaim the federated components into their impersonal, natural state. We defend our boundaries against nullity, against being tipped back into the mindless soup we came from. Nature waits to junk us as we lose way; it listens for the faltering heart and unsheathes vulturous claws. Salvage-men scramble aboard, appraise and bid for the wreck. From the watchtower of his head, my father sees us as the enemy, conniving at the dismantling of his personal state, adjacent powers massing on his frontiers; frowns are his fences.

My mother told me that when she thought she was dying, as the result of complications during her appendectomy (when?), all she thought was, 'I wonder if I shall see Irvin again.'

14.12.70. London. A meeting with Tom Maschler and Michael Sissons about *Who Were You With Last Night?*. Michael Rubinstein has reported adversely, and pompously, about libel. The biggest danger is that Mrs Gregston will claim that the wife in my novel is depicted as the premature seductress of her husband, surely an antique anxiety. Yet there is a problem; some degree of realistic reference to the A6 murder can hardly be denied. After we had finished talking, and Sissons was almost at the door, Tom said, 'Have you got time for a drink?' M.S. was not meant to hear, but did, and said, 'Well, a quick one.' Tom said, 'I thought you were rushing off somewhere.' Sissons, in his gold-rimmed spectacles and fair sideburns has the insecurity of those who come late to youthful fashions. He ducked out, quietly wounded.

At Gareth's office. David Hemmings' agent had had the script of *How About Us?* over the weekend. He called without knowing that I was in the office. 'If only they were all like that,' he said. 'I read so many awful scripts. What a pleasure!'

'Any points at all?' Gareth said.

'Not really, no. I enjoyed it immensely.'

The first return. A significant swing?

The private view. The Gallery was full of people who seemed to

know each other, and not to know me. Why had I come? I have
scarcely seen Jack Beeding, the artist, since he and Babs lived next
to us for a few weeks in Putney, before we bought The Wick. They
(and their two small children) have spent the last six years on Ithaca,
where they built their own house. I asked if he knew Peter and Lal;
he knew people who did, Gavin Lyall and Katharine Whitehorn.
What dark, sensual wit did she not dispense weekly in *The Observer*;
oh the shrewd, amused eyes in her Stylite photograph at the top of
the column! Suddenly there she was, a short white-faced woman,
as if the make-up had been washed off by tears, watery eyes full of
journalistic mock-modesty, no interesting recesses, no alert
humour, only the usual Oxford civility, the usual docile self-righteousness. Somehow we got talking about a famous Red. I admired
him, from the outside; she knew the dirt: he was always denouncing
the Bourgeoisie for its neglect of the aged, while at the same time
attempting to have his mother-in-law's electricity cut off.

She despised Robert Ardrey: 'He talks like a Hollywood
scriptwriter.' (She had no idea who I was.)

I said, 'I like the way Hollywood scriptwriters talk. I certainly
prefer it to the way scientists talk.'

This led me to remark how wise the Catholics were to have a
celibate clergy. 'Really? Why?' The liberal feminist prepared to
bristle (or was a column forming?). 'It makes the priest free of the
most damaging measure of his practical virtue: how he behaves
towards his family.'

'I'd never thought of that.'

'We could all be good,' I said, 'if we were only voices. It's rather
obvious really, isn't it?'

'Like all great ideas,' she said, 'once you think of them.'

'Once somebody else thinks of them,' I said.

'I must look at Jack's pictures.'

Was she glad to get away from me!

Paul went up to London to meet the Hymans and go to the
Spurs/Wolves match and then to stay with my mother. We drove
up from Langham on Saturday night to Tony Becher's fortieth
birthday party. First, we went to Seymour Walk and called to make
sure that P. was safely in Putney. I heard Beetle say, 'You *spoke* to
grandpa?' It was true. The old man had spoken to Irene when she
got to the hospital that afternoon. When she had returned home,
the nurse phoned. Bad news? 'Your husband wants to talk to you.'
The phone gets wheeled round the ward and he took his chance.

Despite the continued discomfort of a tube in his throat, he spoke distinctly: he called Paul 'Pau'.

On the Sunday, he had no memory of having phoned. He was crotchety and taciturn. The one-sidedness of the conversation gave it the style of the nursery.

22.12.70. C.M.R. had the tube removed from his throat yesterday and was able to speak, and complain, more freely. He said that he was being cared for by 'a lot of little people'. The nurses are short; one is Chinese. He and Dr Little did not hit it off: 'Someone should have taught him manners.' My mother explained how much Little had done (she so fears trouble), but the retraction was grudging. This rather alarmingly uninhibited C.M.R. is not uninteresting (as we used to say of a 5-0 trump break) and more of a personality without the bowler hat. The catheter too is out; he may have pulled it. He managed to pass water, not a lot. He drinks and eats less than he should. He spoke in a muddled way for a while, but then said sharply, 'Have I been talking nonsense?' He remembered a bridge date and a dentist's appointment from before the accident. He failed to respond to the name 'Cassius Clay' when his old friend, David Aserman, mentioned it, but later, when my mother alluded to it, he asked the result of the fight. Most characteristic, he said, 'We'll sue…everybody.'

Renford Bambrough was at the Bechers'. He seemed darker than I remembered: had he dyed his hair? He wore a dark suit and waistcoat, white shirt, neat black shoes, rather pointed. The unaltered profile might belong to a worldly cardinal. Since 'Renford' is a first name no one could ever *guess*, its use puts those familiar with it in a kind of club. Quite tall, pockmarked, with alert, hooded eyes, he is now thick through the middle. Someone told us that he was 'a great womaniser in his youth'. You could have fooled me: he always seemed very married to Moira. But then in the 1950s everyone seemed very married to someone.

He looks past you towards some conversational destination which he has already scouted. Not interested in areas unfamiliar to him, he never picnics where there might be ants. He has shifted his philosophical position 'since the days when I taught you'. He no longer concedes the primacy of the mathematical mode. He cleaves to the style of Wittgenstein II and Wisdom. Wisdom has left for Oregon, reportedly because of the sour atmosphere in the Moral Sciences faculty.

Moira said that the venom of the meetings was beyond belief. Were speakers not always ritually mauled? I remember Maurice Cranston almost in tears after a lucid and unassuming paper on John Locke. It was now worse than ever: Renford was demolished almost to the point of despair. His paper was later published and led to 'dozens' of invitations to address societies.

As we stood side by side (not face to face) in the hall at the bottom of the Bechers' stairs, R. told me that he now takes the view that ethical and political questions are best dealt with in the novel. Unsympathetic to Noam Chomsky's leftist attitude to Vietnam, he was fastidious in pointing out that Chomsky's academic achievements did nothing to warrant his radicalism; they were, in fact, of a rather 'conservative, rationalist' order.

Only seven or eight years older than me, Renford is a working class intellectual who has rationalised his own good fortune. He was now 'a little to the right of the centre of the Conservative party'. Like honest John Braine, he has moved from one political wing to the other; and measures society's qualities by his own progress in it. If Braine *is* honest, he is also foolish: he believes that his pocket is part of his body and that natural conclusions can be drawn from filling it.

Chomsky's licence to criticise 'the New Mandarins' derives more directly from his scholarly ideas than Renford will allow. His evidence that America has been miseducated comes from errors in the assumptions governing his own discipline. Academia, he says, affects expertise in fields where certainty is not available, at least not on the premisses advanced. Imagine how eagerly his critics would remind us of Chomsky's intellectual reach, were he to endorse Nixon's foreign – or Agnew's domestic – policies.

Renford's luck is to operate in feeble old England. Would he be as willing to strike stringent attitudes if it really mattered what he said? Like a human adverb, he can modify, but never incorporate, what is essential. The single-minded pursuit of a distant ambition (to be Master of St John's) asks of the world only that it stay stable enough for the goals to remain upstanding. The careerist's youthful radicalism lasts long enough only to procure the slaughter of whatever sacred cows inhabit the field which he wishes to crop. (23.12.70)

The English are fortunate; they do not encourage politicians who take their promises seriously. Failure to deliver on advertised programmes is England's happiest tradition. As a result, there has been no pogrom, proscription or massacre, no tyranny and no commune, for three hundred years. The charges of insincerity flung so ritually in politicians' faces are reminders to them not to do anything significant. Good English housekeepers know that the right place for dust is under the carpet.

C.M.R. to the Sister on Xmas day: 'I'm going to write you some Greek verses – and when I've finished them, I think you should eat them.' It was Sister Thomas, from the Emergency Unit. She had never heard him speak before. She and Fariah and the black Dr Adams came down together, happy with the champagne I had sent them. 'How is "sir"?' the passing staff asked, aware now of C.M.R.'s superior style and accent.

Dr Little seemed so certain of his death that those who talk of other modes of healing become more plausible. Ignorance, faith and chance fill the deserts around the small oases of scientific certainty, and competence. The doctors water the flowers, and weed the beds, but none is sure which particular specimens will survive. Death's door and the public exit swing on the same hinges. Recovery and death are heads and tails; having dodged one, C.M.R. is obliged to the other. After all the agonising, it is strange to realise that he was never in great pain; he is thin, and sore, but he has not *suffered*. Even his depression has lifted; not knowing how bad he had been, he thought that he was sinking, not rising. Now that he has guessed Lucy Long's death (he wept), he understands the seriousness of the accident. Yet he is still confused: he forgets that he no longer lives in Pembridge Square, where he spent his childhood, and he talks of meeting my mother in Ladbroke Grove for dinner. Time's dimensions have collapsed.

A stranger has surfaced where someone familiar went down; he has a more vivid, less trammelled, character than the victim. C.M.R. is not, of course, truly a stranger; merely strange. To be re-born at seventy-one must be an odd experience. He talks of not having much longer, which alarms my mother, as if a man of his age should have no consciousness of mortality. He says that they should learn Italian; that they should write; that they should visit Cyprus again (for the last time). He has an almost epigrammatic form of speech, secret and sly, in some ways more intellectual, and less polite.

'I shall never play bridge again,' he says. My mother is distressed, as if he were renouncing some essential function, but might it not be that he is throwing aside the mental sugar water with which he has, for so long, been diluting his intelligence? There is earnestness in his concentration on 'higher things': a second childhood alerts him to the deviations which fear and ambition forced upon him.

For a while, when things were at their worst, my mother was equally 'liberated' by the accident. She was uninhibited, almost – though decorously – gleeful in her lack of sanctimoniousness. Now apprehensions return; she does not want him home too soon. She fears the clash which may come between an irritable and less controlled C.M.R. and her mother, the 'old lady' whom they (she) so self-righteously imported from Kansas City and who, against all predictions, lives on in their nest. A man back from the dead – his heart stopped on the night of 20 November 1970 – is not likely to be as patiently reticent as the previous Cedric.

30.12.70. Richard Zanuck has been fired by Fox. It now becomes clear that Darryl was behind the torpedoing of *Guilt*. The final thumbs-down came after R.Z.'s trip to Europe to see his father (and his father's mistress). Darryl reminds one of the old Ruhr steel-masters. How can you help admiring the nauseating resolution of a man in his late sixties who embraces the loneliness of throwing away his own son? What self-sufficiency!

The first that Dick Zanuck and David Brown knew of their eviction was when their names were painted out in the parking lot. A quarrel between Dick and Darryl ended with D.Z. asking David Brown what he thought. David said he agreed with Dick. Darryl never spoke to him again. Dick was accused of being responsible for *Tora, Tora, Tora*. In fact, it was Darryl's project. It manifestly shared paternity with *The Longest Day*, with which D.Z. saved Fox the last time it was in a hole. The real bone of contention is said to be Darryl's reportedly Lesbian mistress, who treats him badly. Richard Z. refused to renew her option; hence his father his.

1971

I may pass among the unsuccessful as a success, but no one really successful is deceived. I can supply an ingredient they may occasionally want, but I am not in their club. The quasi-boom in the movies has gone, and with it the semi-golden age in which a diversity of productions was a feasible luxury. In the 1960s, the price of *succès d'estime* was to be *en supplément*; now I am off the menu altogether.

5.1.71. Disappointments are not surprises. Van Eyssen called to say that Columbia were not going to proceed with *Ada*: they might have paid $50,000, but they would not spring to $100,000. Was it disgraceful to decline a job so well paid because it was not extravagantly paid? The real disgrace was to consider accepting it at all.

8.1.71. To London to see Gareth's film, *Unman, Wittering and Zigo*. First I went to Putney hospital. Although his face was glazed with the sweat of his exertions in the physiotherapy room, C.M.R. greeted me in a cheerful, firm voice. He has no memory of Chertsey. He may vaguely recall P. and me visiting him on Xmas day (when a policeman in a Morris 1000 accused me of speeding), but nothing else. He now reads the newspaper. It is an amazing recovery. And I, with my broken finger, proved Marx's *aperçu*: even in personal history, after tragedy farce.

In those days, we were regularly friendly with Jim and Monica Ferman. Jim was still directing TV plays (as they were still called). They came often to The Wick on Sundays. Early in 1971, I left them to play football in the next door garden with Paul and some of the local children. I kept goal. I was so busy playing the coach that I parried a ball without looking at it. I was wearing green goalkeeping gloves, but only my left little finger met the heavy leather ball, which broke the finger so that it hung at a right angle to the others.

I sat in the black leather chair in my room while Monica poured witch-hazel over the Peter Bonetti gloves which I refused to remove. Beetle spoke to Mrs Dr Hall. I should have to go to the hospital for an X-ray. I put my poncho on. A touch was pain. Jim, gentle, kind, unobtrusive, drove me in their Cortina to Colchester General. It has a bad reputation; the wise go to Ipswich. The Fermans had come down in fog. Monica feared a late return. I went into Casualty while Jim parked the Ford away from double yellows.

Two families were waiting, one with four children. No one seemed to want treatment. They were getting drinks from the machine. 'A mixture of tea and coffee,' someone told me. I sat until a Chinese nurse came and asked me questions: name, address, doctor, nature of injury, which hand ('Left'), occupation ('Writer, right-handed'), whether doctor private or not. I had to spell the answers, and then spell the letters too.

Finally Sister came, blue-uniformed, white-crowned, displeased with her staff. She took me into the surgery and said that the time had come to take off this glove. I was not keen. Would she cut it off? She would; P. needed a new pair anyway. As the little finger-stall holding the broken finger came off, Jim gasped 'Oh my God!' I elected not to look. I could feel the sharp pain and imagine the bone protruding backwards through the skin. 'Nurse, you'd better take him down and get him on a trolley.'

The liberated pain made me dizzy. A dark girl led me down a corridor, neither of us too sure where we were going. Sister called out after us. Finally, I was on a trolley, flat, relieved to be powerless. They put a splint under my forearm. I was afraid they were going to manipulate the finger. 'Please don't touch it.' They tied the wrist but didn't move the finger. It seemed as brittle as an icicle.

The Chinese nurse returned and stood behind my head. Was she Chinese? She laughed and shook her head. Hong Kong? Siam? 'Burmese.' 'Really?' 'No.' She refused further questions, suddenly quite ill-humoured. Now it was a question of who should operate. The Casualty Officer came in, swarthy and moustached. An Arab! I called Jim and asked if he was, seriously. 'Probably.'

The Casualty Officer asked me whether I would like him to deal with my finger right away or if I preferred to wait for Mr Hume, 'the Consultant'.

I looked at the man anxiously. Whatever he was, I didn't want to hurt his feelings. But I did want to wait for the Consultant. I said, 'What would you do?'

'Oh,' he said, with a fine smile, 'I'd wait for Mr Hume. Every time.'

'I shall take your wise advice,' I said.

Later. A pretty, fair Austrian girl, ready to laugh at flattery (mine was shameless) came to give me an injection for the pain. 'I'm mad about morphine,' I said. (They had given me some in the Marsden. I liked it so much that they made sure I never had any more.)

'In that case, you'll soon be very happy.'

'Which arm?'

'In your behind.'

She suggested one side; I preferred the other (she would have had me roll on the bad side). 'One buttock's as good as another, I assume.'

She agreed, enjoying the game, such as it was. The pethidine worked its spell quickly. I lay in a licensed cocoon of modest pain and bold irreverence. Jim came in and out, discreet as a lawyer, having phoned The Wick, and so on.

After inspecting the X-ray, they decided on a general anaesthetic. Jim helped to wheel the trolley down the narrow passage to the radiologist's room. That part of the hospital was the old Workhouse, with new paint. I had eaten lunch too recently for them to go ahead immediately. I lay in the casualty theatre and waited. It occurred to me that it would be a pretty irony, after C.M.R.'s experience, if I were now to choke to death while having my little finger set. The anaesthetist came and inserted a vent in the back of my right hand, so that we should not waste the Consultant's time.

While we waited for him, Jim and I talked. I was muzzy. I lamented the lack of affection in modern drama, the reluctance of writers to celebrate what was often the most moving, and constant, element in lasting relationships. Was I making a declaration of friendship? Certainly I was moved by Jim's tenderness. Helplessness made me sentimental, but not tearful. I was surprised at how easy it was to be convincingly brave, at least in petty agony. I was a fountain of jokes; the girls liked me. The Burmese girl, if that is what she was, evidently had some personal problem!

Mr Hume was grey-haired, youngish, comfortingly familiar in a Cambridge sort of way. He asked if I was a violinist. No, a writer; why? Had I been a violinist, he would have had to do something more intricate, and less likely to be successful. As it was, I would have a fully operative little finger, but it would not be of concert standard.

When they decided to get down to business, guessing that the

Fermans would now be going back to London, I said, 'Goodbye, Jim, and many thanks if I don't see you again.' The Consultant and his aides laughed, imagining that I was making a death-bed speech. As I explained, solemnly, the anaesthetic tap was opened. Was there anything I had to do? Nothing.

When I woke, it was half an hour later. My finger was on a bright metal splint, fastened with adhesive tape. The ambulance would take me home. I was wheeled back to my curtained cubicle. The man next door was moaning; he had fallen off a ladder and broken his ankle in the road. We were taken home in the same ambulance. Meanwhile, somewhere a child was crying and crying.

The man with the broken ankle was thirty-three. He wore a striped yellow and orange football jersey. The ambulance man who sat with me had been seventeen years at it. Previously he was a butcher; blood didn't bother him. He couldn't get any help in his shop; one of his delivery boys stole the people's money from where they'd left it for the tradesmen when they went to work. In those days you were supposed to be able to trust people in the country. So that was the last straw. He was very happy now, not that they didn't have some unpleasant jobs, not the blood so much as the filth. The way some old folks lived! They went to collect one old lady to take her to a home and when they saw where she'd been living, you wouldn't believe the state of the place. He told the Superintendent not to put her to bed – 'They had clean sheets and everything waiting for her' – until she'd been put in the bath.

I asked him and his mate to come in for a cup of tea. They said they had better not: the other ambulance was on a job and they had to stick by the radio. Beetle had ten shillings for them, which they pocketed, instantly.

I was high for the rest of the evening. I apologised constantly to Beetle for not having treated her better. I lay propped in bed, with light coming in from the landing. Pau told me that he had kicked the ball off the line after I had parried it with my finger. The next day, he bought me a pot of yellow chrysanthemums. They are in flower in front of me now.

Years earlier, in 1962, Jim Ferman directed a TV adaptation of my novella *The Trouble with England*. I was out of England during the shooting of my script, but Stella Richman, my patron at ATV, sent approving reports and reviews. A year later, I was walking along Bedford Way towards Bumpus bookshop when I saw Ian Bannen, who had starred in my 'play', coming down the street towards me. Who was it who said that the US navy was one in which ships sight each other at dawn and collide at midday? At length, we came face to face. I said to Bannen, 'I think you were in a TV play of mine, and I hear you were very good. I wanted to thank you.'

He said, 'You are…?'

I explained that I was the author of *The Trouble with England*.

He looked like a man who wondered what he had done to deserve this. 'I'm sorry,' he said, 'but Jim Ferman wrote that.'

'Who told you that?'

'He did.' He seemed to see a friend in the empty street and dodged past me.

When I told an American friend of mine about the incident, Harry said, 'You have to face Jim with it. If you don't, you'll ruin your friendship.'

I never did. The friendship endured until that Sunday when Jim so kindly took me to Colchester General Hospital.

After I had gone off with Jim, B. gave Monica and the children tea in the kitchen. Johnjohn asked for jam and B. offered an assortment, including quince jelly. Monica said, 'Oh Beetle, don't tell me you buy quince jelly when you've got a quince tree in the garden!' B. said that M. had been 'very bitchy' (B. had in fact made the jelly from our own quinces). Sarah confirmed the scornful note. Monica had said to me earlier that she liked coming to The Wick so that she could see all the new things we had.

The Fermans' son, Johnjohn, was in the habit of reducing Sarah to tears. She did not cry easily, but Johnjohn rarely failed to hurt her, one way or another. When this happened, again, while I was in Colchester, Beetle was unaccustomedly outspoken in reproaching the boy for behaving 'the way you always do'. Monica was irked. Whatever the reason, my laughable 'Goodbye… if I don't see you again' proved oracular: Jim and Monica never again came to our house.

Had I never bumped into Ian Bannen, might I have made more strenuous efforts to redeem the friendship? It was definitively ruptured many years later, but that will be another story.

January 1971. Lunch with Judy Scott-Fox at Prunier's. She wants to be my agent. Do I want her? I made the wrong decision in going to 'Ziggy'; California is too far away. I am offered nothing in England. Judy promised that the BBC would 'gladly and immediately' commission anything I liked to propose. I wonder; I have never had much of a welcome in the Corporation.

Judy and I went to the Morandi show at Burlington House. Ignoring the lift, we climbed the back stairs. At each half landing were heroic marbles of figures in various stages of despair or exhaustion. They should have taken the lift.

The Morandis lacked the lustrous singularity I remembered. In Rome, they seemed to have a strange radiance, despite their unoiled, unvarnished dullness. On a London January afternoon, they were merely pallid. J. made appreciative noises in front of the landscapes, which interest me least of M.'s work. The influences of Cézanne, Léger, Braque and – in the landscapes – Derain were tastefully present: a laming literacy. I hinted at my views but – *vive le biz!* – avoided being erudite (*boring!*).

In the car, as we went round Eros, I saw Tom M. standing on the corner of Shaftesbury Avenue, bargaining with a taxi driver who was pointing the wrong way. Tom wore his black corduroy suit and looked sallow as he rallied his youthful charm to his mercenary assistance; the only circumstances, I suspect, under which he can still look young.

12.1.71. No word from Warner's. I lay awake last night waiting for the phone to ring because the later it rang, the more likely it would be good news. It didn't ring. This morning, Gareth tells me that John Calley (Warner's No. 2) did not even bring the script with him on the plane. The London man remains enthusiastic, but the prevailing wind hardly flutters the sails of hope.

The fracture of my little finger is a ludicrous obstacle to decisive action. I shall never be the same again! After a session with Mr Hume, in which he exercised the injury beyond the point which polite conversation could anaesthetise, it is clear that it will never straighten entirely, or close completely. I feel ludicrously vulnerable, since I have only one reliable fist. Beetle asks when I last hit anyone. She fails to recognise how often I should like to. This petty impotence is a blow to my corporal rhetoric. Hume said, 'It's a

serious injury.' I look back, with righteous self-pity, on the golden
age when I was physically unblemished.

In the X-ray department. A man with a bandaged head. He had
been going upstairs in a building when someone dropped half a
gallon of paint on him. His suit was Dalmatian with white paint,
but he bore his indignity with adequate humour, Mr Cooper. Next
to me was a builder's mate who had struck his own finger with a
sledgehammer. A shark-toothed lad of seventeen who already had
a bad hand, he had been pissed and hit an oak door; the oak door
won. He was rueful and stupid, with the sort of crass cheek which
will allow him to go on smoking whatever *they* say. One crosses
him out of one's life, but off he goes, pregnant with ungrateful
trouble for some girl, some doctor, some stranger...

The libel expert. He wore a black overcoat and an air of polished
smugness. His eyes were those of an expensive fish. As we waited
together on Michael Sissons' doorstep, I suggested that we evade
the issue in *Who Were You With Last Night?* by re-siting the vexed
scene in the car. By the time M. arrived, in a taxi, and let us in,
there was little to discuss. The house lacked warmth, and the furniture distinction: many books, often in their American editions. Did
we want tea? We did. Evans took off his coat, revealing a fleshier
self, white shirt, crocodile-belted trousers. At once pompous and
complacent, he asked, nervously abrupt, whether I hadn't had something to do with *Lady at the Wheel* and did I know David Conyers?
Not any more. He now calls himself Adrian, not David. E. had been
at Cath's and came down two years after me, in 1956. I had taken
him for a venerable institution; he must actually be younger than I.

Coming out onto Hammersmith Broadway, I was fenced off from
a circus of rush-hour traffic. No taxi; I started out on foot. At first
I outpaced a bus and reached the reckless conclusion that it would
be quickest to walk to Putney hospital. I was committed to this silly
plan when the buses began to overtake me. I waited at one bus stop
and then walked towards the next, at the wrong moment. Finally,
I did catch a bus, for about a minute. I had to walk the last half mile
anyway, cutting across the cemetery in the darkness. Death seems a
banality now. Four runners, spread out, padded past me, white
breath jolting out of them.

C.M.R. has been so near death, so conclusively written off, that it is almost an embarrassment to find him undeniably alive. Yesterday he stood without help. He talks still of learning Italian, perhaps studying geology. Is he to be encouraged when he says that he doesn't want to play bridge again? The closing of the Hamilton, abruptly on New Year's Eve, seems patly symbolic. The club was losing too much money. The old Colonel, who ran it for so long, with a rosebud in his lapel, was 'heartbroken'. The club used to be the Rothschilds' town house. Now the whole area is scheduled for re-development.

At Mr Hume's house, on the Lexden Road. I went to have the metal hook, which served as a splint, removed from my finger, which he taped to its straight neighbour. Pot-plants in the window overlooking a narrow terrace over the road. I took a history of nine-teenth-century medicine from the glassed shelves. It was an era of primo donnish surgeons, for whom speed and dexterity were the vital arts. Discoveries, or at least theories, came so rapidly that such simple notions as asepsis were ignored. The agonies of antique patients were small compensation for the deformity of my little finger. I can no longer shake it at them.

When Mr Hume saw what I was reading, he said that he could offer me something much more interesting: a book by Frederick Treves entitled *The Elephant Man*. It was, in those days, an unknown text by the man who had saved Edward VII's life by insisting on the new king having an appendectomy *before* his coro-nation. 'Impossible! I must go to the Abbey on the appointed day.' 'In that case, Your Majesty, unless you have the operation, you will go in a hearse.'

Treves' success, and subsequent knighthood, led to the social advancement of the medical profession. Previously, General Practitioners called at the back door, like tradesmen. Hume knew about Freddie Treves because he had been a student at the London Hospital, in the Mile End Road. Treves' grandson is a good actor, who impersonated my old headmaster, Skete Workman, in my *After the War*.

It never occurred to me at the time to take Treves as anything but an English name, pronounced (as it is) to rhyme with Reeves, but Carole Angier's biography of Primo Levi mentions a Sephardic Jewish family called Treves (Tre/ves, presumably in Italian). Might Frederick Treves' nerve, in telling his sovereign what was what, have had a Disraelian dimension of shrewd impertinence?

I was properly excited by Treves' book, which contained other stories of Victorian medical practice so gorily appalling that one could rejoice not to have lived before morphine, and Lister. The story of the Elephant Man was so improbably convincing that I immediately saw a movie in it. In due course, long before David Lynch had seen it, I took it to the BBC. That was the end of that.

15.1.71. Mersea, on the marsh, in fog, on a recce for *How About Us?* with Stan, the production manager, and Gareth. A decoy duck lopsided in a pond, a nice symbol of Mike's masochistic humour. We squelched about in weedy mud, apparently an amiable trio. Tonight I am exhausted, as if from wrestling with unangelic strangers. Without money to make the film, we made practical plans for the shooting sequence, discussed angles with fanciful precision. We are like Germany after Versailles: officers without troops, all our conquests are on the map.

Stan might be a regular CSM: a certain roughness disqualifies him from the society of the officers who depend on him. In his early thirties, slightly bow-legged, lively brown eyes, a zeal for information, he would exercise your horse, but would not ride with you. He has a wife, two children, three dogs, two cats, two ponies and a donkey. He took the opportunity to chat with a local Essex estate agent. He thought nineteen thousand for a farmhouse with five and a half acres quite a bargain.

Steve, the accountant, came with us; in his own car. His separate, specific brief was to scout for deals in accommodation. A gawky, dark-eyed man, he was as much a captive of class status as Stan was exempt from it. Lugubrious even when cheerful, you almost expected him to be wearing bicycle clips as he stepped out of his Lancia.

Gareth always remains conscious of his rank. He believes that he detests class distinctions, perhaps because they mean so much to him. Class is the spiritual acne which his brand of socialism is supposed to cure. He was quite terse with Ronnie Geary (who wants to design the picture) until this afternoon, when I alerted him to the fact that Ronnie had been a naval officer. Gareth was a lieutenant in the Somaliland Defence Force, and keen to establish that he outranked Ronnie. Ronnie maintained that a sub-lieutenant in the navy was on a par with a full lieutenant in the army. Gareth first denied it and then solemnly (well, *quite* solemnly) proposed that they count down from Admiral of the Fleet (equals Field Marshal) until they arrived at the true parity.

Ronnie's standing was bolstered by the news of his commission. He paraded his Wellington boots as if they were Nelson's as we walked below HMS *Ganges*, a shore station where he had taught at the end of his National Service. One waited for the sentry to flinch to attention.

Orwell Place. A possibility for Lalling, if we ever get *How About Us?* made. The house is Georgian, approached down a curving drive between iron fences, with an unhappy prospect of modernised cottages and servants' quarters. Beyond these, an open gateway into a gravel circle in front of the big, reddish building. A cedar higher than the three storeys of the house certifies its authenticity. Ronnie had showed me drawings of the place as it had been when the Latchmeres bought it. A Victorian owner had built a whole asymmetrical wing, as high as the original façade. Two big chimneys climbed the whole way to the roof. The ballroom they serve has two fireplaces in the same wall.

Ronnie had advised the elimination of the whole section, but Giles elected to level it off above the ballroom. The fireplaces are deprived of issue; the room is cold. Giles uses it as a playroom. An unfinished portrait of Janet stands on an easel. G. has a team of builders (paid by the hour, says Ronnie) who renovate the places he has bought at the cheapest rate, after which Giles resells. R. complains about his ruthless lack of conscience, both in the purchase and in the style of the renovations, but he was as impressed as he was sickened. Ronnie claims G.L. as a close friend and only mildly resents the advice G.L. cadges from him and the meagreness of his gratitude.

Giles drove a white Ford Zodiac station wagon, black with mud from the tracks which lead to the properties he has, so to say, knocked down to himself. He wore an Irish sweater, twill trousers. His property is large: ample, sloping lawns, rather shaggy, tilt down to a narrow lake which the local angling club first stocked and now pays him to use. He has the cynical modesty of a man who not only gets others to butter his bread for him, but also insists that they remove the crusts.

The house is furnished with the routine machinery of a country mansion: sofas face each other in front of the fire; the shelves bear leather-bound volumes; corner cupboard charged with a china collection. Everything convincingly aged and unostentatious, as if it were exactly what they wanted. Yet the library and the sitting room lack any marked personality. The oil paintings might have come from a rectory sale. Ronnie asked, as we left, if I had spotted the Constable. It was only a little one.

Janet ('Janny'). She had been washing her blonde hair. She wore a Hamlet ensemble: black trousers, flare-sleeved white shirt. Her powdered, puffy face was neither young nor old. They have five children, the oldest seventeen. Still in her mid-thirties, Janet must have had her first child, or at least her husband, while she was still at school. She was hospitable but preoccupied, in a dispassionate way, by a road accident in which a friend had driven her Mini into a telegraph pole. The woman's children were with her, as was the daughter of another friend, who was following in her own car and saw her child flung into the road. 'Nobody knows what happened.' The woman who was driving broke both her ankles and her pelvis. She has had buzzing in her ears and has probably impacted a couple of vertebrae. She has been told to keep her head absolutely still for four days. If she fails, they will put her in a collar. Her pelvis must be kept immobilised too, but she is not in an 'accident bed'. The whole process sounded very British: not so much stiff upper lip as stiff upper half.

Janet has bought a Phillips tape recorder and some cassettes to cheer the victim. Mozart accompanied our coffee and ginger nuts. There was no ready affection between our hosts, but a sort of complicity, as if their passion had cooled into a common propensity to outwit others. They preserved the forms of a proper rural life, but converted them to personal profit. Janet has money from her family. She has lived a passionate youthful adventure, but – cocooned in a long marriage which still leaves her young – she now seems more arrested than stimulated by it.

Unperturbed by the proximity of their tenants, who render them cash, not services, they have had this ancestral-style place only for four years. They view the prospect of selling it without dismay. The lake may be turned into a reservoir, which would bring the water almost to the bottom of the garden. Giles has alternative plans, for a marina, which would lead to the place becoming a hotel. The mess in the house is less that of people who have made themselves at home than of those who wonder if it is worthwhile unpacking since they could be moving any minute.

The swimming pool has neither filtration nor heating. It was built by Giles's chaps and is streaked with new beige cement where cracks have been plugged. It empties, through the plug in the bottom, in fifty minutes and can be refilled in 'about three days'. Behind a Victorian gothic red brick arch, the bedraggled rose garden is garrisoned with plastic statues, black boys and diminutive redskins ('Canadian') sufficiently valuable to have lost one of their number to a rustler: he carted it away in his own wheelbarrow. It was discovered a year later in an Essex garden. The trade was so lucrative that the thief had taken it up full-time.

Marble busts leaned either side of the front door, in approximation to elegance which might be consummated or aborted, according to circumstance. While we were having coffee, the butcher arrived, and expected cash. There was a play at panic, when neither Giles nor Janet had any. Ronnie was driven to volunteer 'some of the folding stuff', but G.L. said to give a cheque ('Never mind whose') and the plebeian creditor was staved off. This charade convinced Gareth of the Latchmeres' pedigree, but to equate lack of the ready with aristocracy seemed too hastily obsequious. G.L. is keen to make a good deal for the use of his premises, while 'Janny' has a kind of soiled innocence which suggests that he might well do the same for her, and that she, wearily, might go along with it, if the price was right. Giles had about him a shrivelled open air manner; he might have been a regular officer with youthful mannerisms and a martial vocabulary, robust camouflage for a spindly character. He drove off at rallying speed along the greasy lanes. He wastes no time in casual geniality; his smiles are rationed like the smokes of someone who is trying to give it up. If he could bring himself to sincerity, he would be as hard as nails.

He showed us a trio of dilapidated cottages, and then a railway-crossing-keeper's cottage on a long uprooted line. The cottage was riddled with tiny rooms, its garden fenced with sleepers. With its romantic, obsolete overtones, it was suitable for Mike and Anna's place, but also useless: the size of the rooms would hamper shooting. Yet the grassed railway line, between wet hedgerows, had a sad charm.

We drove back towards the estuary and stopped at a pub for steaks. On the way, we passed a tall chimney, made of pre-cast concrete hoops, with a ladder up the side. Ronnie dreads heights and wondered who would be willing to climb such a thing. Gareth said he would, if the wind was not too high. After National Service, he burned his formal uniform, he told us, but not the gear he wore in the desert. The SDF was the only force in the British army with native troops supplying all the other ranks. He had a guide who was able to tell, by the traces in the desert, who had been at a given spot, when they had fought, who had been victorious and by what score. His name was, no doubt, Gunga Din.

Ronnie is no longer a naval officer. He failed to attend any of the Reserve's training activities for two and a half years and was discharged for failing to observe one of the duties of a naval officer: 'seek promotion'.

A Severed Head, directed by Dick Clement, is well reviewed this morning. John Russell Taylor admired it so much that he neglected to attach my name to it. Less scrupulous critics gave me some credit. Could it still be as dreadful as I remembered from seeing the rough cut? Last night we took my mother. There was a longish queue at the Curzon. The film was quite funny and, except for Lee Remick and Dickie Attenborough, well-performed. After Sunday's notices, Beetle said, 'You know who'll phone now? Jack Lambert.' I was in Ipswich on Wednesday afternoon, seeing *Patton*, when guess-who called. Full of craven contempt, I longed to draw attention to the coincidence; in fact I welcomed the chance to appear in the literary pages, which I had not done since Auberon Waugh's predictable malice in *The Spectator*.★

12.2.71. At Columbia. A bearded, greying Sean Connery came along the corridor. He greeted Gareth with the shifty modesty a well-known face shows towards those who know it privately. His 'natural' look was one of weary slyness; he invited you to admire the disillusion that sits in his shot-coloured eyes. A star retains his humanity by exercising his conscience in a prison with golden bars, in which he is forbidden its use.

Van Eyssen's office. The fawn leather furniture carries a weight of used cigar smoke and seems exercised beyond its years by a relay of wriggling, explanatory behinds. A crack runs along the plasterboard ceiling, between glamorous John's own inset illumination – worked by a dimmer from the door – and the commonplace fittings that

---

★   Years earlier, I reviewed one of Waugh's jejune novels dismissively. When *Like Men Betrayed* was offered to his hatchet, he chopped it. We never met, but I wrote occasionally for *The Literary Review*.

enlighten his visitors. John has new glasses; they add less to his dignity than to the spruce opportunism which, for all his gadgets and soft-spoken command, he can no more shake off than the saint his halo. Like many executives, he parades his personal allegiance kit: photographs of the wife and child are displayed no less eagerly than his willingness to betray them.

We stayed almost two hours, during which time he gave us his clear attention, except for a call from Dino di Laurentis. 'I adore Dino, but if you give him your little finger...' 'He takes your elbow,' Gareth said. 'He takes your whole *body*,' John van E. said. He made that prospect sound more agreeable than perhaps he intended.

Would one spend any time cajoling such a man into admiration if he lacked power? Self-contempt rises in proportion to the degree of charm and effort you put into deserving the good opinion of someone who does not deserve your own. The real question is, will *What About Us?* make money? Its 'distinction' is taken for granted (i.e. discounted). John compared me with Eric Rohmer, whom he has just backed to make his 'international breakthrough'. John goes to New York today to consult Stanley Schneider, and will let us know by the end of the week. Our chances will probably depend on 'casting up' the picture: Warren or Elliot Gould would swing things. John is 'intrigued' by Caroline Seymour; the grand-nephew of J-C Smuts reacted keenly to Gareth's news that she is the grand-daughter of Moura Budburg. Will that get the picture made? It might. There's no business like it, is there?

On the train to Colchester. I was reading Hardy when a fair young man chucked a chess set on the table between us. After I had glanced up coldly at his arriving rattle, we began to talk, first about Hardy and then about philosophy ('I am a philosopher,' he said) and then we began to play chess. He went to Southampton University, where the professor was MacIver. He announced himself a don *manqué* whose career ended when he flattened (I thought at first that he said 'flattered') one of his teachers, a Roman Catholic called Willis, who had been hired 'by mistake'. He had then 'sold out' and gone into business with a big paper company; he had been doing their 'European side' for five years, spoke French, German, and Swedish. He was now leaving Nayland to go back to his native Yorkshire to start an operation in the North. He has a Norwegian wife; no children, but they are thinking of it 'before the menopause'. 'Whose?' I said.

We played chess for the last twenty minutes of the journey. He was surprised by my orthodox defence. He is also keen on bridge, tennis and squash. Should I regret the departure of someone who shares so many of my interests? He is of another race. Deadly thought, to dismiss people less through pride rather than for want of enthusiasm.

Michael Sissons seems pleased with the new version of *Who Were You With Last Night?*. Through the (enforced) elimination of realistic reference, I have made it both truer and more real. The film of *Ten Rillington Place* reveals the limitations of documentary. By sticking to Ludovic Kennedy's 'facts', Clive Exton debars himself from inhabiting the characters: he cannot share their motives, since their actions are already determined. No illuminating detail arises from imaginative rehearsal. Documentary 'validity' is the endemic falseness in English cinema. The point of such films becomes abstract; instead of a drama, we get the case against capital punishment: illustration and nothing else. I say all this without having seen the picture, but Dickie Attenborough's interview suggests that I am right; he agreed to play Christie only after he had heard that the film would adhere to the book. He would have had nothing to do with 'sensationalism'; it might involve imagination. The murder-obsessed English like their cannibal fare served on a lace doily.

Gareth and I had a meeting with Ned Tanen – a Universal producer who is said to have Authority – at the old MCA offices, 139, Piccadilly, the place where, as Leslie would say, It All Began. MCA fell, in full (gold) leaf, under the anti-trust axe, but the same gilt number marks the spot. A servile commissionaire sat at a wide, deep table as if to symbolise that even the least of Universal's offices is better furnished than the greatest of its rivals. We waited on a long sofa. The antique cabinet on the right-hand wall was the same under which Leslie and I waited to see Jock Jacobsen and Bob Fenn. The latter told us, in a crushing interview, that we were 'no longer news'. He proved his own access to the powerful by making a direct call to Danny Angel. 'Hullo, Danny, how are you?' He thus dared us to say that it was his lack of influence that led us to be unemployed.

Ned Tanen was a youngish, thickset man, dark, with a curved pruning blade of a nose, abrupt but decisive. White-socked feet on the desk (Dick Zanuck always kept his small shoes on) proved him to be short. N.T. was attended by his curate, a man called Brolly, who sat tightly furled between Gareth and me. Gareth remembered him from the old MCA days; he still wore the uniform – dark suit, white shirt, black tie, black shoes – on which Lew Wasserman insisted when he set up the Agency. He also stipulated cigarette case and lighter; no boxes, no matches. Brolly offered the two-handed handshake as well. He had greying hair, pale flesh, an air of plenary indulgence. He spoke as softly as a despot's chamberlain, but had read the script with care and intelligence. He seemed an ally, but an ally without cash or ships: if you win, he was always on your side; if you fail, there is no evidence that he ever committed himself to your cause.

Tanen had been noncommittal to G. on the phone, but now seemed eager and accessible. We made the bullshit speech about not intending any bullshit and promised that Art would not interfere with commerce. We discussed casting and proclaimed our willing-ness to have an American for Mike. Elliott Gould did not excite Tanen; he had made five pictures in the last year.

One of T.'s associates has insistently proclaimed himself a member of my 'fan club' on the coast; he even called me once from California to renew his subscription. I took his involvement to be a stroke of luck, but Gareth told me, almost irritably, that he did nothing but organise orgies.*

The man on trial for his life. He has the feeling that he has put on the show and that everyone is there more to amuse than to accuse him. The period of the trial is divorced from its causes, or its conse-quences. The desire to shine disposes the prisoner to be more argumentative than aggressive or – which would make for the worst show of all – defensive and frightened. Oscar Wilde is the exem-plary case of the defendant as performer; and we know what that unfortunate movement led to. Wisdom, as opposed to wit, would have advised a quite different line, but it would have entailed renouncing the opportunity to be a star.

Why do people tell the truth? Again and again they condemn themselves with needless garrulity. They prefer to take their one chance to be the centre of attention rather than to save their necks in silence. A man on trial for his life often finds himself free for the first time when he stands in the dock. He will never again be shown

* Tanen's wife later deserted him for the man who made her husband's shirts.

to better advantage, never be invited more fully to explain himself, and never be so important. The court and the public are taught to 'speak his language'. The victim remains a voiceless object; life trumps history.

An acquitted man leaves the court, they say, 'without a stain on his character'. He also leaves it somehow ignominiously, disappointed, wilted, unfulfilled; he has appeared in the wrong dream and he has convoked images he must now disown. His nakedness is denied a climax. He returns to his family diminished, a civilian exempted from battle.

Whereas an innocent man is 'dismissed from the case', the convicted criminal is entitled to make a final speech; this curtain call affords him a chance for gracious remorse or furious eloquence. If he stays in character, he earns better notices than if bitterness or cowardice corrodes his statement. If he becomes 'emotional', the court will listen without pity or solemnity, but should he 'control himself', and put a telling gloss on the course of the trial, the judge may respond with courtesy that is almost complimentary, even if the charge demands severity. To interrupt, to denounce drama as farce, to challenge the good faith or competence of the court, abuse the witnesses, yawn at the judge – *bref*, to dissent from the human community altogether – requires the self-destructiveness of a fool, or of a saint.

We learn to defer to those whose opinions, if not crucial to our fortunes, would neither entertain nor detain us for a moment.

We have no telephone at Lagardelle. We go down to the Hôtel Scholly in Siorac to hear from London. A call from Gareth informed me that things are worse *chez* Columbia; they can do nothing till July: *dinero*. Sad? I went back to my cooling *chocolat* and stale Kougloff elated at the prospect of an uninterrupted stay down here.

Nouveau Roman. In the little bar of the hotel, barely six metres by six, where every corner was in use, every quarter of the walls filled, and only the beige lino in front of the varnished bar was free, she waited while the shower scourged the square which had been sunny on her arrival. There were four tables with pink, grey and green cloths inscribed with leafy white patterns. One was wedged against the ice-cream cooler under shelves which held the scoops (in a small champagne bucket) and a blue tin of wafers. On the second shelf were upturned sundae dishes and a glass cylinder of cornets on a long metal pedestal. The lowest cornets protruded, three of them, like udders.

Next to the cylinder was a list of the specialities of the hotel, yellow with slanting black letters highlighted in white: *foie gras truffé; pâté de foie gras; omelette aux truffes; poulet aux cèpes; confit d'oie; omelette flambée; crêpes du patron; omelette Norvégienne*. Underneath a list of summer ice cream flavours; next to it, a citation from the *Union Touristique du Périgord*. And in the corner, the telephone cabinet: frosted glass panels, kipper-brown wooden frame. On top were candlesticks, an old oil lamp and many wooden bowls of a modern, vulgar design. More of them lined the lintel shelf along the wall until they met the coppers over the kitchen door, coppers which yielded to brass candlesticks and a little candle-holder with a brass handle; these then gave way to bottles as the shelf passed the line of the wooden-railed bar.

Bottles were thicker over the glassed cupboard containing private keys and were then reinforced to form fours with more bottles stationed behind the bar proper. Upturned Johnny Walker, cognac, Black and White, were to the left of the double-doored wooden fridge with its chrome handles and hinges, on top of which were more bottles: port, cassis, Fernet-Branca, Kirsch, Sirop de Citron, in front of champagne buckets inside champagne buckets, a square, squat cylinder of gas, straws and half a bottle of Bergerac *blanc*. In the recess above the fridge was another shelf with a dirty red check border. This held a parade of long-standing minerals and fruit juices. In the middle, a Black and White ashtray with the usual pair of perky Scotties on it and above them a wooden-faced clock, in the rustic style, with bark edging and gilt Roman numerals. At one corner of the recess was a clog, with a moneybox slot in it, and at the other a painted clog with room for a midget's foot. The moneybox carried a windmill, the other a church among trees. To the right of the fridge, more upturned bottles: Ricard, Pernod, Pernod, Berger, an empty 'shoe' and then Captain's Rum. Behind them, upright and less recklessly exposed, more bottles, above them shelves of glasses, one devoted to decanters, three Ricard jugs of brown pottery and two of the same below, with a variety of glasses.

At the left end of the bar was the *caisse*, armed with a spike for bills and a little operations table where the bill for each guest could be inspected, according to the table he occupied. In the corner was a telephone exchange which buzzed fiercely for an incoming call and rang shrilly when anyone put down the phone in the little cabin with its white wall-phone, sloping lectern, breathless privacy. To the right of the bar, steps went up to the second dining room, unused in winter, with yellow shutters closed across its long windows. The wall opposite the kitchen contained the fireplace, surmounted by a mirror in an oak frame with full-length pillars; old coach-lamps on either side promised alternative forms of lighting to the fluorescent fittings, one long above the bar, two shorter nearer the door, which gave a white formality to the evening. Between a coach-lamp and the door to the second dining room was a board giving the prices of the drinks; below that, a cogged lever for extracting corks. On the mantelpiece were two pairs of salt and pepper, the top of a cona in a metal frame, two holders in a 'Cona-Bar', one occupied by a glass pot, and a spare mustard. The lintel shelf on this wall had several copper vessels, some earthenware beer jugs, dolls in celluloid prisons, one brass and one pewter candlestick and a handsome pot with a green and yellow glaze.

A wooden display cabinet with glass windows offered to anyone on tiptoe (it was hung directly under the lintel shelf) the products of the region, including not only a pleasant local white wine, some tins of *pâté* in amber wrappings, but also some bleakly blanched geese, under evident sentence, and a branch-antlered deer whose head rose above shelf level. Few parts of the walls were free of burdens; there were maps of France and of the district and another of the valley of the Dordogne on the back of the cash desk. *Man Spricht Deutsch* was announced above a short timetable of arrivals and departures of trains. *Les cigarettes sont payables de suite.*

The fourth wall was almost all curtained glass doors, but a black metal postcard rack contained folkloric cards. A chef's white jacket hung on a hook between it and the *cabine téléphonique*. The other small section of wall next to the door warned minors not to drink and repeated the *tarif des consommations*. Elsewhere were prints of local life, boys with dogs, a truffling sow, a crone preparing a meal (fish); above, a little house '*au bon coin*'. A barometer by the door: *Variable*.

To the left of the hotel, below the terrace with its rustic railing, and its *glycine* trained along the line of the gutter, a narrow road descended towards a tunnel under the railway. Above, was a stone embankment, level with the expanse of the little square. It carried a confident wooden chef, *en silhouette*, who was holding an announcement '*Ici On Mange Bien*'. In summer, there would be tables and wooden chairs and a row of plants, each with its little tube for watering. Cars parked on the far side, where a privet hedge divided the tarmac from the railway line. A white P on a blue ground carried small print to say that *Poids Lourds* were forbidden. He was not going to come, was he?

In the kitchen, first thing in the morning, the *sous-chef* scrubs down the wooden surfaces with a brush and a bar of carbolic soap. In the afternoon, they make preparations for the next day. Today (19.2.71) they were cleaning a fat *poulet* with which Sunday's *bouchées à la reine* will be packed. A band of round, orange, unlaid eggs were extruded and put on the edge of the centre table.

I called Putney to make sure that Paul and Sarah were all right, and to hear how C.M.R. was. My mother told me how tired she was. Dad is going daily to the Woolfson for physiotherapy. 'He hates it.' Mentally, he is still 'very childish'. I suppose that this means that he is crying, as he did before I left, at any emotional crux. Irene had stood by his bedside at Chertsey and said, 'I'd sooner he just stayed like this' (than die). Now the miracle of his recovery is not good enough, though the doctors are amazed by it. She is exhausted by his helplessness, and embarrassed by him in front of strangers.

22.2.71. Over a poor line, the message from Gareth that Columbia had reluctantly and – if I heard right – 'with much love' decided not to do *How About Us?*. It is no shock, scarcely even a disappointment. What do I really want? It is nice to be featured in *The Sunday Times* literary pages, but who reads them with any attention? I am conscious of six years (at least) devoted to the making of money, and movies, and of the poverty of my achievement. I have all the houses we can use, and a full stomach. Excellence remains the only reputable target and I am more likely to hit it with a novel than with a film. Film is abjectly subject to compromise when, as now, the front office is in a panic. (David Deutsch said to me, 'You are a luxury item'.)

We are at the end of an age of cinema which may not have yielded golden fruits but which did allow a variety of directors and writers to produce a range of work. The new stringency tightens its strings. Full-frontal vulgarity is now with us, and will grow more grossly assertive. Movie companies will become more demanding and less indulgent. The new Philistines will call God whatever strikes box office fire, and will bend the knee to nothing else. This is perhaps the end of theatrical cinema; the cassette will be enormously successful, and pervasive.

Madame Scholly: '*Quand j'étais jeune, j'avais deux passions: le cinéma et le patinage artistique*'. She named the stars, starting with Jeanette Macdonald (above all, she liked operetta); then Joan Crawford, Olivia de 'aviland, Jean *Artur*, Barbara Stanwyck (with an emphatic 'w'). The only man she mentioned was Nelson Eddy. Had anyone ever made a film in Siorac? In 1943; some actors from the *Comédie Française*. I had never heard of them; they had, she said, all been *balayés* from the *Union d'Artistes*. She cannot forget what the '*Fridolins*' did; she reports gloatingly that her seven-year-old grandson came home from school to tell her that a film about '*les Boches*' was going to be on the *télé*.

Judd: 'I had to choose between him and Bob Bolt. I chose Bob Bolt. Does that make me his enemy? Does that have to mean I'm his enemy?' Judd's money was made out of soda fountains. 'But you don't make actresses running soda-fountains. At least I never did. I love England. I love it. If it had Californian weather, it'd run forever' (or, 'I'd put money into it'). 'Know what bad times are in the movies? Because I'll tell you: when you can't talk a hypocrite into backing art any more.'

The policeman's story. They came when the alarm went on a stormy night; the dining room doors blew open. The Dedham man, David, was in uniform, his blue drenched black by the torrents he had motorcycled through. The plainclothed CID man, Frank, had come by car from Colchester. D. was young, big, bearded; he deferred (without deference) to Frank, an able, slightly troubled man. Four a.m., they accepted apologetic whisky and sat with me (in my Mexico City poncho) at the kitchen table.

The ethics of interrogation troubled Frank. He said that he would drop in a tape which he had done on which, in a court case, he had imitated fourteen different accents. He had also used his mimicry on the telephone, but was wary of overdoing it. He accepted the privileges of the correctly spoken, whom he mimicked smartly (especially the way they said 'back'). Richard Burton had played cricket with him, at Heathrow, and encouraged his dramatic ambitions; seriously? Who can say?

Frank's skill as an interrogator. He notices things; the shape of a man's speech affects his thought; get accurate hold of the form and you are on your way to the content. The 'sympathy' between cop and robber is a kind of symmetry. You get the impression that the policeman catches a man, or finds proof of his guilt, most frequently after he has decided on the criminal. He can find out only what he 'knows' already. Scientists too work back from a solution to its problem.

The routine of making the last witness the first suspect suggests the need for an immediate focus, the theory of a solution. Frank told of a man brought in after a number of children had been assaulted in the Castle Park. Frank was convinced that this was the man. Frank admitted that he had 'used every means' he knew, including a threat to beat him all round the room. He said that he would tell the man's wife and children (?), ruin his reputation, 'ekcetera'. The man denied everything. He would have to be released; there was no evidence. Finally, Frank put his head down on the table, on his hands, and began to sob. He says he was faking. The man watched him for a time and then he came and put his arm around him and said gently, 'It's all right, it's all right; I'll tell you all about it.'

Frank asked if I thought he acted wrongly. He insisted that it was a ruse, that he had not been genuine, but he was in front of another policeman (and of himself, on duty). What gave him the idea of affecting tears? Was he distressed by the thought of the victims, and of the victims-to-be? Unlikely. By failure? Possibly. Or by frustration, both ambitious and emotional – a kind of childish disappointment which appealed, with inadvertent aptitude, to the dammed emotions of the guilty man? The capping irony: this tender complicity was converted abruptly into an indictment. This echoes the moment when the desire of the man for the child, an enveloping craving, is transformed to violence by the victim's terror and incomprehension.

What is the relationship between brutality and fondness, between attention and victimisation? By appearing impotent and *in need*, Frank unmasked the criminal as a child *like himself*. A man who had been able to harden himself in the face of a policeman – that father-figure who *deserved* to be deceived – was driven to comfort someone who appeared in the same condition as himself, an overgrown child. Frank wondered if he had been wrong to use such tactics. As a protector of kids, one could congratulate him on his cunning; but he could not excuse himself. He sometimes feared that he was 'becoming schizophrenic'.

A Member of the Public. A detective, determined to find the man who was molesting children, begins to hang around a playground and to impersonate a sex criminal, in order to 'get into his skin'. He succeeds to such good effect that he doubles for the man he is hunting. He finds himself incapable of sex with his wife or of rapport with his children: he cannot bathe them or put them to bed. His alienness makes them so foreign to him that he sees them (and they him?) as a stranger. Any wish for affection becomes a kind of assault; he feels he has to defend himself. Their offered embraces seem almost obscene, a provocation. Now the clinching interview would have electric possibilities. The final breakdown into confession slips the guilt, like manacles, onto the prisoner who would only incidentally, *co*-incidentally, be the actual child-molester. The policeman is *relieved of the crime*; like MacHeath, he is at one moment headed for the gallows, at the next ennobled (cf. benighted and be knighted).

Another 'trick' Frank told me. A man came running into the police station to say that his mate, a milkman, had been banged on the head and had a hundred and fifty quid, his total takings, stolen from him. It was five in the morning. Frank hurried to the house and found the milkman holding his head. They brought him to the station and gave him a cup of tea and asked him about the incident. It seemed fishy, but the suggestion of a put-up job might be wrong, and lead to serious trouble. Frank talked generally about how difficult things were, how hard to cope with rising prices, and so on. He said that a policeman was only an ordinary bloke and they all had their problems.

He also remarked how strange it was that there had been two dozen milk bottles in the area by the front door and none had been knocked over in the struggle. The man cocked an eyebrow at that; but said nothing. Then there was the question of which way the assailant had run off. Frank had noticed that the pavement was glistening with rain, on which any foot made a distinct mark, yet there was no sign of the stranger's print. Was it perhaps *now* that Frank began to lament how short of money he was, and how little policemen were paid? Suddenly the man put his head down in his hands; it was all over. Where was the money? In the man's car; they went and found it. He was charged with theft and dismissed; he comes up at the next sessions.

Frank had again acted in an ambivalent drama. The thief saw himself as a victim (of assault) and believed that he could play the victim's part, but Frank 'criticised' his performance crushingly. As a result, the thief lost faith in his talent; thrown back on his own inadequacy, he gave up the role of the innocent. His make-up had not sufficiently disguised him. He renounced acting and accepted that he was a failure.

How singular that both Frank's cases ended with a man with his head in his hands: once the accused; once the accuser! He told me that, if I were a suspect, he would ask very direct questions. I was not the sort of person on whom an oblique approach would work; I would see through cunning questions where I might not be able to counter straightforward ones.

As for him, I put him down as a man who needed the licence of authority to vent his inventive aggressions on others. The entertainer and the policeman have much in common (no wonder there are so many convincing cops on TV); they need excuses not to be themselves, and the immunity of paid performance.

Tunis; 2.71. The Arab smile: a slight narrowing of the eyes from the bottom upwards, a look almost Etruscan in its unkindled warmth, a greeting apparently focused on the single recipient, who is alone in the gaze of the smiler.

Colchester 3, Leeds United 2.

Scipio Nasica argued for tolerating the continued existence of Carthage, but the unargued reiterations of Cato finally bored the Senate into ruthless measures. Darlington suggests that the elimination of Punic competition resulted in the facile enrichment of Rome by the mere force of arms. This led to the (moral) ruin of a republic which had been held together by the industry of its citizens; they were now companions only in greed. Darlington makes this a grandiose example of the benign effect of competition and pluralism.

Does the economic dominance of 'the West' bear comparison with Roman acquisitiveness? The lead which western technology enjoys over the barbarians supplies a kind of force, and arms a vanity, not dissimilar to that which enabled Rome to hold down its empire, by trumping any conceivable 'alternative'.

Arthur Miller said of the character in *A View from the Bridge* that he 'allowed himself to be fully known'. Thomas Hardy's call on our respect (no synonym for admiration) depends on a similar willingness. Henry James's friendly contempt for Hardy (he went so far as to call him 'good') suggests an aversion from self-revelation. H.J. preferred artfully fabricated personality. His idea of The Novel was at war with that of Hardy, who accepted – relied on – the impurity of literary creations and for whom life was not to be reformed by aesthetics. Hardy never traded the gaucheness of his sentiments, and resentments, for the manners of a Jamesian cosmopolite. He was the man who would *not* come to dinner.

D.H.L. hurried to London and advertised the primacy of the blood. He wrote loud copy for a philosophy which had no roots. Hardy maintained his residential provincialism. Avoiding Lawrence's vagrant modernity, Hardy remained almost Wesleyan in his sermon-ising vocabulary and Latinate decorum. When he shook his fist at the Almighty, his heresy was faithful to the cadences of *Hymns Ancient and Modern*. He never flapped the cloak of genius in a whirl-wind of his own making.

Since D.H.L. could not get far in England, he went too far, else-where. *Lady Chatterley's Lover* was a home thought from abroad; *Tristia* in the form of a slap in the face. Hardy too resented dispar-agement by London, but where Lawrence chose peripatetic prophecy, Hardy stayed at home and moped. Lawrence despaired of England; Hardy of himself. D.H.L.'s poems are self-assertive, self-aggrandizing, frantically free. Hardy's own to bondage. An Anglo-Saxon Zarathustra, Lawrence ran for Messiah. Only very late, and in private, did he confess disillusionment with all that Nietzschean stuff, which is more than Nietzsche did, unless embracing that cab-horse was a confession.

Like Albert Speer, D.H.L. left penitence too late; his rant was already too catchy for apology to neutralise it. Mortality manifest in his ailing lungs, Lawrence sublimated the death-wish into violent passion for life. Like the valetudinarian Nietzsche, he made a virtue of the strength that was denied him.

Hardy's socially bruised sensibility chewed off more than he could bite. He can observe, and envy, virility (in Sergeant Troy); but he is too honest to impersonate it with conviction. Lawrence, Hemingway, Mailer are no more genuinely manly, but artful in seeming to be. Hardy is enough of a man to play the female part. Virility in Hardy's characters (Troy, Fess Derrimer) is seen from the point of view of the truncheoned *victim*. He cannot *quite* bring himself to breach the established decorum of the Victorian world. It beats him, as it beat Jude, into retreat.

When Lawrence declared that Sergeant Troy 'understands' Bathsheba, he implied that she does not understand herself, or her tragedy. Bathsheba's emancipation is briefly social, never sexual. In the end, she settles with, and for, Gabriel Oak, as Hardy did with his second, unloved, wife.

D.H.L. claims that Hardy's characters are not much bothered about money. In fact, they are obsessed, and controlled, by it. As long as marriage was central, as it is in Hardy, how could he say goodbye to social proprieties? Since then, things *have* changed. The decline began with the po-faced rehabilitation of *Lady Chatterley's Lover*. What had been written to shock and appal was declared, perjuriously, to be a great English sermon. D.H.L. was transformed by *bien pensant* humbug into Jeremy Taylor.

The dismantling of Lawrence proceeded with the filmifying of *Women in Love*. Larry Kramer, the screenwriter, was naïve enough to think that to jettison the verbosity (i.e. the poetry) did nothing to damage the 'story'. The poor man was so proud of his work that he canvassed Frank Leavis for endorsement.

The post-traumatic response to Fascism has been to reject its ethics and digest its aesthetics. The rhetoric of gesture and the art of display create a 'morality' of narcissism. Its trick is to promise – as Hitler did the Germans – what cannot be supplied, *except in the form of desires* (hence the circulation of *Playboy*, pornography as truth). Our 'culture' substitutes the demand for liberty for liberty itself; it replaces happiness with the *right* to happiness, discrimination – in the accurate sense – with tolerance, in the sense of indifference. This playboy Fascism takes its cue from Speer, whose pillars of light were thrillingly dramatic, but were not pillars, and supported only dreams. They hid the emptiness they filled; showbiz has the same office.

Cambridge in 1950. The newcomer was confronted with a pigeon-hole crammed with societies soliciting his custom. So eager was this canvass that no future seemed unavailable. He might choose to be Arab (what *are* 'Majlis'?) or Christian, socialist or canoeist; he might prefer Scottish dancing to golf, or put Conservatism above Mumming; should he care for Judo, he could tumble to at once; if he wanted to row, an oar was waiting for him; nothing for the mind or for the spirit would be denied him. It was as if his whole past were now irrelevant; only future desires and ambitions were of consequence. What a release from the pinched preoccupations of childhood! What a hope!

Firsts. On a visit to the G.-L.s' country house, M. notices a small painting the proceeds of which could enable him to 'do what he wants' for the rest of his life. D. encourages him to steal it, but he daren't. Cf. Tattingstone and Lady R. 'The Catholic family.' The house is reached by way of a branch line, later derelict.

Basil Brain, aka A.J.A. What was once a passion had become a profession. He was now a better philosopher, in the sense that he was seldom demonstrably wrong, but he was much less interesting, since he scarcely ever affected to be right. Loaded with honours, and popular fame, he no longer had the urge to change an audience more comfortable when applauding than when listening to him. His first wife had been a plain Jewish refugee, who worshipped intelligence; his second was a glib American screenwriter who liked only the Sheffield steeliness of his prose. Elegant, and acid, she was against the War in Vietnam, but has accepted Basil's increasing Toryism. She is drawn to the smart company, to which he affords *entrée*, and which her politics deplore. Basil finds her as attractive as her ideas are shallow; that is (part of) what attracts him.

Delenda est Carthago. Are you *sure*? The modest law of the jungle: wiser to submit than to fight to the death. Murder is a strictly human crime, unappetising to the most savage, if sated, carnivore. The conservation of enemies is a prudent economy; it keeps reflexes in order. Those who fear nothing become sluggish.

Rather than surrender to Caesar's detestable *clementia*, the pious, and priggish, descendant of the great Cato committed suicide in the African province which his ancestor had insisted that Rome annex. The legendary Brutus, who secured the eviction of the Tarquins, had a descendant – Shakespeare's noblest of them all – who exacted 48 per cent annual, compound interest from the Cypriots whom he was sent to govern, *en passant*, after the assassination of the scourge of Rome, who had acquired Gaul because he needed to pay off his overdraft.

The end of Ideology seems a happy destination. Does it also mean the end of checks beyond those of arms, the abolition of limits? Will it also lead (betcha!) to the end of dialogue as a sublime battleground, and so procure the Armageddon which the advent of an 'irreligious' age is said to render less likely? When doctrine is digested into cant, expect denunciation and anathema. With the dissolution of formal confrontation, the two sides will be driven either to open force or, one of them, to surrender.

Uninhibited by some universalising ideology, however spurious, why should men not go to the limit and destroy what they lack the mission to convert? A world without Christianity or Marxism is as much without hope as it is without illusions.

Another Woman. The unconscious, half-naked girl in the emergency unit – the priest and the doctor by the (defunct) coffee machine – the ex-philosopher who comes to visit the dying man (a dog called Fido?) – conversation about life after death – the giggling nurses and the unconscious patient (hairy legs) – the dance in the hall near the emergency unit on the night he is admitted – is he too in a DJ? – the circulating couples waltzing behind the silencing plate glass, ONE-two-three, ONE-two-three, ONE-two-three – the mentally defective patient with the harmonica bracketed to his wheelchair – the inquest (?) – did the old friend, the ex-philo., have an affair with the wife?

One day, before *Two for the Road*, I was in S.D.'s flat (we were listening to Nichols and May) when John Kohn, an overweight, graceless producer in his early forties, burst in as if urgently obliged to tell us this joke. 'This director – fag, right? – got married and went on honeymoon with his bride. When they got back home, he made her stay in bed while he brought her a breakfast tray, flowers on it, the newspaper, everything he could think of. She smiled at him and said, "Oh whatever-his-name-was, no one could be nicer to me than you are. If only you could fuck."' The often-told story was that Kohn was impotent.

Stanley is a child of the 1930s. He grew up in North Carolina with a mother whom, for years, he did not acknowledge and a father who is never mentioned. He escaped at the age of sixteen and went to NYC, where he became a dancer. Like my father, he found in dancing an art which did not require you to be an artist. It demanded energy; it supplied company. The snobbery of which he later accused Adelle, and of which earlier friends acquit him, influenced S.D.'s sexual more than his social ambitions. He acquired women as evidence of what he could afford: they were his costume jewellery. He admires those who have previously belonged to others, if the provenance is impressive. When Sinatra heard that Adelle was to marry Stanley, he sent her a telegram: NOT HIM. He could hardly have made S. happier.

S.D. now advocates films that are 'personal'. Ashamed, maybe, by falling down on *Staircase*, and influenced by Lindsay Anderson, who spent some weeks with him and his new lady at Cap Ferrat after the Cannes Festival where S.D. was a judge influential in securing the Grand Prix for *If*,★ he sat down and wrote an original screenplay. Would I come round and read it?

Stanley's new house is in Montpelier Square and boasts a lift. It has been revamped for his new woman. David Hicks made a classy drawing room out of Hyde Park Gardens; some more modern spirit has made Montpelier Square into a showroom for primary-coloured plastics. Money has been spent, but not on anything of value. The Cycladic figure in the 'bar', where I sat down to his script, is a reproduction from the BM.

Stanley's story is 'autobiographical', but it lacks a credible central figure: selves too require invention. He imagines himself a lawyer who suddenly cries 'The bottom has fallen out' and flies off to Denmark where, after a dive to the bottom of the barrel, he discovers a new woman and self-sufficiency. The central emptiness betokened the sickness of those who have nothing left to bring up.

Gwenda David's Viking evening party in Hampstead. Kingsley Amis and Gavin Lyall were engaged in a protracted discussion about guns. Lyall said that Amis had confused repeater and automatic, assuming them to be the same thing under different names. In fact a repeater meant only a magazine rifle, anything which did not require reloading between shots. An automatic fired again and again as long as you kept the trigger pressed. Amis huffed and snorted like a revenant Evelyn Waugh and finally cried out, 'Good heavens, I've *fired* the things,' and went into a clicking and banging representation of an infantryman.

Amis proceeded to a fulsome and well-read appreciation of Lyall's *Shooting Script*, which I happened to have read on a BOAC flight. Both men demonstrated condescending ignorance of the practicalities of film-making. K.A. did a script of *I Want It Now* for Stanley Donen, who told him, after Kingsley has sounded off about the shittiness of movies, that he now had a chance to put his money where his mouth was (in the ancient world, it is said, the mouth was the first pocket, in which case people did *literally* put their money where it was). Amis was more modern: he put the money where his wallet was.

★ I observed later that the trouble with Lindsay was that *If* was followed by too many buts. He was not amused.

Stanley considered that he had done nothing but type out the novel in screenplay form. What a surprise! It is hardly K.A.'s style to detect flaws in his own work and put them right. Men with his vanity may not need the cash, but there is something despicable in taking the *petit cadeau* and not coming through. Amis was entertaining on the Welsh; welshing is quite his thing.

I left in the rain, hoping for a taxi with a familiar childishness learnt from my father, who used to talk of 'the Raphael taxi'. He often had good fortune in conjuring cabs in downpours. I remember one lurching out of a cobbled alley behind Gray's Inn Road, its availability flaring in the gloom, a present from the Absurd to my father's idiot pride. There was no taxi for me. I ran to Hampstead tube station, panted for a ticket, and waited and waited for a train. I thought to change at Charing X, but it was soon obvious that I could never make Liverpool Street for the last Colchester train. I got off at Euston and raced up to the main concourse to find a cab. The station was enormous and deserted. It wore an air of face-lifted modernity, all agreeable lettering, a refurbished ghost, without the previous polite personality. Arrows indicated inter-station buses and hotel advice. There was nothing about taxis. Oh yes, there was: I was pointed downwards and ran down the stairs and along a curving tunnel to the rank. At least there *was* a taxi. He doubted if he could make Liverpool Street in the remaining six minutes to midnight. 'Could we discuss it as we go along?' I may not believe in God, but I retain faith in cabbies' ability to arrest chronology.

He did it too. At a minute to midnight, we seemed about to arrive at Highbury, but at midnight itself I was pounding along the platform. I sat gasping in a first-class compartment with a couple already *très bien installés*. 'Only just made it,' I blurted out, as the train jolted on its way. 'You're lucky,' they said. 'We only just missed the last one.'

I was about to start a new script and called S.D. to say that I cannot devote time to his film, which Columbia was apparently willing to back, if he was ready by July. I was prepared to be generous with advice; and, if he would wait till I had finished, I would do what I could. This was taken, as it was intended, as a sign-off. Beetle and I had to go to Bordeaux to collect the car and intended to spend a couple of nights in Paris. S.D. said that we should use his and Barbara's flat on the Ile de la Cité; we'd be crazy not to. We went to Montpelier Square to collect the keys one evening after dinner.

B. and S. were entertaining a stockbroker and his wife to dinner; they were helping him to collect evidence against Adelle for the divorce case. Stanley introduced the man as 'someone who makes money for us'.

Barbara resented our easy acceptance of the Paris flat, which she suggested was 'hers'. I had understood that S. took it for the shooting of *Staircase* which, for tax reasons (Rex's and Burton's) had had to be shot in Paris. In the end, we were given the keys and elaborate instructions about where to find the telephone and the maid, but were so embarrassed by Barbara's grudging charity that we went and stayed at the *Raphael*.

Stanley reproached me on our return; they had tried to call us several times. I said that I gathered that Barbara was unhappy about our having the place. 'And anyway it didn't seem worth it for one night.' 'You were there two nights,' S. said. He sounded quite peeved, although the maid had had appendicitis and the whole flat was in mourning.

Some time later: S.D. has grown a beard again. His film is not being made. Falling among artists (Lindsay and co!) has maimed a talent which flourished among Philistines. S.D. is like the clever copy-writer who became rich on Madison Avenue and then got ulcers after giving it all up to 'do what he really wanted', which he couldn't. S.D. was a rich and capable director of entertainments; he is now crucifying himself for the sake of 'art'. It would have been better to do *Hello, Dolly*. His native exuberance has been corrupted, à la H.J., by European pretentiousness.

Antonioni's snob appeal persuades actors to take parts which, in dispassionate circumstances, they would dismiss as 'not there'. The parts which Sarah Miles and even Vanessa Redgrave play in *Blow Up* may have their place in the context of the completed film, but they lack individual substance. Actors like to be treated as intellectuals, as long it doesn't entail having to be intelligent. Directors too: by persuading actors of the overall merit of his work, M.A. can eliminate tracts of dialogue from his scripts. This economy has aesthetic consequences: the film becomes abstract. The artist paints self-portraits not because it spares him the need for a model but also because it leaves him with no extraneous responsibility: he need please only himself. If he becomes a *name*, he can treat others as mercilessly as he did himself: his signature becomes the flattery he might otherwise have to deliver. An actor sits, or walks, or speaks, for a famous director in similar style: his reward is not to say 'look what I did' but 'look what I was in'.

In the dark sheds where the plastic sheets are dried, the smell of camphor.

Catullus, in early manhood, could have had access to young slave girls whose subservience he, like any Roman, did not question. He may even have shared them with his father. When he goes to Rome, he has had no known, no famous experience, none with an 'equal'. For G.V.C. all his equals must be superiors; Rome is a society for aspirants and dominators. One can imagine C.'s prose resembling Byron's Ravenna journal. When Caesar went east, ambition made him agree to be 'queen of Bithynia'; Catullus merely failed to get rich. Memmius' honesty as governor was the last straw C. could have wished to draw.

Peter Lorre: what a display of versatility he made it always to be the same!

For Catullus. Strange to have been so moved by laughter – the throaty, uninhibited laughter of a woman (the line of whose throat and thrown back chin I seem absolutely to see) – that I was convinced at once, believe it or not, of her *moral* worth. Was it simply that I was on the street of the rich, infected by the aura of importance which their mansions radiate, and that I wished upon that delicious, gushing sound a superb authority that made me want nothing so much as to be its cause? Success and pleasure could be joined, if I could but whisper in her ear and have her throw back her head, stretch that throat, produce – at my sole prompting – those cadences of golden contempt.

The street door opened and she came out. Not tall, she was beautiful; hair brushed back in many curls from forehead and temples, eyes glittering in the sun, huge and sly as she looked back towards those following her. She was used to followers. Their reluctance, or their clumsiness, or some splintered memory, seemed to change her mood from complicity to disdain. She ceased laughing and looks down the street; at me. I was fifty paces from her, yet she looked as if she expected me to understand her mood. And I did; I understood her; I consumed her with my eyes and my heart as if she were naked. I *loved* her.

In the same moment, I swear it, I shot her a look of contempt, as if she were a whore. I turned, trembling, down towards the forum. I heard her call, harsh and impatient, to one of her slaves, or friends, 'We're going to be late, you fool!' I shuddered to think of, and envied, the humiliations of those subject to her personal malice.

When I looked back from the bottom of the slope, her party had turned in the opposite direction. Cicero was coming up from the forum, busy in one of those intimate, earnest discussions which begged to be overheard. The sauntering patrician beside him agreed, with urgent boredom, to M.T.C.'s ingratiating highmindedness. Poor Tully! No dupe has keener perceptions; none aspires more eloquently to the nobility which the noble have long abandoned. If only the old families had a tenth of the qualities which M.T.C. engraves on their walls. He hates Clodius not only because C. rubbishes his policies but – much more! – because he won't take M.T.C. seriously as a *gentleman*. P.C. is the crude proof that, under their po-faced amiability, the Best People regard Tully as a nice old upstart who has never known real power or standing. He sings them sentimental lullabies about their unselfish purposes and persuades himself that the good old days are just around the corner.

M.T.C. loves the language, but never notices where it leads him. Ever since he prosecuted Verres, he has been afraid of the facts (e.g. that he made early enemies of the Metelli). He knows, but cannot face the fact, that there isn't a family in Rome that he would consent to dine with which is not tarred by the Verrine brush. As for Clodia's laughter, he lives across the street from her and must hear it all the time, and guess (wish?) that he is its target.

*

Two weeks later, I was taken to meet her. I scowled like a child; I disapproved like an idiot; I thought she was loathsome. When she laughed, I was scalded. I told myself that I wanted to leave, and stayed. Why? I hated the place; the opulent confidence of the guests. I tried to coax one of the slave girls to smile; I wanted her to appreciate that I despised the company and shared her longing for a different, straighter world. I craved her complicity so much that I wanted to bend her down, with my straight arm pressing her neck to the floor and a clutch of her Asian hair in my hand, and fuck her, hard, in the ass. When she smiled, which of my ambitions was it that she smiled at?

Publius came up to me, his handsome spoilt face creased with left-over laughter from something a friend had said. He saw the girl I was looking at and put his arm around her too. She smiled and wriggled; his attentions were more pleasing, or more commanding, than mine.

'You look a bit broody,' he said to me, fondling the girl. 'Don't you know anybody?'

'No,' I said.

'And, by God, you sound pleased not to!'

'Is there anyone worth knowing?'

'That's *all* there is,' he said. 'I know! Gaius Catullus, am I right?' He studied me as if we were old friends. 'From Verona.'

'Come to see the sights,' I said.

'And here they all are, I'm afraid! Have you met my sister?'

'I've seen her,' I said.

'You should meet her. She likes poets. Preferably for breakfast.'

'Is she what she eats?' I said. 'She must be immortal. If her diet includes Marcus T.!'

Publius decided to laugh; he was shriller than she was, but had the same lordly confidence. He could remove his eyes from the company and still be sure of their attention, and devotion. He had no fear of people; it amused him to be dangerous. Only a man sure of his friends could choose to be so offensive to them.

When I had finished the poem, it was, in spite of my intentions, against my friends Furius and Aurelius that I felt abiding bitterness. As for C., I was so seized by longing that I had to see her again. My denunciation of her might have been a love letter. I was excited, as if given a new lease of hope. My love poems, on the other hand, filled me with despair; abuse made me tender. What pleasure in the rehearsal of places and epithets! What richness in the trajectory of words! If one wishes oneself dead, it is for the luxury of being ubiquitous.

The Wisemans asked us to dinner on Friday night. We drove to town on Thursday, after Stee was in bed. Oh the stomach-churning deceits of family life! We dined at the Angus Steak House in Dorset House, which has cannibalised the old restaurant where my mother and I once had lunch adjacent to Bertrand Russell and his son, Conrad. ('Would my knowledge of Greek help me to learn Sanskrit?' he asked his father. 'No, I think really your knowledge of *Welsh* would be of greater assistance.') In those days, the restaurant was small and genteel and catered largely to the tenants. There was a blue-rinsed manageress and aged waiters. Dorset House, like England, still has much the same façade, the same porter's desk, the

carpeted hall with the 1930s cinema foyer lighting, the marble steps
to narrow lifts, but the Steak House, with its hellish red plush, has
banished the sea-green gentility of the old Restaurant where they
did a very good ham in madeira sauce, with excellent purée potatoes (five bob, including soup and pudding). Smoked salmon was
2/6d extra; we never had it.

The Steak House is much larger; it has taken over some shops
backing onto Baker Street. Though empty when we arrived, amid
a jangle of fire bells heading north, it had an air of expectant business. All modern public places approximate to a twenty-four-hour
day. We move towards the total relativity of space'n'time: an eternal
now.

I lunched on a sandwich in Shepherd's Market, after a visit to
Heinitz and then to Glanville, who sat amid fallen fruit from his
neighbour's huge pear tree, composing a piece on the resurgence
of wingers. I was due at Cape at 4.30 and dawdled at Maples where
(of all places) they had an exhibition of modern design: multi-screen
projections, spheres, soggy furniture. They were selling the *sacco*
chairs I saw with B. in Paris. Young art students and graduates were
sitting round in them. A very pretty girl at the 'Brides' desk was in
charge. What were they filled with? 'Little balls.' 'I bet you get a
lot of bright jokes about *that*.' 'We do.' The furniture was very
sociable: we were all soon talking.

We were at Cape to discuss the obsequies of Bookshop 85, into
which I had put a good deal of money. Tom was in shirtsleeves.
There was a message for me to call Jo Janni; Tom squirmed with
impatient jealousy. Jenefer came in to take the post. As she left, with
instructions from Tom, I said, 'And put the kettle on, love.' 'Do
you want tea or coffee?' 'Tea.' 'It'll be from the machine.' 'Great,'
I said. 'I'll pay.' 'You can pay for mine too,' Tom said.

The meeting proceeded. Venetia (Pollock) was grey and drawn.
Her son is in UCH (too ill for a private room), after gastro-enteritis
left him almost completely dehydrated and demineralised. I cheered
her up with accurate and acid comments on Tom's motives and on
the ill-researched origins of the shop, and its failure. As when playing
the hand at bridge, first mistakes are usually irretrievable. Not only
was the shop badly sited (at 85 Regent's Park Road) but Tom had
hired a 'hip' manager who over-ordered unreadable and expensive
books and (even before I became involved) gave the place an irre-
ducible financial 'hump'.

Our mood favoured closure. Tom, as a publisher, feared the consequent ridicule. Anyone would think he had never had a failure. I quoted Brian Marber: 'In the Stock Exchange they say that taking a loss is like having a good shit. You always feel better afterwards.' I paraded a showbiz brazenness which I never display in showbiz, where I prefer to play the intellectual parachutist.

I had an (ultimately futile) idea for saving the shop by asking 'friends' to invest £200 each, which they could recoup in purchases over a period of time. Since it meant that he would get something for nothing (i.e. my secretaries' help), Tom eagerly accepted. He apologised for his own lack of ideas. He had a headache, the result of 'crying babies and no sleep'.

'Tough luck,' I said.

Going downstairs, I explained to Venetia: 'For twelve years I've listened to Tom bitching about my excessive domesticity and showing no understanding of our problems. I hope the baby cries non-stop for a year.'

Venetia, I learned later, is dying of cancer.

The Wisemans live in Arkwright Road, which runs at a steep angle to the Finchley Road. The house is red brick, Victorian: the sort of place where you imagine German emigrés living, toiling up the many stone steps to the front door with arms full of voluminous arguments from the library. Inside the house was big; white rooms with spotlights in the high ceilings. The furniture was sparse, and discreet. Who would guess that Tom once drove a leopardskin-lined car and was the journalistic bane of the Rank Organisation?

We ate late; avocado and shrimp, fricassee of veal, jacket potatoes, cheese, fruit. We were finishing the main course when 'John' phoned. 'Come round,' Tom said, 'Freddie Raphael is here.' Poor Beetle! The incidental pains of being a writer's wife!

John was Fowles. He and his wife, with whom Malou had recently stayed for a week, but whose name she could not remember (Elizabeth), were just back from the Frankfurt Book Fair. John was in cords, loose shirt, neckerchief: an unkempt Henry James. His beard is less virile than bristly; his teeth are the colour of good agricultural land. He seems gentle, mildly regretful, full of useless sighs at the follies of a society he cannot like but dares not attack. Frankfurt was 'awful, 75 per cent pornography; like Cannes'. Why did he go? He was asked by his German publishers. He has the soured complacency of the Best Seller who feels out of things because his books do so well. He had brought some aquavit which tasted of pears and lighter fluid. Elizabeth was unsmiling. She has a twenty-year-old son by a former marriage, but is unable to have any more. Tom told me that this was a source of great regret to John, though I remember, at the time of *The Aristos* (a title taken, consciously or not, from a no less precious work by Frederick Rolfe, Baron Corvo), asking John if he had any children. He affected surprise at my question. How could he have children after advocating population control? If Elizabeth smiles, it is as if it were against her principles. She talks of 'him' in italicised inverted commas as heavy as shackles. She is '*his*' driver; if it weren't for her, '*he*' would never leave the house.

Fowles' success seems to come to him rusted with irony; it sustains his vanity, but not his pride. We lamented the state of English films; we mourned the decline of the novel; we worried about the future of art. We went home.

Stanley Price told me that he worked with J. Miller on *Take a Girl Like You*. He replaced George Melly (now about to be the film critic of *The Observer*). He rewrote the whole script with Jonathan's eager encouragement and participation. When Hal Chester returned from America, he told J.M. that Stanley had 'taken all the cock out of the story'. As he saw it, the thing was about the man with the third biggest cock in the world. Jonathan agreed with him. Stanley was fired. Melly returned with all the lines S.P. had cut. The script was restored to its previous state.

'Know who that is over there? Leach.'
   'Who's Leach?'
   'Howard Leach. The man with the deductible girl? In the famous case?'
   A proofreader will, ten to one, change the last two question marks to full-stops. But *hear* (and act) the exchange and it has an inquisitive inflection.

The director. Because he looks very anxious, people take him for an artist. He will accept the job of gilding the lily with absolute confidence that he can embellish that overrated flower. Given the chance, he will set Beethoven to music.

It can be easy to find someone to pander to one's pleasure; rarer to find exactly the right person to cause you pain.

'Love the country? Sometimes I see the landscape like those pictures you find in the *Rue de l'Ecole de Médecine*, lurid illustrations of diseases. Trees are like cancers which have burst through the skin; rocks are calcified eruptions; the whole of the earth twisted and grassed with gangrene.'

28.2.71. At the Scholly. We drove there for me to take a call from an Israeli producer. As we parked, we were adjacent to a ponderous vehicle with Parisian plates. A man in his late fifties and a woman, of about forty, were sitting in it. They looked unhappy.

We waited in the Scholly bar. After a while, the couple came in. They drank *porto*. The man, lined and sallow, had a slice of *tarte maison*. After I had spoken to 'Londres' (which turned out to be Cologne), the man remarked, in English, on the shortcomings of the French telephones. I suggested politely that all telephone services were alike. No; he cited American, German and English as superior. The woman sat against the wall, a tremulous smile on her faintly swollen face; glaucous eyes, tender and sad, observed the scene as if she were not present. After a while, the man called for his bill. He was going back to his house, near Doissat. 'She' had to go on a journey (perhaps they had come for her to catch the train). Would we like to come to Le Mondiol next day '*prendre un Whisky*'?

Stee was playing all this time with two of the little glass dogs they give away with Total petrol. When the man said goodbye, with courteous tenderness, to the woman (who still had time to kill before her train), she rose from her corner and tumbled a quartet of new glass dogs among those that Stee already had. With a flush, as if embarrassed and pained and amused all in one, she smiled, said nothing, and walked through the kitchen towards the hotel itself.

The man explained how to find his house and went into the square for his car. Madame Scholly informed me of what I had long guessed: '*La femme que vous avez rencontrée aujourd'hui est sa petite amie. Demain vous allez rencontrer sa femme.*'

The track was long and rough, through pine woods hedged by stacks of felled timber. A notice warned: *Propriété Privée*. A car was parked outside strong new gates. The staff did not drive in. The courtyard was grey gravel, with two tall trees leafless in the winter wind. A few gritty snowflakes swirled. A maid came out in a thin white overall. I leaned out. '*Le Mondiol?*' '*Oui, monsieur.*' She tugged a bell pull high on the house wall.

The long narrow building pointed towards Doissat, on the far side of the valley, over to the right. Beneath a low stone wall were rose gardens, bleak in the snowy light, and the basin for a new swimming pool. It had been built, the owner told us, for a tenth of the price of ours. It looked it.

His wife was slim, silver-haired, with protruding blue-grey eyes. She showed none of the heavy weariness I expected of someone reported to have had a recent heart attack. Her house was as neat as a brochure; the perfection of deadness. Everything might have been picked from a catalogue; all numbingly correct. Every door fitted; every tile shone; every velvet chair was flawlessly napped; every surface gleamed. It was as lively as any funeral director could have made it.

Stee was afraid of the woman who tried so promptly to seduce him with sweets. His uncertainty turned into greed; one could not blame him, but I was angry, with him and with them. They gave us champagne and boudoir biscuits. We never asked them back.

If the sentence passed on the Basque nationalists at Burgos is not commuted, how should one resist the logic that maintains Franco to be their murderer? If he were assassinated, it might be justice. But if his death becomes proper, the consequences are incalculable. His courtiers would even the score and the prospect of civil war increase, unless (perhaps) the assassin were a foreigner.

Edward Hyams 'justifies' the ideal assassin by saying that he expected to perish in the attempt. Unfortunately (perhaps), the common modern assumption that no one acts singly will make sure that an opportunity will be taken to drown many others in the same bag. The lone, conscientious assassin is defined out of the realm of practical possibility by the prevailing rhetoric of politics.

Why did the Homeric gods laugh? Because they knew they were immortal and that men were not, and knew it. Once men were prepared to believe His word, that Faith brought immortality, God had to keep a straight face. It was that kind of a joke.

On Ios:
Do you think that perhaps it tripped
And fell, that triangle,
That alpha in the doorway
Of the sunken church?

Do you think had we got there
A minute sooner we might have seen it
Drop like a cat, quick as a glance
And lie there still?

Are we all it needs, do you suppose,
To kill the movement in the world,
Frighten the eyes and deaden the life
In nimble, silent light?

There is this glass everywhere,
Our heels crackle and leave wounded;
We walked later along the beach,
And never guessed the glass.

We feel the hardness, hear the noise;
The glass traps that crash and bite,
But break the fragile, soundless pane
That leaping has dropped, like a cat.

At the Venezia, after seeing *Five Easy Pieces* (not a good film, but one that tries to be good). Behind me, a man was pleading with a girl. Not easy to tell his age, but evident what he wanted. He protested the honesty of his desires, and the gentlemanliness with which he was furthering them. She declared the respect she had, until now, felt for him. She regretted that she did not feel, yes, 'that way about him'. How old were they? I couldn't see. He declared that she was the most attractive girl he had seen in, yes again, 'a million years'. She told him both that she was engaged and that she was going to see her 'mother-in-law' over Easter (logically possible as old Ewing used to say, or bray). Patient, but callous, she had first met her companion, she reminded him, across a casualty desk. Soon she went out to the loo and I could see a tallish woman, in her early thirties, in a black trouser suit; little make-up, eyes rimmed with mascara, a dulled, chilly look about her. When, eventually, she came back, the conversation resumed. He told her of his commercial prowess; he had been important in negotiations between Hawker-Siddeley and some foreign government. He had told them exactly what was what. 'But what am I talking about all this for?'

   The girl met his wheedling boldness with patient aversion. Her nursing experience made her frigidly indulgent. Nurses can seldom resist the offer of a square meal. Jo tells of a director who wanted sex so badly one night, in Weymouth, that he was driven (no doubt in a unit car) to pick up male nurses from Salisbury hospital.

Box and Cox:
   'The intellectual flatters himself – hence his guilt, his obsessive (as in commercial) *interest* – that an abstract doctrine triggered the Holocaust. And – dare we whisper? – Art itself. Steiner can't bear for the chapter to close on Art before it has had the chance to redeem itself. The unimportance of the specific, singular instance enables us to make history out of murder, statistics out of sadism. Pornography too takes no account of ordinary human limits. It ignores any part of life which lacks sexual or perverse suggestiveness. In this sense, it's very scientific: as Malraux saw, it has neither *tempora* nor *mores*. Isn't what Steiner fears above all that its aesthetic makes absolutely absurd – makes into the stuff of *farce* – the fate of the European culture which he sees six million Jews as impersonating *and suffering for*? Forget Art and they too are forgotten. His abiding use for fiction is Proustian: the defeat of time. What makes Tynan, intellectually his manifest inferior, into the – let's postulate – his polar opposite?'
   'Do you know Ken?'
   'I'm not talking about any *particular* Tynan here –'
   'Ah, *a* Tynan!'
   'Thematically, he's someone who resents not the loss of a valuable past but his failure – the bastard! – to belong to it. Steiner plays the legitimate heir to European culture here, the man with a line of achievement, and family, behind him. Where he is the noble Pretender, Tynan is the shameless (but ambitious) Edgar who debunks the claims of legitimacy –'
   'Edmund. The bastard.'
   'Of course: wants a world in which family bonds are no longer redeemable at Pa! Whereas for Steiner, the father –'
   'Exactly.'
   'Means *value*; whereas for Tynan paternity involves false exclusiveness, a value-façade applied, like make-up, with no beautifying effect, to social institutions. Property/propriety makes sex a part of the *order*, rather than – as he would like – of the *disorder* of things. Betrayal of the "partner" – like that of one's country – is a cardinal sin in the bourgeois world. Tynan's adolescent fantasies of kings and pageants – the *Sinister Street* syndrome – gave way to a revolutionary vision of a naked world: no false institutions, no modesty, bereft of the personal salvation of legitimacy. The delegitimisation of the legitimate becomes his mission. K.T.'s ideal emperor has no clothes,

but Ken – *qua* critic – can promise him that nakedness is the fanciest dress. Careerism and the cult of fashion afford K.T. a sort of just cause: revenge in the name of Man gives the dignity of logic to ill-tempered desire.'

'Meanwhile – '

'Absolutely: Steiner seeks redemption; he hopes to shame the guilty by finding them – his supreme contempt – unable to be *sentenced* adequately in words. Symbolically, he turns his back on them; Tynan, to shame *his* enemies, turns his front, and dares them to find him *different*, or themselves better because they are, when they manifestly aren't.'

'Steiner sees Tynan – '

'Indeed: as the man who favours degradation. He rightly remembers the force of the pornographic imagination in fleshing out, and licensing, the brutal fantasies realised by the Nazis. He dreads the lack of artistic – i.e. ethical – restraint on the imagination. *Tout est possible* is a horrible possibility! He accuses the pornographer – the modern prophet – of "doing our imagining for us", but might he not more accurately say, "doing our imagining *to* us"? Surviving Jews of a certain age are torn between the desire to find a "meaning" for the Holocaust and the urge to proclaim its senselessness. At once to be associated with it, as victim, and to proceed beyond it, so as to be able to judge its perpetrators and learn something from its somehow despised victims. To find a meaning for death has to be an essentially religious preoccupation. The scientific correlative could only be to find a *cure* for it.'

For Cavafy:
Who are these people disembarking?
Why are they marching with drums and banners,
Who have survived where others failed
And have now come home?

They were fighting in a distant place
And now have been released
And are marching through the city
With their drums and banners.

These were our soldiers, our men.
Can't you recognise the faces?
Meepos gnoridzete ta prosopa ton;
They fought our war, and lost it, for us.

And now, after all these years, *tosa chronia*,
They are marching through streets new to them,
With drums beating, banners flying.
Why does no one cheer or recognise them?

Where are their families and their dogs?
Why are they marching in steel lines,
And why are their banners flying?
What are they going to do to us, poor things?

Box: 'Steiner's preferred province is ingenious puzzlement. He dreads a world comprised only of *problems*. Difficulties are resolved by metaphors; problems by solutions. Hence he cannot welcome a world without difficulties. What would he do in it? Stinks!'
    'Whereas Tynan – '

Arnold Wesker in *The Sunday Times* office: 'Why does someone like Freddie Raphael review books? Surely he doesn't need the money.' Later, when I was there, he said that he had recently been down to the East End again, surveying the ranks of Pakistanis who now live there. He couldn't help wondering, he said, if another Arnold Wesker would be found among them.
    He was in a shirt slashed to the navel, revealing a chest so ostentatiously hairy that it lacked only a WELCOME on the mat. He was imbibing journalistic atmosphere with the dedicated wrongheadedness of a small boy learning to be a doctor by sitting in the waiting room. He talked about directors, and shows which had had more than one. *The Royal Hunt of the Sun*, he said, was unique in having had its two elements – the Incas and the *Conquistadores* – rehearse their sections separately. When John Peter mentioned *The Caucasian Circle of Chalk*, I said, 'I believe that it was originally rehearsed as two semi-circles which were only joined together at the dress rehearsal when they fitted together like *that*!' Arnold failed to hear. John Whitley had to repeat the story. Arnold's ear is tuned to receive only his own voice.

Box and Cox: 'I disgree! The claim that science is unwarrantedly powerful is a reactionary view; it re-arranges the overstuffed furniture of metaphysics. Leach's assault on the family seems reckless, not to say brutal – we *know* that families are not the guilt-machines he labels them – and yet in disestablishing the theocentricity which they incorporate, he has a point. Families engender many of our weaknesses, and crutch them. If it's cruel to deny people palliatives, it's right to *prescribe* their emancipation. To extricate man from needless terrors is the historical result, but never the practical job, of science. We cling to the darkness – *love* of the dark is as common as fear of it – as we cling to concealment, and silence, its black cloak. Man may reach a time when sexuality is no longer his central pleasure, and his consolation. If our lives are lengthened – and there you have *the* challenge of scientific *ethics* – i.e. that's as ethical as science can ever be –'

'Got it. I think.'

'The claws of marriage, sharpened by jealousy and dread, will be pared away. Chemistry may solve – or better *dis*-solve – neuroses which Freud imagined could be treated only by lengthy analysis. This took place within – and was a function of – *the old vocabulary*. In mental operations too there can be sepsis! *Can't* there? Progress is the transformation of moral problems into practical ones. A successful retroactive contraceptive will render the Right to Life campaign superfluous; it will not be an *argument*, but an answer. Scientific advances in domains previously mandated by moral laws, and lords, will render existing ethical categories as senseless as the dread of eclipses or the fear of black cats. The ultimate efficient NHS will free us of the need, and desire, for immortality: following mundane prescriptions is the modern way of telling one's rosary. And then we shall have to face the force of Wittgenstein's equivalence of ethics and aesthetics. Conduct changes; art changes. The novel is no exception. The new language will not be disposed to make novels in the style we now admire. What law ever had to be passed against epic verse?'

Cox: 'I've been thinking…'

'And I agree: what the Nazis did may have been serious – as when we talk of "serious crimes", but the error of the powers who opposed them was in thinking that they were to be taken seriously, as if their fatuous ideology and their legitimised greed issued from something *deep*. An opponent who did not fear them would have laughed at them as we laugh at petulant children.'

'Didn't Nabokov…?'

'Of course he did. In *Invitation to a Beheading*.'

'Where the condemned man –'

'Laughed at the executioner –'

'Monsieur Pierre.'

'The very same! And the whole crew were reduced to cyphers,

like the court cards in –'
    '*Alice Through the Looking-Glass.*'
    'Steiner frightens himself – in Bluebeard's *cathedral*, you might say
– by conjuring up a vaulted, Grimm/Gothic gospel of magic
purposes and spells in which he can be a *scholar* of Nazi intentions
and motives. This sentimental search for men who can be forced to
the logical duelling floor and made to test their mettle against the
Musketeer of Humanity and Truth is essentially Quixotic. It reveals
the unwillingness of survivors to register the triviality of the brute
they have escaped. The monster's want of motives of any deep
interest whatever is much more alarming than the purposeful
méchanceté with which Steiner wants to equip it (in fact to make
himself a Heracles, wrestling with muscular shadows). The most
horrifying feature of Nazism is that *nothing* "lies behind it"; the lies
are all in front. The insistence that diabolic arguments must moti-
vate diabolic acts leads to the literature of the sacred criminal, the
divine idiot, the superb brute. In this line of argument, Nazism finds
its involuntary apologists: they are more ingenious at finding
warrants for Nazism than the Nazis were.'

They took three stones – the size of black olives his wife said – out
of his kidney. When he came round, they were waiting for him on
the bedside table. 'Very poor taste,' she said. She wore a long suede
coat with a fur hem, a longish skirt, black turtle-necked sweater.
Her pretty breasts and handsome head still recommend her, but the
once fine eyes are sunk in contractions of wrinkled skin, cheeks like
shrivelling peaches. Married to her lover, the eager adulteress dwindles into the dutiful wife.

March. I was uneasy about going to Lagardelle. I asked Beetle again
and again whether she was looking forward to it. She was. The
Smiths were to follow us. An enormous amount could be done. I
was tired; I would paint and read and take it easy for a couple of
weeks. The drive was unrelaxed; Rennie-Roberts was supposed to
have balanced the wheels and checked the tyres of the Mercedes,
but it had lost its stability. It seemed to shift and slide on the polished
road, as if on wet rails. I drove with constant apprehension. Every
time a car approached us on a country road I feared we might sidle
into it. Not until the second day did I think to ease some of the air
out of the tyres, reducing them to the recommended pressure.
    We stayed on the Loire overnight, near the Château de
Chaumont. The blossom was out, almond and lilac, polished by

showers which had now passed. Stee found a stick 'gun' on the steep path between rooty trees. We ate well; we had a neat suite; things were fine.

They seemed fine at home too. The weather was dull at first, but everything worked. There was still a mess in the apartment, where Crestani had left everything unfinished: the walls were slashed with electric wires, carpentry half-done. The usual phone calls brought some action: the arrival of Villafranca, Crestani's troubleshooter, with his insolent servility. They had not been paid, so there was some justice in their sloth, but the work was badly done and no deadline had been met. Had they been paid, we should have been conned; since they had not, we lacked authority. However, the plasterer came, and then the electrician; the apartment was incomplete but, by the Thursday, habitable.

On Friday I drove to Bordeaux for Jack and Isabel. We needed the help. On the way back, we stopped for lunch in Castillon, at the *Auberge Basque*, a standard unrefined meal, twelve francs. Jack was apprehensive (he dislikes 'messed up food'), but ate thoroughly. I was anxious that they enjoy France and prepared to be annoyed if they did not.

We had great heat during their first week. Much was accomplished. Our neighbour Norbert took me across country to find someone to shift the earth which Crestani had dumped on the field below the house. Three brothers ran a tractor business. They were out when we arrived. Norbert stood and waited. A woman helper put us on the list of jobs, but said that they were all due to go to St Amand-de-Coly on the Monday morning. We started home and came across the essential brother heading home through the woods. We boarded the panting tractor as it halted in front of the Mercedes. Norbert waited until inertia brought surrender; he would come on Monday, *before* St Amand-de-Coly.

All weekend we worked to clear the bank of weed and sod. Jack worked tirelessly, up at six, in bed when it was too dark to continue. The sweltering heat did not stop him. On Monday, no one came. I went again with Norbert, after lunch, to find out why: the digger had broken down. They would come the next day; a promise was a promise, they promised. We ordered stakes to mark the field. The swimming pool had been fenced for the winter by the *menuisier*, to stop Norbert's sheep drowning in it. The stakes and wire could be cannibalised for the field.

The digger arrived the next morning, with M. Lemaire on board, a handsome young man of thirty. He worked steadily – no drinks or breaks – bringing the earth and tipping it through the gap in the wall onto the steep slope down to the pool. His tyres were smooth and he handled the tractor with less skill than Jack (an expert) was willing to admire, but the job got done. The tyres were filled with water, Jack said, otherwise he would never have made any ground.

In under three hours he had done all he was willing to do and almost all we wanted done. The earth on the slope now had to be smoothed by hand and planted with grass seed. On the Saturday we bought many plants in Sarlat and came back happy with plans. We even swam in the cold and mucky pool from which the soggy poly-styrene plaques (the winter cover) had been laboriously removed.

On Sunday evening, we were on the terrace outside the sitting room when the trees were violently agitated, as if a child were seeking to dislodge an obstinate ball. The air grew cloudy, yellow-brown. The cyclone was fierce and yet so localised that its margins were as definite as a room's. Stee's inflated yellow pool went bowling down the steps. Jack caught it as it whirled by. We took the violent rainstorm that followed as a blessing; the lawn needed a shower.

The slabs had arrived for the terrace I had planned. We unloaded most of them from the *remorque* before we left for dinner. I had promised to call Pau again, at Bedales (we had a bad line when we spoke) and, not wanting to impose on Madame Scholly again, we set off to dine in Les Eyzies. The threat of a further storm seemed remote.

It took a long time to get through to England, but we had a good meal in the genteel dining room of the *Glycines*. We took the call in a bathroom which housed the hooded *cabine téléphonique*. Pau was again hard to hear, but he seemed to be saying that everything was 'fab'. Ouf! We were well across the Dordogne, on our way home, before the first intimations of trouble. The road was steaming; leaves began to speckle the surface; then twigs; then branches. The mild mist thickened till you could hardly see. The road was ribbed with debris. We turned up our little *chemin* and the surface was matted with green. I dropped Beetle by the back door and drove into the *grange*. When I came out, the grass was very wet.

By the back door, in the flower bed were thick white crusts, grimy in the half-light. In the kitchen, the furniture had been pushed back. Jack's face, red as if embarrassed, shone from behind a barri-cade of chairs. The sitting room was flooded too. They had had a savage hailstorm. They said it had lasted three-quarters of an hour (actually it was twenty minutes). So fierce had been the bombardment that Jack thought someone was throwing stones. If they had opened the kitchen door, which he almost did, they would never have shut it again. They had cleared up pretty well. We went to bed with no great sense of disaster, even though flowers had been decapitated and carpets drenched. The radio in the flat was out of action; water had gone through the sitting room floor.

The next day revealed the ruin of all our earlier work around the pool. There was a breach in the wall above the pool, into which they had been promising for months to insert a long log, on a bed of cement, to make a seat. All the accumulated water from the melted hail had cascaded through the gap, driving loose earth down the steep slope, over the low cement wall, across the '*plage*' (a pavement without a margin) and into the pool. It was now a sullen porridge. So was Jack. My 'Morning, Jack!' drew no happy response. He had tried to tackle the sludge, but the job was beyond him. The earth on the slope, scored by the torrents which had invaded it on the centre and on both flanks, was heavy as plasticine. The surviving plants were smothered in mud. We scraped the mud from the stones and sluiced them with bucket after bucket of sour water.

By lunch-time, the surround was clear, but the Smiths were still bewildered and resentful. They were children on an abortive picnic. My own mood, which might have been similar if theirs had been different, was doggedly cheerful. I arranged for *Piscines Aquitaine*, from Le Bugue, to come and drain the pool. Work began that evening.

The terrace was a major task still ahead of us. I was determined to get it done. The mason came and started on the cement base on which I proposed to lay thin plaques of limestone. To avoid an excessive amount of cement, we decided to use hard core from the ruined house behind the new barn. I assumed that it too belonged to the new complex, including the *grange*, which I bought from M. Cabanne (40,000 francs). We took wheelbarrow-loads of stones and poured soft cement over them. That evening, old M. Barrat came down from the farm. The formality of his manner, the alteration in his usually deferential stance, was a decisive warning: the stones which I had appropriated were not, he said, mine. The ruined house was his. He was not concerned about the stones, but with the question of ownership. Everyone, it seemed, had been soured by the weather. I was angrily resolved to appear unchanged. I smoothed the old man with a fine show of trust: I did not doubt his word, I told him, and I had no wish to inspect the village records, as he proposed. (In fact, he was wrong, as we discovered later.)

The remaining days of the Smiths were without joy. The terrace got done, but I never recaptured the camaraderie which Jack and I enjoyed when we set the fence around the new field. He held the pickets and I smashed them home with our new sledgehammer. He relied on my eye and assumed my strength. I drew a dividend of pleasure from his confidence. We worked together on the terrace too, but with no illusion of virile comradeship; we just did it.

There was more rain. We ate at the Scholly a couple of nights later, but every drop of rain rattled my nerves. We drove the Smiths into Bordeaux on Friday afternoon and were glad to put them on the plane. Our too comfortable reliance on Jack was dissipated. The strain of worrying about his feelings elicited rueful contempt. Yet he had worked hard, and cleverly, at the variety of problems the property presented. His cry of 'We're winning' became folkloric. Determined to be grateful, I gave him a good present and wrote a warm note, but I regretted finding there was no one on whom one can *always* rely. I worked on, single-minded and single-handed, laying thick stone slabs on the big terrace. The stones were back-breaking and little Stee helped me loyally. On one occasion, I stopped for a rest. We sat for a while and then Stee said, 'I think I've had enough of this.' I said, 'Thanks for your help. Off you go then.' 'Enough *resting*,' he said. Not bad for a three-year-old!

Herb Ross. He and Jo came down to Langham in Jo's Jaguar. Very tall, bespectacled, with a lot of brown curls, he wore a generously skirted suede overcoat and shook hands like a recently arrived cowboy. Choreographer and 'stager', he became a director only recently. Yet he had all the assurance, and trappings, of an established figure. His suite at the Dorchester was full of flowers and warm with welcomes. He listened intelligently to my ideas for *The Driver's Seat* (Muriel Spark's twig-thin novel), but made few contributions. Did he make *any*?

A week later, at Prunier's, Richard Gregson said that Herb had been 'as gay as a bird'. Now he had a wife, the ex-ballet-dancer Norah Kaye. A lady of between thirty-five and sixty, she had a plump bird's face and the balanced, careful walk of a dancer who has just dismounted. Ross padded about the suite in bare feet. His film *The Owl and the Pussycat* was running at the Curzon. From what I saw on TV, it was appalling, but the figures were good. When Herb's *Goodbye, Mr Chips* came out, it was rather a flop. 'A case of "Goodbye Chips, Mister",' I quipped. That was not warmly received either.

Bill Goldman. I had taken him the key of Seymour Walk, which Stanley begged of me because he could not find anywhere for Goldman to put his family while the two men worked on a script. Having just had the house decorated, we were not keen to let it, but the sentimental urge to do Stanley a good turn was seconded by the prospect of profit. The Goldmans were about to go to Venice and had no time to look elsewhere, but they clearly found our house too small, and unpretentious. They kept silent, and the key. While they were in Venice, someone found them what they wanted. Now they were embarrassed by the long hesitation. Afraid we were offended, S.D. himself became evasive. Anyone would think we had thrust the house at him.

The Goldmans never mentioned it when we dined with them at Carlo's Place (an excellent dinner, complete with 'extras' which were lisped at us by the Martiniquesque waiter). As they dropped us at Seymour Walk, Bill spoke of our 'darling little house'. His wife, one of those wide-smiling, unspoilt girls who wear black pants and shine with unchanged happiness no matter the topic, came from Texas; she was so determinedly cheerful and charming that she had no personality whatever. Goldman had reserves, I guess, of sour wit and malice; congeniality suited him badly. He is sharp, but charmless, craving money and Oscars. He and his brother, James, won in successive years. James and his landlord, who won with *The Producers*, got it in the same year, which had to be a record: two people at the same address.

After the première of *Sunday, Bloody Sunday*, Gareth said, 'It has a message. Half a loaf is better than none. That's worth thinking about.'

Beetle: 'I agree with you. It *is* worth thinking about. For just about thirty seconds.'

The first night was supposed to be 'informal', but the names of those attending twinkled on luminous tape above the Swiss Center. A crowd bulged out around the entrance to the cinema. From the laborious opening sequence, the film was a confusion of ingratiation and solemnity: standard Schlesinger. The time span is awkward, from one Friday to the Sunday week, so that the climax is not at the weekend one expects. Clever deception, or the result of clinging to a slick title?

The noble homosexual doctor is played by Peter Finch, who appeared, happily pissed, at the party at Trat Est, 125 Chancery Lane. The doctor has not the smallest vice, except a certain impatience

with patients. The 'adult' quality so admired by the critics is
procured by omitting the pleasure of (homo)sexuality in favour of
wistful dolefulness on everyone's part. The joys of domination and
submission are ignored, though the desire to *possess* is emphasised.
The suffering is merely the absence of triumph; it lacks the partic-
ularisation which goes with acknowledgement of the petty, the
childish, the passionate. The elimination of spite and pain (different
from suffering) means that force is removed from the 'characters';
they turn into vases for the display of Schlesinger's flowering
conceit. It is an adult film without any adults in it. Nothing discred-
itable is ever disclosed about anyone. The flashbacks, with their
sentimental banality, offered a clue to the flat, uncreative nature of
the film-makers. My reaction, and Beetle's, was not an afterthought;
it began early in the screening. The film reproaches 'society' in so
understanding a style that no one is finally expected to do anything
about anything. Everyone suffers, but no one does anything wrong.
How comfortable all the discomfort turns out to be!

John was very amiable at the party. 'Quite the best film you've
been in,' I said. 'I wasn't in it,' he said. I meant, of course, that I
could see him in all the performances. He has cut off his trendy side-
boards and has new, businesslike glasses; he is a responsible director,
a serious artist. Long gone, maybe, are the days when, in hysterical
frustration, he would fling open the windows of his Peel Street
house (always decribed as an 'upper-and-a-downer') and shriek
obscenities at the neighbours.

9.7.71. I lunched with Clive; muscular quail. He sat next to Roman
Polanski at John's first night. Halfway through the film, Roman
nudged Clive and made the time-honoured gesture: wanker.

Fear shakes everybody down. They pay their blackmail in smiles.

Since France, Jack has become moody; he works no less hard, but
he is greedy for grievances. He is testy with the children. Last week
he and Isabel were on holiday. Jack returned at the beginning of
the week in genial spirits, but yesterday afternoon he was in the
kitchen with a fresh grievance: he would be grateful, he told Beetle,
if we would ask Paul what he meant by asking him, 'What have you
been doing in the last couple of days?' A civil question had been
hotly twisted into a slur. 'No one's ever accused me of having a lazy
character.'

I left the kitchen. Cowardice or disdain? Between wise appeasement and self-reliant indignation, we spent a miserable time concocting crushing speeches and then censoring them. We understood and forgave; we accused and condemned. Jack is a big baby: he resents children who mess up the garden, and distract attention from him. Said to be a great man for the ladies, as game as Mellors, he is also jealous, spiteful and pettish.

No sooner do we have a small domestic disaster than we are convinced our lives are falling apart. Elsa Morante wrote a novel about a family that disintegrated on the death of one servant on whom, quite unconsciously, everything depended. The garden ceases to be the delight which he has made it and is transformed into a burden, just as life itself – constituted of bills and tax demands relating to past years – begins to be lived backwards: one is busier planning the past than the future. The Revenue wants to know about dates in 1966; the accountant, Mr Whines, whose wife died of cancer, expects me to supply dates from my diary. What diary? The weight of expectations, of pay, devotion, diplomacy, extinguish one's flame. I become a persecuted figure who cannot even read a book. The world discovers a bruise and presses on it. In the middle of this comes a call from Murray ('Who's for tennis?') and then a pale entreaty from Beetle to cope with Jack, who continues to brood on Pau's innocent words.

I went directly to him and quickly guessed the secret: he imagined that Paul had repeated something which *we* had said. What is more dificult than being convincingly innocent? I think I succeeded (he is now in the kitchen, chatting gaily) by telling him that I rarely raise the wages of those with whom I am displeased. Everything in the garden is now lovely again.

18.7.71. I went to Pinewood to see Norman Jewison. Jets scored straight burns on the bright sky; the trees below them were silver-green in the over-exposing sun. N.J. had sent his driver, a silver-haired man in a blue sailor hat, with mottled, elderly hands. He picked me up outside the bank in Sloane Street. We went out along the M4. I used to go via Western Avenue. The driver told me that Basil Dearden died recently; he always preferred the old way. The driver's son has married a Spanish girl; they have a hotel in Irun. He himself has married a second time and has a young family. Such men often disown their earlier children and make their new indifference a fault in them.

Jewison has offices in the grandest section of the old club house. His secretary took me across to the cutting room. We walked beside the covered way where, when Leslie and I were under contract, Tony Wright and Jill Ireland and Maureen Swanson might be met, at the height of their brief fame. The brickwork is the colour of crushed raspberries. We walked in the heat towards the lot where the sets for *Cleopatra* once stood. A gryphon stood white on the skyline. The secretary had seen *Cleopatra* twice, once recently, at the Odeon Marble Arch, in the company of about three dozen people. She had never seen *L'Avventura*, of which I was reminded by one of the galleries in the main building.

Jewison wore a crumpled white denim outfit over a dark brown shirt, open to the hairy chest, metal necklace, half-glasses, face crumpled as if from staring at some artificial sun. The curtains of the cutting room were drawn. I was introduced to the editor and the musical supervisor; the assistant editor didn't rate. Reel twelve of *Fiddler on the Roof* was on the movieola: the scene of the wedding interrupted by the Cossacks. They have started cutting the negative which redoubles the tension. Tiredness had thinned them all. Their conversation seemed more the rehearsal of objections already heard than a debate on present issues. One square on the squared lino floor was bright yellow.

'Ba-dee, ba-dee, ba-dee, ba-dee; we're missing a beat in there somewhere,' N.J. said. He gave me the glance of secret impatience and public lordship common to directors who, engaged on one project, are courting a new writer, with whom they hope (as usual) to do something unusual. It contains a combination of apology and self-assurance. N.J. is able – the credits are there – but he has the habit of repetitiousness, of self-exhorting sloganeering, so manifest in Schlesinger. A long analysis of one of the *Fiddler* scenes began, and ended twenty minutes later, with 'What we want to see are the faces.'

Between displays of inexhaustible patience, the editor was planting his intention to spend Monday afternoon at the dentist. After a series of final silences, we left the eternal night of the cutting room. The efforts to give it individuality made it resemble all the rooms from which they had tried to distinguish it: the clipboard of letters from UA, the facetious postcard, the yellowing cartoon. We walked back in the sunshine, late but strong, past a young girl in tailored – but not *well*-tailored – pants, through the main doors into a lobby where trophies, several won by Jo Janni Productions, are still displayed.

N.J. had a big, light office. I was introduced to Pat Palmer, a close-clipped, red-haired American who produces with/for N.J. His contribution to our conversation was to nod intelligently. N.J. renewed our conversation almost exactly where it started a few months ago. He was fascinated by Africa and he wanted to tell our story – whatever it was – through the eyes of two mercenaries. One of them should be intelligent, a very bright guy who had been maybe in Vietnam and had come to the conclusion that everyone was full of shit. He would do things strictly for the money. He would persist in this to a certain point, see that things were not so simple, and then be killed (or something like that) to ironic effect.

This generalised approach, typical of the movies, fills me with dread. It is a recipe for lifelessness and melodrama. You get 'characters' who are slaves to the 'story', created solely to deck a predetermined triumph and without obstinate life of their own. There will be no friction between individual and predicament. We shall have party-line propaganda, with The Industry standing in for The Party.

The walls were placarded with N.J.'s awards, a variety of bold, blatant, banal badges and certificates. He brought in five or six broad boards with cuttings stuck on them, mostly from the Congo. At one time he wanted to do the story of Lumumba, but he decided against having only a black hero. He considered Lumumba's story 'tragic', but he had a detached attitude to 'the material', like a designer who hesitates between making some exotic stuff into a dress or a trouser-suit. He sees ignoble motives everywhere (and isn't afraid to bad-mouth 'The West'), but no true sympathies; as J.R.S. treats society – as a series of scandals – so does N.J. see History.

When I challenged the idea that 'everyone is full of shit' (I maintained it was inverted sentimentality), he conceded the point. He makes concessions to maintain his position, not because he is willing to alter it. He talks of 'them' with the ritual indignation of the artist entangled in an industry, but success makes him condone what he condemns. Our discussion, at once circular and disjointed, decided nothing, not least because UA had 'passed' on the subject, having bought three others. No promise of backing could be offered. He knew I hated treatments, but perhaps in this case... Why didn't we both think about the whole thing in the next few weeks? In other words, he had no deal to offer.

They called a car for me, from a nearby company. The silver-haired driver, in a blue cap, had a sticker from a Royal Garden Party on his windscreen. He had taken some old Commodore the previous day. People were only invited, he said, because they had applied to go. The idea that it was an honour was a complete fraud;

it was all silly snobbery. N.J.'s car had sported a similar sticker; he had been to the Palace the previous afternoon.

Richard's Things. End: Kate finds the lipstick which the girl left in the hotel. She draws a mouth on her dressing table mirror, pulls a wing of cold glass against her face, and kisses it. A triple mirror, of course. The girl's tail lights are lost among others. FADE OUT.

The Child Molester. After the case is over, Strike, the Detective-Sergeant, goes back to the park to make sure that all is well. A child playing by the swings shrieks and shrieks. He is unable to calm her. People look strangely at him.

Elisabeth Ayrton told us that when Wittgenstein was staying with Dr Bevan during his last illness, Mrs Bevan made him a birthday cake. 'Many happy returns,' she said, as she brought it in. 'Would you care to reconsider that statement?' Wittgenstein said (or is said to have said). Can a wish be a statement?

Imagine a 'private' language on one page which is said to be translated *en regard*. At what point, having no direct knowledge of it, would we say 'This can't be a translation'? And on what grounds? Suppose that what looks like dialogue is opposed by solid paragraphs; questions by statements. When do we say 'I don't believe this is a version of that'? Could we *ever* do so with a 'truly' private language? Wouldn't it be untranslatable? What the demand seems to be for is a language which corresponds not only to the experience of a sensation but one which echoes its logical form so exactly as to have the same status, that is of *unshareability*.

T.E. Lawrence was the implement of imperial policy at a time when it was becoming necessary to camouflage greed as principle. His enthusiasm was deplored in Whitehall less for its hypocrisy than for its sincerity. He took the Arabs seriously; in this, to his masters, lay his want of seriousness. Had his Arabophilia been merely perverse, they might have shown it lordly tolerance; had it been boys he admired, he would have been in good company; had it been political manoeuvre, even better. But passionate partisanship led him to make fools of those who were used to making others theirs. The British have always distrusted their allies more than their enemies. The imperialist always knows that it is in the ranks of his subjects that his greatest danger lies. When auxiliaries realise how much their masters depend on them, they wonder why they remain subservient. The British in India survived a mutiny; but the Great War, in which Indians fought in their ranks, proved the first solvent of their authority. The deception of the Arabs, to which Lawrence took verbose exception, was nothing out of the usual in British foreign policy. Had not a hundred native princes been duped, from the Ganges to the Niger? T.E.L. was guilty of the one sin no official Englishman could forgive: he took things personally. Perhaps he did inflate the valour and the moral qualities of the Arab leaders; perhaps he did attach undue significance to the chivalry of those who make a virtue of cutting each other's throats. But he had given them his word. When the British haggled over honouring it, it was as if they were disowning the bastard; and so they were.

Private languages. Can we imagine a *written* private language and, facing it, a translation into a public language? Would there come a point where we said, 'I'm beginning to get the hang of it', like a code, or Spanish? The 'problem' of privacy is not a problem of access. To be truly private a language would have to be not 'difficult', but *impossible*, to learn. One could not find the key through the user's negligence, nor even with his connivance.

Bleeding Harry. A plan to spring a bank robber in order to get the loot off him. He has not escaped, he has 'been escaped'.

I wrote a screenplay based on this idea a few years later. Fox liked it and I was introduced to a young man who had just directed his first (TV) film: *Duel.* I was gracious to the debutant Spielberg and he was about to do my movie, which I called *Roses, Roses…*, but elected to do *Jaws* instead. Such are career moves.

A word does not mean what one *thinks* it means; the privacy or rareness of one's thoughts does nothing to lend private or rare meaning to one's expression of them. Take 'I have a feeling': can one imagine someone 'needing' a new, private word for this intimation? If he had one, would it contribute to a kind of secret dossier on his internal states? Doesn't it all come down to a quasi-tautology: if it is private, it's not a language, and if it's a language, it can't be private?

Do we perhaps *fear* a private language, like the secret weapon of a linguistic Gyges? Suppose we 'knew' that X. had evolved such a notation? Should we regard him with admiration or apprehension or what? What would we expect that he might now be able to do or say? Our fear would be of an alternative world, to which we could gain no access. The private world becomes, in that case, *unscientific*: given enough private languages (if the motion *meant* anything), the common basis of our world-view would be sapped. What would 'our' *mean* if my language had no rapport with yours, and no prospect of translation into it?

Before their car had even passed the gates, I knew that we should never have asked them down. I first met Ivan when I played bridge with him and Richard Bird (who might the fourth have been?) at Jordan's Yard in my first year at Cambridge. Already a graduate, he wore a maroon velvet jacket and lived with a mistress, the boss-eyed Bess, a tweedy, bouncy girl with whom, later, I went (with small appetite) to a point-to-point at Cottenham. When we got back, we went up to their room. Ivan wasn't there. Bess crouched on the bed, gleaming. I fled her expectations.

At first he had lived downstairs, where there was a piano and a big round table at which, at weekends, several of us gathered for John Brickell's cooking. Iv-arn (we pronounced him as if he had to be Russian, although his father was, in fact, a QC) had a drawling, Chekhovian style; Idelson and idleness suggested languor, but he was a clever mathematician (and a chess Blue). Bess told me that she had 'taught him all he knew'. His drawling style failed to reveal how much that was, in any department.

Our bridge fourth was sometimes Peter R., a Trinity mathematician. I went punting with him one summer afternoon in 1951. We caught a couple of student teachers. In the evening, to improve the occcasion, we took them to a dance at a Caledonian Ball beyond the Catholic Church: the only available music. Kilted enthusiasts did a sword dance and really said 'Hoots!'. My teacher proved passionate, up to a decided point: she opened her mouth under my kiss, but her tongue evaded mine. I took her to the train in the morning. She had come to my rooms in 3rd Court for breakfast, but nothing more. Maud?

P. had a refugee accent and the habit of putting his hand down the front of his trousers and, after prolonged rummaging, extracting his fingers and sniffing them. I never liked him, but did not know how to reject his importunity.

That first year, 5, Jordan's Yard had the decided silence of an unofficial library. Ivan's piano-playing brought a note of autumnal elegy; it was always November with him. Later the house became loud with jazz, and snaked with skeins of wire imported by Gordon Pask as he set about transforming the world through the construction of extensive machines. Transistors had not been invented; his prototypical computers spread all over the upper floor, each element apparently wired to all the others in a congeries of multicoloured spaghetti. Gordon was the very type of the mad inventor. When he spoke of 'negative feedback', he seemed in at the birth of a new language.

It was rumoured that Gordon's doctoral thesis began, 'As I have said before…' He lived on marmalade and aspirin tablets. He denied that they were addictive; he ought to know because he took fifty a day. It avoided having to interrupt his work by going to the dentist. His teeth were like carious, unaligned tombstones in a desecrated churchyard. He would come stumbling, blinking slowly, into the kitchen where Beetle and I slept on a single mattress among the spoil of the previous evening's meal. 'Sorry, my dears, must just get some marmalade.'

He worked thirty-six-hour days, sometimes forty-eight; nature's days were not long enough. He kept himself going on benzedrine until he collapsed. He was alleged to use his doctorate – not in medicine – to procure prescription drugs. He offered them before lunch, like cigarettes, blinking slowly, blue eyes protruding like rare eggs in the charmingly unsavoury nest of his face. He decorated the downstairs room with a mural: a city of viaducts, shops and cafés inhabited by a spindly population given to tall hats and upward extension. This room became public; you could rarely be alone in it. Posnan, Tony Becher, Rein van Dijk and a succession of *au pair* girls or foreign students stayed in or passed through it. Tony, who had no home to go to, spent the vacs at J.'s Y. and became more of an habitué than I, to my covert jealousy. John Brickell, who had been the landlord *inter pares*, became – though passive – more proprietorial. He would banish or discountenance individuals, but did not try to dominate the company. If he deplored the Sunday freeloaders, he cooked the meals which attracted them. He relished the Bohemian reputation which bought them to his narrow, but open, door.

The house seemed to be sustained by its bulging wallpaper. The woodwork buckled like stale biscuits in a damp larder. The stairs were as yielding as Uriah Heep. One consoled oneself that it would not be far to the ground. The weight of the house might be bruising, but no more crushing than a heap of wastepaper. When the place was full (I remember a crammed party for the *Ballet Rambert*), it seemed less a structure than a sort of lathe-and-plaster overcoat, bulked out by those inside it.

Nothing was forbidden, though not everyone was welcome. John was an albinoesque arbiter, secretive and vigilant, especially when the first foreign girls (often Swedes) came to live there. Bunks were installed upstairs when Monick ('she's a tonic/ she's super-sonic') and Rosa moved in. John was said to enjoy watching one of them dress, and undress. It did not occur to me that it might give her pleasure too.

I do not remember Ivan departing; he simply disappeared. The next generation had no appetite for bridge or reflective pursuits; even philosophy, which became the in-game, was only a sly variant of conversation, punctuated with Wittgensteinian hand-signals. The days when the house had been a refuge, yielded to louder decadence. Queenie and Kenneth came, and stayed in the vac. She was the great, diminutive Cambridge actress of the time. As she and I walked away one evening, I asked if she would take a character part in *Lady at the Wheel*, the musical comedy which Leslie Bricusse and I had just written. She winced, a prize too solemn to be recruited to mere entertainment. Recently she sent us a postcard 'Shall we ever see you again?' We did not reply.

I saw Ivan again only a few years ago at Crockford's. He was not markedly amiable. Since Crockford's closed, I have played little bridge. Two weeks ago, Miss ('*Pommes frites*') Pomfret, Jack Lambert's secretary, called from *The Sunday Times*' 'lit-ry department' to say that they had been called by an old Cambridge friend of mine, a Mr Idelson. He 'wanted to get in touch'.

His telephone exchange is MOGador; it sounded exotic; it is outer Epsom. I assumed that if he had a *purpose* in contacting me, it was sentimental. He did not disabuse me: he said that a psychologist had told him that forty-two was the age for revisiting the past. I invited them for the day on Sunday, having spoken a couple of times to his wife, Eva, who had a drawling diction which, with wishful fancy, I thought might conceal a quicker wit. Ivan's remembered, velvety femininity (it was still there in his speech) led me to imagine him with some wise and sensual mate. He now runs a business consultancy, dealing with storage and distribution. He employs a dozen people, has offices in Horsham – the eponymous spot for a sell-out and a phoney – and famous clients, including Unilever.

Before they came down, I alerted Roger, thinking that Ivan might supply the means for him to escape from his precarious position in the plastics factory. He and Katie would come to tea. Eva had said that she and Ivan had two children, eight and five, but they could always leave them behind. I told her that we liked to meet people's children, unless they were sick or destructive.

We expected them to be late; they were early. We had speculated on their car; I guessed a Rover. It was a petrol-injection Triumph, rather guttural. Was I filled with apprehension as soon as I saw them? Perhaps it was not until Eva got out. She was short and stiff. She wore a Sherlock Holmes cape. A chiffon scarf girdled the tight bun into which she had drawn her hair. The sharp, definite face had unblinking currant eyes and an entry-wound of a mouth, ragged with distaste, strict as a Board School. Nicholas was eight, darkly handsome, but lopsided; shy, not modest. Tamara wore a purple dress, green tights, pretty buckle shoes. She had red spots across her forehead, like the apotropaic markings of some species of timid predator. I greeted them like bad news, with as good a grace as I could contrive.

When the children went up to the playroom, I warned him against touching the electric typewriter. 'I'm afraid,' Ivan said, 'forbidding Nicky to do things usually has the opposite effect.' When he discovered that the projection room was locked, it became the target of his obsessions.

Eva went to Oxford, and read PPE. Ivan drank St Raphael. 'A French apéritif,' he explained to Eva. No cosmopolite she; she drank sherry. She was so stiff, so ungentle, so curdled. In the bedroom, she had said to Beetle, 'Do your children eat you?' 'No.' 'Mine eat me.' I achieved miracles of wilful courtesy. Nicky and Tamara informed Beetle ('*Beetle*!' Eva said, implying *ugh*) that they did not eat lamb. They would have ravioli.

The early afternoon was very long. However, Ivan buys a lot of books and had read mine. I kept wondering why exactly they had come (empty-handed, of course). Ivan had mentioned on the telephone a man called David Spencer-Brown. I recalled a wispy, donnish figure who used to play bridge at Crockford's. He treated every deal as a protracted problem; he did not play with you, you were merely present. A mathematician and a chess player, he lived in Cambridge, had taught philosophy at Oxford and had now become an author who printed his own books. He had recently 'published' a sort of novel: *Only Two Can Play This Game*.

I assumed that Ivan was merely being conversational, but soon after lunch he produced a leaflet advertising the novel. I asked genially if I could be sent a copy. Ivan said, 'Surely *The Sunday Times* has plenty of copies.'

The brochure suggested a parody of W.'s *Philosophical Investigations*. I said it seemed a little callow. The fuse was a broken 'betrothal'. The pain of disappointment led S.-B. to speculate on the nature of love and on the shallowness of positivism. Beetle pointed out something Fowles-like in the vatic musings; callowness and self-importance in tandem. I ironised without malice, but I had, I supposed, spiked Ivan's mission.

Ivan wore a tweed sports jacket, grey flannels with turn-ups, an open-necked shirt and knotted silk square. His business makes him a psychiatrist to sick companies. His brother, Francis, is a speculator who lives in Switzerland. He had been standing to make so much money out of shares that he removed himself to Australia, but Australia was inconvenient, unless you wanted to be in Australia, so he relocated to Zurich, where Ivan once went to a good strip show. Francis is solitary, though sociable, and very rich. Ivan is now out to emulate him; his business needs a thousand a week to run comfortably. They have already secured a hefty consultancy from a Japanese company, four of whose engineers will join them in January. He said the odd surprising thing, for instance, 'The customer is the most important member of the firm.'

How could this be applied to the cinema, I wondered? In the 1940s and 1950s, I suggested, when the middle-aged had nothing to entertain them at home, they went to the movies, while their teenage children stayed and necked in peace. When TV came in in a big way, the parents preferred to stay comfortably at home. The kids were obliged to go to the cinema for uninterrupted necking. Now the young wanted to fuck. Why not, therefore, project the movies on the ceiling? There was no need for seats; the floor could be specially upholstered so that the film could be watched from the prone position. Those who directed the ceiling (or panoptical) films would soon have serious articles devoted to them, hailing them as engineers of a new popular art. Those who complained that the mattress-houses were hot-beds of vice would be howled down as philistines.

Eva was not amused. She said that the young were far more puri-

tanical than we imagined. Their *au pair* did not want to go to bed
with her young man. She seemed to be warning me against any rash
investment in The Horizontals. She believed that a home is somewhere to get out of; she goes to Ivan's office to do the books.
Recently she accompanied him to Bournemouth on a conference.
They had a free suite. She no longer found it 'absurd in principle
to flirt with sixty-year-old men, in a mild way'. She was, I thought,
lucky to get them. But how lucky were they?

When Roger and Katie arrived, the tedium was diluted, but I
was sorry to have invited them to so dud an occasion. Eva talked in
her exact, uninteresting way, assertive of her intelligence in the style
of women who have lost faith in their looks. She seemed at least
fifty but she told me that she was born in 1933: younger than I then!
Was she English? Yes. Her father was invited by Sir Jules Thorn to
come to England from Vienna in 1925; he had not fled, he had left.
Her cold, apprehensive eyes promised superiority to the subsequent,
refugee rabble. Her face, nevertheless, had an accent. She hated her
son; she was determined to do nothing to control him or to please
him. He chased Charlie (our Labrador) as if she were a nanny. He
asked me continually to open the projection room. How shameful
to hate a child not yet nine! Yet it's easier to hate children than
adults: one is made a child again oneself, capable of brutality and
vindictiveness, mutable and malicious. When Roger and Katie left,
soon after six, we hoped the Idelsons would follow. They did not.

Beetle went to put Stee – who had already been reduced to tears
– to bed, if only to make him safe from sly cruelty. Nicholas wanted
to watch Morecombe and Wise at 7.25. I was determined that they
should leave before then. They did not, in fact, go till after eight,
but the telly remained off. I claimed that it would disturb Stee. I
asked coldly whether they were hungry; there had been no thanks
for lunch, nor politeness over tea. We went to the playroom where
Nicholas had destroyed Stee's cardboard house. The family watched
while Ivan and I played ping-pong. I won 2-1. Would they now
go? Timid as her brother was wild, but no less unnerving, Tamara
was terrified of the spiral staircase in the tower which led up to the
playroom door; she had to be carried up or have her hand held.

Eva left us to sort out the children. Ivan removed Tamara, who
was crying that he was pressing her tummy, while I went in search
of Nicky, who had disappeared. I found him at the top of the secret
stairs to the projection room, hidden behind one of the sack chairs
which he had dragged up with him. He refused to come down. I
was patient, calm and persistent, icily. I said that if he came down

he could turn out all the lights in the playroom, or see if he could without making a mistake. The challenge was beyond him and the lure insufficient. He declined. I insisted. He came. They all settled down again in the kitchen.

By the time Beetle came downstairs, Nicky had lost his sandals; he said that the dog had taken them. Charlie never takes anything. I found the missing sandals. The boy was by now wearing a pair of Sarah's jeans; his own shorts had been muddied in a fall which he blamed, of course, on the blameless Charlie. Eva made a big show of rubbing the dried mud out over the basin. I doubted if it would do much harm. 'It might dirty the Raphaels' chairs, or even the Idelsons' car,' she said, in her calculatedly consonantal way.

Now Nicholas lost his boot, between the house and the garage. It turned out that he had run up the spiral stairs and flung it onto the roof of the walkway. I climbed over in the wet and retrieved it. Ivan had opted out of everything.

Their car farted reluctantly. For a grim, hilarious moment, we imagined that they might claim a night's stay.

After they had left, I called Roger and Katie. When she answered the phone, I said, 'Katie, I love you.'

She said, 'You've made my evening.'

Patrick Sergeant: much of the wealth of Swiss banks comes from the investment by them of secret money deposited by the Nazis, and by their victims. Only by knowing the number of daddy's account can cash be reclaimed, even by those with clear title. Much of the money was smuggled in by those who later died, in raids or in the camps. No one can now lay claim to it.

Another story: after the bank raid on Barclay's Marylebone branch, customers were asked to come and claim compensation for whatever had been in their safety deposit boxes. Although promised immunity by the police, only ten per cent came forward.

Tennis at Hall Road is to end in February. We knew that the axe was going to fall, but kept picking the cherries. Patrick gives himself great airs as the head of the 'syndicate', as Peter Rendel (a Lloyd's man) unfailingly calls it. Patrick's chauffeur carries in his bag from the Jaguar. Patrick and Ferdy Mount – a *Daily Mail* leader-writing O.E. of modest vanity – are not slow to call a ball out. Last week, I accused them of behaving 'like the Syrian B team'. Laughingly, of course.

I called Queenie, guilty at our failure to respond to their postcard during the summer. Ken is in Chicago for the next two and a half weeks. She is low, but managed a bright tone. She considers that she has been a 'coward'. Why didn't she write a book?, I asked; everyone else does. She denied the talent. 'God,' I said, 'you haven't become modest, have you, suddenly?' We spoke as if we were dead. No, as if she were. From me, a mixture of sympathy and vindictiveness.

She said, 'How's Beetle?'

'All right. Fine.'

'She always was.'

'We all failed to be nice to each other,' I said.

'We didn't know how,' she said.

4.12.71. A week waiting for Michael Sissons to read *April, June and November*. I wrote a review; I read Wittgenstein; I played squash with Roger. All the time I was waiting for Sissons' rented praise. (Yet if he recommended another book to me, would I read it?) He said that he would 'be back' to me by the end of the week. At three p.m. on Friday afternoon, I called him, from tennis. He was in conference. I asked that he call me at Slazenger's at ten past four, after my lesson. I read Penrose's *Picasso* as I waited for Frank Wild. It was a dark afternoon, but F. was slow to put on the lights. Do I enjoy his lessons?

The school closes on 18 February. The demolition men were there yesterday, loitering ominously behind the yellow, opaque windows of the gallery overlooking the brick and steel court. Patrick has heard of a covered court somewhere up near Highgate. Coulsdon?

Frank won't go to Queen's (too snobbish), but where else can he teach every day in an English winter? I went through my routine motions, hardly raising a sweat. It was a dutiful pleasure. Perhaps he has taught me more than I think; I hope so. After my shower, I sat in the dressing room. At 4.25, I heard the telephone ring. Frank answered; first puzzled, then irritated. I picked up the extension. 'Hallo, hallo, platforma, platforma, calling you from out of London – over. Platforma, platforma, hallo, hallo.' A madman? A joke? Certainly not Michael Sissons. I called A.D. Peters at 4.30 and left a message. I took a cab to Marks in Edgware Road and bought a caramel-coloured cardigan for my father's birthday. My cabbie was Jewish, an eager reader. I deposited my parcels at Seymour Walk. Should I phone Sissons once more? I did, and was put through.

A stammer of excuses: as I imagined, he had had a marital crisis. He had not been able to read the book. My week of anxiety had been pointless. I was benign, understanding, and furious.

Had he made a ten-second phone call, on Monday, I might have been spared all my petty anguish.

Lunch with Rachel. She spent the summer in Wales, with a troupe of actors led by Jane A. She was the common servant until her revolt infuriated those who were using her. Sheila Allen left early. Miss A. was planning to make a film of *The Story of O*. Did Rachel covet the part? Jane A. lives with a hustler who talked some woman in Wales into leaving her family and giving Jane all her money. Rachel was due to meet this woman after lunch. They are planning to make a documentary about 'the Wren set'. This, if I heard correctly, is a community which dresses up as wrens and have a murder cult. Oh boy. For a moment, I thought they dressed up as WRNS.

Yesterday (5.12.71) was my father's birthday. I sent my parents my tickets for the press show of *Fiddler On The Roof*. Beetle and I drove down to Bedales to see Paul and Sarah. The eunuchoid proprietor of the Old Manor House restaurant in Midhurst made us welcome for an early lunch. Sarah had to be back at 2.15 for the performance of the Christmas play. It was a mini-oratorio; musically ambitious but dramatically wooden, conducted by Snuggs, who – so Paul told me – had made an anti-Semitic remark in class. It boiled down to 'waking up' P. with the remark, re Balshazzar and Daniel, 'This ought to interest you, it's about your ancestors.' Hardly the Hitlerian jibe of the season.

P. is apprehensive lest I alert anyone to our Jewishness, though it seems no great secret. Some people are much teased. He asked Beetle not to wear her mink in the school grounds: 'Some people think we're millionaires.' I never thought to embarrass my children with riches, of all things.

I stood awkwardly for the carols. I cannot sing the words; Beetle can, and does. The local vicar, in undress uniform, said that there would be a silver collection for Shelter. He asked, with deep-socketed sincerity, that we spend a moment in prayer for those whom Shelter was meant to help. He paraded the usual worldwide skeletons so dear to the sado-masochism of accusing piety: India, Pakistan, all those places for whom this would *not* be a happy Christmas. Everyone closed their eyes in humble embarrassment. Afterwards I asked a soliciting Bedalian where the Shelter money was likely to go. With artless candour, he said, 'England. It's a strictly UK charity.' Must the good always lie?

It would be nice to give more than two cheers for Bedales. The staff lack fire: Slack is foxy, G.P. unctuous, Snuggs two-faced. Despite my bold Philippic at the last parents' meeting, about the lack of a washing machine (I offered to supply one), nothing has changed. One of the parents who had called me 'the *enfant terrible*' greeted me with 'While shepherds washed their socks by night'. Not bad. I smiled coldly. Nevertheless, P. and S. are happy: Paul said to me, 'It's a dream come true.' If they dredge up minor grievances, they seem little distressed by them.

We drove back to Langham in sporadic fog and good spirits, despite Beetle's cold. I had asked Jack to go to Ipswich to get tickets for the Manchester United game. Isabel had a cold, feared asthma; he couldn't leave her. I drove to Ipswich at 10 a.m., expecting a long queue. There was none; I got four tickets and was home by eleven. This afternoon I started work on *Richard's Things*. I also wrote a letter to Michael Sissons.

Van Gogh: not a day without a line. What seems a declaration of worthy devotion to his art is also the confession that he will not give a full day to mere life. Addiction is paraded as duty.

Sissons phoned. He liked the novel but not my letter. He was 'bugged' by my schoolmasterly tone. The fact that he did not do what he said he would do has been let slide. The truth is that he works for me and he must take the strain. Meanwhile, the 'smashing' quality of the novel is lost in pettiness. He chides me for alluding to the break-up of a twelve-year marriage as 'personal troubles'. Should I commiserate? If we are not friends (and we are not), why should I even be told? I want service, not excuses.

10.12.71. A meeting with Sissons at noon. There had been only three of us at tennis: Janering, Mount and I. The three-sided game generated some tension by the end. I led, lagged and finally served two aces to equalise. We all had fourteen points when Frank ambled accusingly onto the court with a basket of balls ready for his next pupil.

Sissons is so sandy, so pale, so English. Long hair, drooping moustache and American jargon cannot conceal cold calculation. He had told his wife, 'I can't believe that I cannot make someone

happier than I make you.' He acknowledged the accuracy of my
account of amateur soccer. He formed a team called Thames-siders
(catchy?) from which he recently retired. Alan Sharpe (also red-
headed) was his centre-half. He was unimpressed by Valentine
Mitchell's wish to reprint *The Limits of Love* as a Modern Jewish
Classic. 'Ten per cent of two thousand copies,' he said. When I
mentioned that Tom had told me that *Who Were You With Last
Night?* was 'selling nicely', he said, 'If he calls that selling nicely, my
cock's a kipper.' He brags of knowing everyone; does anyone brag
of knowing him?

Lunch at Grosvenor House with pen-friend Daniel Stern. I haven't
been there since I used to have free lunches with Cyril Ross.* It has
been gutted and revamped and could be any modern hotel
anywhere. I waited in the lobby, trying to attach Stern's likely face
to those seated around me. I stood up; I walked around; I was
ignored. Then he came along, from the elevators, slim, dark, not
tall, more a salesman to look at than an artist, although apart from
being a novelist he was, in fact, until the age of thirty-one a professional cellist. He wore a lead-coloured suit. His face has a kind of
practised roundness; he avoided striking sharp attitudes. I did my
best to seem pleased to meet him, but his slickness inhibited warmth
as it exacted its counterfeit. He was scandalised by the vehemence
of my fracture with Tom Guinzburg; not the way, he said, that he
had been brought up as a nice Jewish boy. His new book is called
The Rose Rabbi.

He had taken a job at Warner's, but California had not agreed
with him, or at least not with his wife. Still on full salary, they were
living in the Rue Payenne, in a studio owned by Rodrigo
Moynihan. He offered inside information – so and so was doing the
new Mordecai Richler, somebody else had a deal at Universal – like
a secret agent proving his access to privileged sources. He had seen
Bernard Malamud the previous evening; he knew Vassili Vassilikos
in Paris. He did his own publicity; and how. I asked if *Miss America*

* Cyril was the self-made chairman of Swears and Wells, a large Oxford Street
furriers. He wanted to be a novelist and I was appointed his tutor. He gave me
twenty-five quid and a good lunch for taking him seriously, and I was grateful.
One day he asked if I remembered the 'Victory Services Club' during the war.
It was at the top of Edgware Road. I did. 'I built that,' he said, 'and gave it to
them. Eisenhower and Montgomery used to go there.' 'Did you meet them?'
I asked. 'Coupla times,' he said, 'but to tell you the truth, I don't much go for
the *goyim*.'

had been based on personal experience. 'Painful personal experience,' he said. His wife said to him when they married, 'You had plenty of wild oats, so don't think I'm going to be understanding. If I catch you, I'll shoot you. Bang.' The prisoner boasts of his gaoler's flattering ruthlessness.

A dying philosopher is manipulated by scheming acolytes. Like Russell, his name grows more powerful as he gets older. It becomes a separate force to which he must cling like a Jamesian hero who loses his soul to his own shadow, and walks in fear of it; a sick prince with a stern bodyguard. Stronger than he is, his shadow drags him where he dreads to go. He contrives an incognito *fugue* during which he revels in casting no shadow at all. Recaptured, the shadow makes sure he doesn't get away again by dragging him over a cliff. Then it goes back, fat with imposture, and signs a will in which the Great Liberal endorses Mao and what all else.

Clear sunny day, haze in its clarity. Queues at the Colchester ground, funnelling politely into the narrow slots. At half-time, a shakoed band from a boys'n'girls club: girls with reddened legs, boys all sizes, from toddler to red-headed furtive smokers (as they lounged in front of us during the first half). Floodlights brought on fuzzy evening. Peterborough scored; the match seemed lost; then Colchester equalised. Paul and I raced back to the car. He might have won (nearly fourteen), had he not taken a wrong turning, which he refused to correct at my call. Curiously, the match passed unmentioned in the football results, like a dream.

A man sits in a bourgeois dining room, reading a book. The door is unlocked with all the rattling ceremony of a cell door being unbarred. The governor announces to the man that his term is over. The prisoner breaks down and cries. The governor is pitilessly liberating: he cannot stay. The prisoner's name is Lyman.

The Public School as Magic Mountain. A novel-essay in which the boys stay endlessly at school, become generals and judges, criminals and rebels. The School Spirit. Proles as oiks; intellectuals as 'professionals'.

Fifteen years later, I wrote *School Play*, a film based on this *donnée*. Directed by Jim Cellan-Jones, with whom I had been at

Charterhouse, it starred Denholm Elliot, Jeremy Kemp, Tim Piggot-Smith, Michael Kitchen and Jenny Agutter. It was widely admired, but never repeated. The top people at the BBC realised, *après coup*, that it was a metaphor for England and, not least, the BBC. The most enduring of the myths about the English is that they can take a joke; so they can, as long as it is not against themselves.

1972

2.1.72. A perfect Sunday; hard to say why. It was dull and chilly, grey enough to create the common glumness. Yet we were in good humour. After tea, I started to make collages. Soon Paul, Sarah, and Stee were all in my room cutting up magazines. It was the family scene I most frequently imagine: no demands, only an energetic eagerness, a fury to create and enjoy.

In the evening, I called my mother, who had been out to dinner when I called on New Year's Eve. 'Our New Year hasn't begun very well,' she said. 'Oh dear. Why?' 'Jock died last night.' It hadn't prevented my parents from going out to dinner, but now it demanded sympathy, almost apology.

I used to play tennis regularly with Jock and Pamela when I was in my late teens and early twenties. Max Stewart made up a four every Sunday morning. I played singles a few times with Pamela during the week. She was then a pretty girl in her early thirties. Jock soon put a stop to our innocent assignations. She had never occurred to me as a sexual possibility, but Jock had been made a fool of by one wife and was not to be cuckolded again. His wariness did not prevent him from soliciting my company. He liked to play *L'Attaque*, a board game with military connotations. I would take my set across to Somerville House from time to time.

During the war, Jock had been an officer in the King's Own Scottish Borderers. He spoke little of his experiences in battle. He told me that he had killed only one man himself, very late in the day. His squadron of armoured cars was already inside Germany when he had to go into a house which was suspected of harbouring a sniper. There were dark steps leading to the cellar. He went down, bent over, checking with his dirk for trip wires (there had been casualties from booby traps). The man hidden in the cellar (who was presumably out of ammunition) tried to club him with a swinging blow from his rifle. Because Jock was bent double, the blow missed him. He straightened up with his dagger ahead of him and took the man in the solar plexus, killing him almost instantly.

Jock was also keen on stamps. He gave me his collection of Americans; they were rare, but not as valuable as Stanley Gibbons' catalogue led me to think, on account of their imperfections. His generosity was a function, perhaps, of the loss of his own son, whom his first wife had turned against him. When Jock was ill with cancer, the son never came to see him. He also had a daughter, in Australia, who lived with her mother after the loud divorce. Would he really have wanted them to come and live with him and Pamela at Manor Fields? Would Pamela? They led a hermetic existence. Jock let no one into his wife's life; she let no one into their flat. She cleaned it herself. My parents never dined there. When my father was in hospital, did they ever invite Irene to a meal?

The two couples played bridge every Saturday night and affected a close friendship, but Jock rarely, if ever, asked Cedric to play golf (Jews were not welcome at Royal Wimbledon). He ignored him, bowler-hatted both, on the station platform on workday mornings. The hospitality on Saturday nights was rigidly reciprocal: whisky ('The old Mahogany') for all but my father, who drank 'squash', and cheesy biscuits. Jock always played with C.M.R. There was no exogamous flirting, but Jock was a compulsive maker of risqué remarks. His marriage to a pretty girl gave him a vanity so shameless than he assumed his own handsomeness, and the licence it supplied. He worshipped the sun. In the summer, he lay on a deckchair on the lawn. It was understood that no one was welcome to approach him. The measure of good manners was that you conformed to his convenience. In winter, he basked under a sun-lamp for so many minutes, or hours, a day.

After he made a lot of money from Hampton Gold shares (a tip my father forgot to pass on to me), he bought himself an Alvis. He and Pamela took the opportunity to buy their flat in Manor Fields, when the freehold was offered, as did my parents.*

Jock and Pamela had been several times to the Caribbean. Jock

---

* My father borrowed £1,500 from me to complete the purchase. When I came to write the cheque, he said, 'You might make it 2,000 while you're at it.' Years before, when I wanted a mortgage, he would not guarantee it. I made it 1,500.

enjoyed saucy conversations with the local girls. He spoke of one 'very pretty, sexy darkie' who wore a white dress. When she walked away into the night, she disappeared except for her dress which could be seen oscillating deliciously in the void.

Roger and a colleague had to sort through the personal effects of an employee whose car was crushed by an articulated lorry. There were no secrets, but his papers were covered in blood. Some of his things were in a plastic folder. The blood was still wet and unclotted. Shreds of tobacco stuck to it. They threw his Masonic Rulebook into the incinerator. It too was covered with blood. The Lodge called next day and asked for it.

31.1.72. A rare Monday in London; a day of new people. I drove over snow and ice to Colchester station, skidding helplessly at the entrance to Boxted Straight Road. Luckily, no one was coming. I stamped the platform waiting for the train in the fur hat which Stuart Lyons gave me a couple of years ago, a relic of Huston's *The Kremlin Letter*.

Judy Scott-Fox and I lunched with Alan Pakula at the Connaught Grill. He was slightly late, a not tall, sandy-red bearded man, with emphatic blue eyes. He was nervous, a compromise whose transition from producer to director was signalled by the juxtaposition of orthodox collar and Mayfair tie and creative hair on his jaw. He has just had a big success with *Klute*. Acclaim and money have rejuvenated him. He produced for some years for Robert Mulligan and made a happy living in California. He is reading *April, June and November*, but fished for alternative things we might do. General enthusiasm is the producer's easiest form of preliminary payment; it doesn't cost a thing. We talked the restaurant empty, but the wine waiter remained benevolent; I had procured easy approval by selecting a '61 Burgundy, one of the cheapest on the list, but – he let me believe – one of the best.

What they call 'a good meeting' ended with A.P. suggesting that he drive down to see us next week. Columbia have provided him with a car and a driver. By then he will have finished my novel. We taxied back to Savile Row, where the William Morris office is, in time to see three black labourers drill industriously into a water main. It gushed an uncontrollable fountain, which they leaped back to admire. It played all afternoon.

I waited for Jack Clayton while Judy dealt with her busy list of calls. He arrived at four, having telephoned to say that he was having car trouble. He parked in the street where it said NO PARKING and handed the keys to Judy. Clayton has a halo of baldness surrounded by long grey hair through which he continually combs his hands. His eyes are large and blue-grey, of a compelling, vacuous intensity.

We sat in Bob Shapiro's office and, talking generalities, loitered on the frontier of *Gatsby*. We began by demolishing his rivals: Losey, Kubrick, etc. Truman Capote had failed to deliver the *Gatsby* he was after; Clayton did not criticise him, but preferred to sympathise: 'He is rather ill.' Shall we be reading of T.C.'s death shortly? Was there anything in Capote's script that could be useful? 'Nothing.' He had done an efficient translation from prose to script; had he been a lesser name, they would have accused him of phoning it in. How much of our meeting was a discussion and how much an audition? There is a job and it is in C.'s gift. One goes about getting something by assuming that one already has it; that is the evidence that one hasn't.★

Clayton asked if I knew Long Island society. Truman had taken him around. It was much the same as it was in Scott's day. My only experience of such people was when I knew Bill Fine. His wedding at Fleur Cowles' Albany apartment, two or three or four years ago, might as well have been in East Egg. I went alone, wondering as I always do when alone, why I was doing what I so little wanted to do. Fleur Cowles Mayer is now all purple and powder. Arbiter of taste, painter of screens, designer of frivolities, she has a dusty, dated elegance, like a much-married Miss Havisham, less jilted than obsolete. She once edited a magazine called *Show*, which was one of the first to include 'inserts'. A *New Yorker* cartoon showed a young

★ After the failure, as it turned out, of *Gatsby*, Clayton made postponement his only art form. He wore his hair in a ponytail and often caressed its length. His Indian wife was beautiful and blessed him with a cosmopolitan air. It seems that he acquired his refinement by association. Much later, I heard how he had rented a house on Benedict Canyon owned by Ken Annakin, a veteran English director long resident in California. After a while, Annakin told Clayton that he was sorry but he would have to give him notice: he wanted to sell the house. Jack said that he would buy it, at the asking price. Annakin was surprised, and pleased. Clayton made just one stipulation: he would pay the price only if the house was left exactly as it was. K.A. said that he wanted only to take some personal items, books, pictures, records. 'No, no,' Clayton said, 'if I'm going to pay the full price, I want the house left exactly as it is now. Exactly.' K.A. wanted the money and accepted the condition.

author boasting, 'I once had something in *Show*, but it fell out.' Fleur survived her extravagances thanks to her husbands' money. She was the friend, and the pander, of the famous. She gave them the conviction that they had good taste with the only proof they could understand: she made them pay handsomely for what had then to be handsome.

For a time, Adelle Donen was billed in *The Evening Standard* as one of London's best hostesses. Stanley supplied a suite of titled nonentities and complacent celebrities who could be relied on not to take offence at a free meal. The first time I heard him speak, Stanley was on the telephone to Adelle. 'If I can't get the Duke of Westminster,' he was saying, 'will the Duke of Marlborough do?' Mrs Cowles had been in the business long before Adelle. In a world where the resonance of a man's name determines how close a friend he is, she waited to have you identified like a bank clerk confirming a customer's credit. She paid out in smiles or turned away, in a cloud of *Cologne*, should you not merit further attention. She had the capacity to be at once the most gushing and the most snobbish of her own guests.

Her apartment must have had solid walls, but my memory is of canvas screens, overlapping like the rugs on a hypochondriac's nervous bed. It might be sumptuous but you would not have been surprised to see the bailiffs: too many ornaments, too many apprehensions.

Bill Fine was a handsome Jew in his early forties. As publisher of *Harper's Bazaar*, he lacked nothing in grace or standing, but he had the shifty cordiality of a man who had proved everything except his courage or his honour. He had lately abandoned a long marriage. I was the only person in front of whom he felt obliged to shame; it was an uncashable bond between us. The rest of them were socialites; there was scarcely an American in the room who had not voted Goldwater. You were not required to be the same as they were, but it was unwise to be different. If you had money, you were in. Disapproval of poverty was the only permitted vanity. The poor were decidedly *not* always with us, or with us at all. Their condition was diagnosed as want of energy. The world might be cruel; it was never unjust. Among such people did Bill and Susan kneel to an Anglican priest, empurpled like an emperor, while he poured over them a sermon glutinous enough to double as *Béarnaise*. Among gaudy silks and Second Empire bibelots, he praised the simple resolution which, in a world rancid with cynicism, had led these two young people to plight their troth in a religious ceremony, however unpretentious, however lacking in ostentation. Bill had told me that his first wife had been his childhood sweetheart. The priest, with his swinging cross and halter, was administering as impious a sacrament as love could devise or money excuse. Those who joined him in prayer for our friends would as easily have passed through the eye of a needle as remembered the words of a single hymn, in no matter what faith.

Never mind. Mrs Cowles Meyer was a great hostess. Her lunch would banish embarrassment and restore our faith in worldly things. After the priest had finally run out of unction, we filed under a narrow doorway into an inner drawing room where the buffet was to be served. Mrs Cowles Meyer disappeared, re-appeared, disappeared and re-re-appeared. A disaster had occurred. Mr Fu – 'My genius of a Chinese cook' – the incomparable, legendary Mr Fu had left two turkeys in the oven on silver platters. Absorbed in the creation of other culinary marvels, he had neglected the temperature. The platters had melted, deluging the lower turkey with silver rain; the higher was merely incinerated. Overcome by shame and unable to face his loss of face, Mr Fu had fled Mrs Cowles Meyer's employ. We had shredded lettuce for lunch.

As I left, I found myself next to an elderly American producer, whose wealth was founded on Batman and Robin. I lamented that we had not tasted the fabled fruits of Mr Fu. 'I don't believe Mr Fu even *exists*,' he said. 'You *always* get lettuce for lunch at Fleur's. She serves the worst food in London.'

On the way out of Albany, I called in to see Terry Stamp. He lived in a book-lined pad, all red wallpaper and white marble busts, a cockney boy got up by a smart tailor, richly out of water, but swimmingly content.

At the Axelrods'. I loitered in Eaton Square, fearing to be too early. The street door was opened by a listless girl in a blue cotton dress and white collar. 'Mr Axelrod? Would you take the lift at the back of the building and go up to the third floor?' The hall narrowed to a passage covered with grey figured wallpaper lit by Odeon brackets. The lift opened directly into the flat. I was reminded of when I went to collect Jo Janni at Penelope Gilliatt's place at 90, Central Park West.

There were plenty of people already *chez* Axelrod. Anxiety had made for perfect timing. I was greeted eagerly by a small knitted woman with a freckled, wide-eyed face. I tried to remember who she was. She reminded me of Maria, the little Sicilian who worked for us in Seymour Walk. Might she have achieved some miraculous translation? It was Malou Wiseman, disguised with fresh suntan from a skiing holiday. Tom confessed, with his weary, melting smile, that he had skied for the first time. 'You have to be willing to risk your life.' 'And to look ridiculous.' 'And to look ridiculous.' '*La condition humaine*,' I said.

The guest of honour was James ('Jim') Jones. The author of *From Here to Eternity* was wizened in a grey check suit, like a cowboy warned off the saddle. I was introduced to Kirk Douglas; it was like meeting the Taj Mahal. You looked, but there wasn't anything to say that hadn't been said before.

The apartment was littered with collections: snuff boxes and empty liquor flasks, each of which might have been drained personally by our host. The Axelrods have let the house to a banker, but they have tranferred their pictures. We might have been in some touring company whose sets could be thrown together in any location. The show of elegant, tasteful treasures was a kind of pleading declaration, as if our hosts feared some cosmic Customs Officer might be about to assess them for duty.

I greeted Alan Pakula like an old friend; to meet the same person twice in a day forges a rare bond. We stood about the party like Homeric Gods, in but not of the society we patronised. He was about to go to *Alpha Beta* at the Royal Court; it has suffered the fall in esteem that follows too grand a premium. Everyone you meet at a cocktail party seems to conspire, secretly, against the pretensions of the occasion. Mordecai Richler was so bent and squat and overweight that he might have been auditioning for Quasimodo. He managed to be affable; his dyed black-haired wife, with her Irish blue eyes and brave mouth (as if she were rehearsing widowhood) was positively keen. They are returning to Canada after eighteen years in London. *St Urbain's Horseman* sold 'five or six thousand' in the UK, which probably means four and a half. Mordecai thought that his publishers had gone too deliberately for the Jewish market; it was like Spinoza looking for a job at Marks. Ready to become a character, M. has consented to be middle-aged; he is going to teach one day a week somewhere near Montreal. Tall with independent deference, his wife towers below him. She was once married to Stanley Mann; Mordecai captured her in a bold, traumatic (for S.M.) raid. Stanley then became a victim and the friend of victims: his Putney flat was a comfort station of the cross for those undergoing marital crucifixion. He went into analysis, wrote indifferent scripts, and re-married. Stanley made a recovery, of a kind, but Mordecai was never seen to smile again. He is a humorous writer, but a humourless man: he is in the funny business.

Andrew Sinclair arrived, long face vertical with mordant vanity; his film of *Under Milk Wood* has just opened. There had been six rave reviews, he told me. 'I was talking about you only today. I was saying that you and I and Jonathan Miller were the three most *exposed* people in London.' 'Yes,' I thought, 'but Jonathan is more exposed than I, if only because he is exposed to me.' Andrew said, 'My publisher, Tony Godwin, tells me I'm for the chop this time. My book's in proof, but he's shown it to a few people and he says I'm for the chop. They can't stand versatility and they can't stand you being prolific.' He was married for a long time to a Frenchwoman called Marianne; for many years they had no children and gave the impression of leading a very modern life. Then they had a child; two years later they parted. He sees the boy 'occasionally'. Now married to the movies, his publishing house, Lorrimer, is his baby: 'It's my contribution to the educational process.' He is as full of himself as any director who has delivered himself of his work, prouder of his tricks than of his achievements: 'I had Burton in Wales for two days, two *days*, but you'd swear he was in every scene.' He managed the deception by panning through black: 'You'd never believe it wasn't all the same shot.' An American in a tartan jacket, peeled face bracketed together by college-boy spectacles, attacked Andrew with prepared praise and I stepped clear.

Someone had failed to close the lift door. Waiting for it, I was trapped with a couple of young Hambros. I was reminded of *The Exterminating Angel*. The girl denied having seen it, but latched so sociably onto my synopsis that it almost persuaded me she had. George folded a big book of Toulouse-Lautrec drawings, which was standing on a hoop-backed chair, splayed on its spine, and disclosed a door which opened onto elegant, but dark, stairs. It was like being despatched down a Georgian laundry chute.

Clive Donner phoned to say that he was keen to do *Who Were You With Last Night?* He had a producer in mind: Stu Lyons. Promising! Clive booked lunch at Odin's, which is near him. Stu had broken his leg while serving at tennis; he honoured Clive's invitation by coming, in a limousine and on crutches, from Walton-on-Thames. We lunched until dark. We were the only people left in the restaurant and still no one, certainly not Clive, had called for the bill. A writer does not pay for lunch when there is a director *and* a producer at the table. Nor, in Clive's case, does the man who issued the invitation. If Stu imagined himself a guest (since he knew nothing of the project we had in mind until it was explained to him), he realised, eventually, that he would have to be a paying guest or risk being there at dinner time. He paid and went painfully on his way. The project did not get any further.

Edmund Wilson on Bomarzo in the *NYRB*. He emphasises its sinister qualities, as if it were some corrupt blot on Italy's *bella figura*. No doubt the Orsini who ordered its construction was an unsavoury figure; disfigured himself, he disfigured the landscape to be seen from his dark castle. But isn't the effect of his soured imagination less curdling than Wilson suggests? When we visited the place, seven years ago, Paul and Sarah ran and played among the grotesque statuary without nightmarish consequence. The softening effect of moss and lichen and the indifferent beauty of the site mitigated wilful horror.

But even if the petrified malevolence of Bomarzo were to assault the visitor, would it really be so Medusan? Orsini's bitter jests come almost as a tart relief after the blandness of humanist elegance and divine proportions. One reads often enough of the stiletto-ridden plots and poisonous intrigues of the Borgias, their greedy desires and intricate malice, but how rarely they have a visual correlative! Bomarzo vindicates a curious humanity; Renaissance loftiness is, like the stone giant, turned on its head. The monsters, like Greek satyr-plays, supply a gnomic gloss on standard solemnities. Bomarzo's beastliness is a spicy condiment for the fish-fleshed marbles of Italy's lesser masters; it reminds us of dark places which even the greatest are never commissioned to plumb. The sculptures are as comic as they are horrible, as endearing as loathsome. How much more cruel is rape or a ripping battle than the tortured expressions on all those dying Jesuses or the pious excruciations of saints and martyrs? The contrivances of Christian sado-masochism add smugness to gloating. They placard a violence more defined, more disagreeable and, perhaps, more perverse than Bomarzo's. The contortions of the giant are not imposed by a vindictive scheme; they are the routines of all-in wrestling performed by lapiths (its playfulness hints that no one really gets hurt): we are watching some fanciful show, not an execution. What is missing is any affectation of morality or justice. The hunchback refused to see the world through the straight eyes of those who imagined there were such things as just deserts. It is not the barbarity that alarms us, if it does, but the impudent implication that our idea of beauty (and goodness) is both blinkered and arbitrary. Bomarzo's celebration of ugli-ness is a liberty, and a scandal. If it is repulsive (I did not see it so), it is scarcely obscene, still less didactic: it invites us neither to commit cruelties nor to venerate them, as Christian art does. Void of love, it does not incite to hatred; romantic (since it admits no limits), it is not diabolical. Was Bomarzo the setting for orgies? It fails to encourage them. It is too reassuring, too cosy: it belongs to comedy. Who would not prefer to have a picnic at Bomarzo than under the eyes of the Vatican statuary with its plaster of Paris parts? Any imag-ination which pays no homage to prevailing *mores* affronts the pious; it puts scripture to the question, rather than allowing it all the answers.

When the bastard claims to be as good as the established line, he starts to subvert it. All claims to equality are meant to overthrow equivalences. In the well-born bastard and the blue-blooded freak, privileged resentment lends energy to the mechanics of revenge; the insider-outsider knows the language which he is debarred from speaking.

Yvonne Mitchell's Riviera house is advertised for sale in *Country Life*. Bernard S. told me that there had been an article about it in *Ideal Home*. It looked beautiful: the shutters, the pool, the L-shaped drawing room, the local tiles, ochre and black, rare and elegant. The article gave the gushing impression of a creative, thoughtful house-hold, with his and hers studies. The only child, a daughter, went to the village school and was, no doubt, bilingual. *Bref*, an idyll. Yet the more one looked at the happy pictures, the less one wanted the place. Wispy-bearded, sockless Monsey is an onion disguised as a sage. Y. – all trousers and keen eyes – is the intelligent actress who can be relied on to put down the author. Every phrase in their praise seemed to breach the impression it was calculated to give. The article said that there were rumours of the Monseys' return to the UK but 'roots went deep'; since the only land attached to the villa is a paved yard, one wonders how easy they have been to sink.

Tom Wiseman now reveals that the contented pair are on the point of splitting up. Derek has found himself a young girl; Y. is returning to the stage. One could imagine a story in which the calm description of the house – apparently no more than an inventory – would tell the reader that the happy couple was on the point of rupture and that their child was woeful with dread.

Bernard S. spent eight days in Ian Smith's Rhodesia, representing
the African National Congress. He stayed at a big multi-racial hotel
(the Jameson?), unlike Lord Goodman, whom he despises. He was
not harassed, but isolated: no one would give him an office or find
him secretarial help. When he applied to an agency, the woman
said, 'You're a very dangerous man, Mr Sheridan; I shall tell my
husband when he gets home.' When B. told his African friends, they
advised him to notify the Secret Police at once, and tell them what
he was doing in Rhodesia, before they got to know of it from a
hostile source. No advocate in Salisbury would represent his clients,
who face the death penalty. Nor are there any African advocates,
though three Africans are qualified to plead in the courts.

B. declares his difficulties without self-pity or alarm. Being a solicitor dispenses him from taking things personally. Although he
changed his name, which might have been a professional liability,
he shows no reluctance to commit himself on his clients' behalf, nor
has he any apprehensions of unpopularity: he is almost amused by
the fear which contact with him appears to have created, not least
in the landlord whose offices he rented. The liberal is able to move
relatively free of bullying because he is white: he relies on the privileges he aims to abrogate. A huge (black?) policeman, busy ripping
down posters outside the ANC office, had the grace to look
ashamed, when B. challenged him, tremulously, and mumbled that
he was only carrying out orders. B. had hoped to go into the 'Tribal
Trust Lands', but admission is at the discretion of the District Com-
missioner. In any case, the distances were too great for the value of
the possible interviews. He fears returning to Salisbury, where he
might be arrested; he is off to Nairobi for further evidence. He
despises Goodman for having placed more importance on getting
an agreement with Smith than on what agreement he got. B. does
good unobtrusively and without hope of reward. Well-informed,
he refuses cynicism; he knows that there is much jockeying for position among groups dispensing aid, comfort and counsel to the
Africans; if he has no comfortable solutions, he is slow to despise or
condemn: he concedes the limited good faith of some of the white
farmers. Only Ian Smith and his gang are without scruple or honour.
The white voter may be narrow-minded and self-serving, but he
has no conscious intention to break his word. The women are more
venomous than the men, more vindictive towards the dissident and
more repressive towards the African. When B. did manage to find a
secretary, she was a white divorcée with three children who couldn't
afford to turn down the extra cash: he paid well over the odds.

The Driver's Seat. Recent events prove that whoever is in it, it is never the writer. Two weeks ago, bags packed, I was ready to fly to America, when Jo Janni cancelled, on the grounds that I would not agree to stay more than five days: good films, he insists, can be made only through protracted seances. He oscillated between anger and pacifying indulgence. The choice of Herb Ross as director is at the bottom of our dificulties. If I didn't like him, Jo offered to find someone else. But Paramount like him, which is why Jo 'chose' him. Herb imagined that his commercial success was so certain that he could afford to play the class market. The failure of his Candice Bergen piece has breached his self-confidence. He blames the writer, in whom 'I had faith and who, at the critical moment, was unable to answer the questions'. Yet in May, when he was here, and shooting already completed, he said he had made 'a pretty inter-esting picture'. It's not the writer who has failed him, but the audience. Now he sees that the Spark novel cannot be improved by anodyne sugar, but he fears to make the sour film that it would otherwise be. He has enough taste to flinch from the vulgar, but not enough to cleave to the artistic.

8.2.72. Beetle looked for a while at a Flemish altarpiece and then said, 'Mind you, I get jolly fed up with Christ.'

C.M.R. re Pat Cotter, one of Job's more regular comforters, 'He's very nearly the nicest man in the world, but not quite.'

David G. Fluent but not eloquent, well-dressed but never smart, he moves easily in a range of milieux. He constantly improves himself, but never gets any better: you could not accuse him of being a Jew, nor suspect him of being a Gentile.

INTERIOR/EXTERIOR. Arrival at the hotel. Girl crying in the lobby. Ramon. The room, shutters. Call from the Studio. Cancellation/postponement. Driver coming for him; but doesn't. Walk; the gallery and the girl in the bookshop. 'Don't I know you?' CALIFORNIA TIME.

Fragments can be more suggestive than what survives intact: a few lines from a lost Euripides excite the imagination like a spell. Splinters of the ancient world needle fantasies. Classicists listen to taps and creaks from behind the tacked arras of time, believing that wit and diligence can unscramble its lost codes.

6.9.72. Murder of the Israeli athletes at Munich. Shocked? Yes. In spite of everything, we still expect happy endings. When struck by 'tragedy' – now a synonym for death, not a poetic form of it – modernism is unarmed to sound a worthy alarm or mourn the dead. Old music and old rhetoric supply the bandages to staunch the void with obsolete decency. For the rest, the death of the Israelis is an embarrassment, a damned spot on new upholstery. Death is not a recognised event. Who recalls that the Olympics began in the funeral rites of heroes? Today, whatever disfigures a design, or a timetable, is worse than a crime: it's a nuisance. The Olympics go on not as a gesture against inhumanity but as a concession to it.

13.10.72. J.W.L. is as obstinately uxorious as he is middlebrow. He tells you that he is glad that he didn't go to university, and only then do you realise how much of a handicap he must find it. His uxoriousness is less than unalloyed. We first met him *en famille* by chance, ten years ago. I had just been taken on as a reviewer by *The Sunday Times*. At a lunch thoughtfully contrived by my father, I was introduced to Pat Murphy, then the deputy editor or so. I was wondering how I could bring the subject round to books when he said, 'Jack Lambert, our literary editor, asked me to ask you whether you'd be interested in doing something for us.' It was my undergraduate dream delivered by hand. Not long before, in the hope of a job reviewing fiction, I had been to see Karl Miller at *The New Statesman*. His modest sportsjacket did not quite conceal the full Leavisite uniform. I had published eight novels, but he asked me what qualifications I thought I had for reviewing fiction. Given a volume of Fromm on which to audition my competence, I did not feel the vocation.

Just before I was to begin my first fortnightly batch for the *ST*, we went to Paris for the weekend. To my silly pleasure, I saw Jack (whom I had met by this time) boarding the same plane. At Orly, while we were waiting for our luggage, he sauntered over, a look of inquisitive apprehension in his basilisk eye. I was gratified: I had a beautiful wife to introduce. Beetle and I seemed sophisticated cosmopolites; he was encumbered with a wife and a trio of adolescents whose unguardedness might let him down. Never upright, he had the anatomy of a snooper who suspected himself. At Customs, he patrolled between us and his too ordinary family. He attached undue significance to his new recruit, as though he were the one on trial.

We met them again in St Germain des Prés, and a more genial occasion developed. We went to eat at Brasserie Lipp (upstairs, of course); Jack's French was not exceptional and he was as alien to the Parisian literary world as I was. He was, I suppose, in his middle forties: a young man, as the obituaries say. He had a sort of hangdog lordliness. Catharine beamed with polished candour: she announced the domesticity which he preferred to keep secret. She had intended to be an actress but met Jack and her mind was made up. It was just before the war. He once told me how he had gone to Paris soon after their engagement. With an involuntary wink (he had a hooded, twitchy eye), he recounted how, in agreeably emancipated company, he had done the rounds of the brothels, which were officially sanctioned in those days. Because of Catharine, he had refrained from the delights. I suspect that all his life he has eaten more menus than meals. He aped freedoms he did not live: 'Thumb it in softly,' was a favourite phrase; 'a quick crouch' another. What the war did for people!

When I began to work for the literary pages, he was tactfully avuncular: he liked my jokes, but pruned their enthusiasm. He encouraged receptive catholicity, the right attitude in a literary journalist. I held the position of fortnightly reviewer for almost two years. In the freezing February of 1963 we went to Le Rouret, near Grasse. I was so anxious to keep my job that I offered to fly home every two weeks to collect my batch. BEA flew them out and I took delivery at Niçe airport.*

Soon after I began to write for the paper, Leonard Russell, the Arts supremo, asked me to contribute to a whimsical series of 'Conversations with the Dead'. My exchanges with Wittgenstein were well received and I corrected the proof. Then the series was abruptly aborted, after Enoch Powell's chat with Disraeli. I was not to blame, but my name had been advertised and I felt humiliated. Leonard Russell attempted to renege on the payment, which was to have been a fat two hundred and fifty pounds: he offered a kill-fee of seventy-five. I demanded the full fee promised in his letter.

---

*   I had to drive down in the afternoon traffic. One day I was a minute or two late at the Douane and the official refused to give me what I could see on a shelf behind him. I had become mildly, and now recklessly, fluent in French and was unwise enough to say, '*On n'est pas en Algérie, quoi?*' His face became incandescent and he stormed out of the room. I asked another functionary to give me my books, but it was beyond his station. Could he get the first man to return? '*Il est en colère, monsieur. Vous devez vous excuser.*' '*Volontiers. Mais il n'est pas ici.*' '*Je ferai ce que je peux.*' The official returned, his redness reduced to amber, and agreed to shake my hand. Then he gave me my books. I left pretending to have triumphed.

He asked if I could produce any evidence, although he must have had a carbon copy on file. Otherwise, he advised me to abate my indignation, especially if I wanted to go on writing for the paper. It was a choice between prudent capitulation and dangerous defiance. I searched and searched and finally found his original letter among the dense detritus on my desk. I sent him a photostat and was paid in full. His concession was coldly gracious. I continued to write for the paper.

None of this impaired my relationship with Jack, but I had discovered that if he was a sort of friend, he was no sort of ally. He and Catharine visited us in Langham after I ceased to be a regular critic. Our exchange of letters, in the summer of 1964, after we had decided to go to Rome for the winter, was cordial: he asked if I would become a contributor on single books, an elevation of a kind. And so it continued.

That summer on Ios there came a telegram from John Schlesinger, saying that *Darling* was to go into production. Later, in Rome, came a handwritten letter which informed me of the treacherous hiring of Edna O'Brien, to 'touch up' the script. Her mushy innovations were later excised, expensively. I became a successful screenwriter, with the unreliable glitter of reflected glory: I was the saddle on which Christie and Schlesinger rode to their triumph, well-paid for being successfully sat upon.*

We invited Jack and Catharine to the 'thrash' (as he would put it) for *Darling* at the Dorchester. I asked Jack as my public father, as it were; I never imagined that he might be insecure in louche company: I was inviting a disinterested keeper to have tea with the chimps. If I supposed that I was revealing the vanity of the vulgar, I had, somewhat devilishly, taken him to the pinnacle of the temple.

In 1967, at a Cape party, just before the publication of *Orchestra and Beginners*, Jack uttered an early warning about the reception of my novel. I had won the Oscar and become too successful: 'You should,' he told me, 'no longer expect to be reviewed on your merits.' That spring, my introduction to *Two for the Road* had been on the front of the *Weekend Review* in the *ST*. My amusing words had not been amiably received by the critics, though my fellow-writers congratulated me on my outspokenness: the bonhomie of the herd towards a scapegoat-elect.

---

* In Rome, John asked me to go into a press conference at the Hotel Parco dei Principi with him, because I spoke so well. I said, 'I'm tired of playing the elephant to your Hannibal.'

I had laid myself open and the chop was not long delayed.
Paranoia was not my only augur: during that noisy summer, I read
in a film monthly, obscure enough to be mantic, that my stock was
due for a fall. I duly fell. Jack told us that he had sent back the review
of *Orchestra and Beginners* to be rewritten; he had, at least, put it at
the top of the column. Last year, I met the reviewer, Monty
Haltrecht, whom I had once praised, at the Festival Hall. Full of
smiles, he had taken up a career as a male model. He bore me no
ill-will for the things he had said about me (trust a Jew to slaughter
a Jew) and drew my attention to a nice little review of *Who Were
You With Last Night?* in that night's *Evening Standard*. He also said
that no one paid attention to book reviews any more; or to books,
for that matter. I had the impression that he had hoped to recommend himself to me by the disagreeable things he said about my
novel. Randy adolescents advertise their lust by declaring how they
hate girls, or boys.

I assumed for years, indeed until very recently, that Jack's
prescient warning had been calculated to soften the blow. I realise
now that it was part of it. His sense of imminent thunder was acute
because it rumbled his own wounds: he had been a bright young
man, and might still be bright, but was no longer young, nor much
of a man. He had the plumped handsomeness that lies, slightly, about
its weight. If he had Don Juan's dreams, they were never realised:
he came of a repressed class and a repressed time.

His father was Cornish, a dealer in the specialised field of salvaged
goods: he disposed of insurers' remnants. The market was
dominated by Jews, of whom he spoke with the admiring malice
of a gentleman unwilling to concede that he was as commercial
as the next man: his idea of unfair competition was any sort of
competition at all.

One day, after some broadcast, I had lunch with Jack (or rather
he with me) at Scott's in Leicester Square. On our way from B.H.
he told me – it must have been soon after the Six Day War – that
the Jews were beginning to get a bit above themselves again: a nice
use of 'again'. I took it, or chose to take it, as another genial,
premonitory whisper. Now I wonder if all the warnings were not
threats: he has a thorough ambivalence, does our friend Jack. He
was in the navy during the war and came out a hero: DSC and all.
Yet I think of him, affectionately, as a coward: when you are in a
corner with him, you are on your own. Doubtless he did brave
things; somebody must have seen him. No one could ever have seen
me do anything brave. In that sense, he will always have it over me.

It is no pleasure to say that he came out of the navy both a hero and a wreck. There are friendly witnesses: he had a speech impediment so severe that he could hardly utter.

Catharine had chosen him when he was strong; she cherished him now that he was weak. With her help, he conquered his disability. He had edited trade papers before the war: *The Fruit Grower* had been his apex. He also auditioned, successfully, in other trades, such as the Arts, in *The Spectator*. After the war, he had little problem in joining *The Sunday Times* (whose most renowned editor, Denis Hamilton, was notorious for coming the old soldier: he was known as 'Major, major'). It was assumed that Jack was as ambitious as he was able: he was thought of as a future editor. Did he decline to be a contender out of modesty or out of fear? He was still talked of as a vigorous candidate for Ivor Brown's place as drama critic on *The Observer*, a throne usurped by Ken Tynan.

How the Lamberts came to stay with us this summer in Lagardelle, it is not easy to say. I suppose it was, in part, because *April, June and November* was coming out in October. When they accepted, it seemed a mark of favour. Beetle suggested a week they should come; I promised that they would not be exposed to a surfeit of Raphaels: they could use the flat for a holiday and see us when they wanted. I suggested that they fly Air France, which was offering a week's free use of a car. That kind of freedom was not, in the event, free enough: they would come by rail. I was less than easy at the prospect of unwheeled guests.

The first part of the summer was hot and delicious. I worked with panicky energy scripting *The Death of the Fox*, a 'best-selling' novel about Sir Walter Ralegh, which Dick Z. and David Brown had bought on impulse and then discovered to be a flowery dog. They took me to lunch at *Les Ambassadeurs* and flattered me into saving their bacon.★

The Lamberts sent a telegram saying that they were arriving at Souillac, the less convenient of the stations I had mentioned. I went, in good time, to start the Mercedes to go and get them. It was a hot, blue day; the swimming pool was full (since we did not yet have

---

★ When I had delivered my first draft, they sent me a three-page telegram saying that it was the best thing that the studio (WB) had ever had. I never heard another word. A few years later, I was in L.A. on another project and asked John Calley whatever happened to *Death of the Fox*. 'Was that a great script!' he said. 'That was a great script.' 'Is that why I never heard another word?' 'Freddie,' he said, 'who the fuck is Sir Walter Ralegh?'

running water, it had to be trucked in, eighty-four loads of it, from Sarlat); the place looked perfect. The car was dead. I ran to the Barats and we tried to start the engine with jump-leads. Nothing. Finally, Norbert lent me his Renault 16 (what neighbour in England would lend me his car?) and Paul and I set off. We passed the château of Montfort, where a well-boiled hitch-hiker flagged us. I addressed him in French (we were in a French car) and only after a few minutes' comedy discovered him to be English, in the limbo between school and university.

At Souillac we bought the *ST*; Paul had something he wanted to see. We had time for coffee at the station before the long, long train slid in from the north. (Will anything ever be as long as the freight trains which cross the Middle West?)

The Lamberts lumbered towards us with huge luggage. When Catharine came to The Wick for the day, she would arrive in town clothes and then go to change into 'something more comfortable'. She was stately but never chic. Now both of them looked hot, swollen, glazed and puffy, like over-risen loaves. One of their suit-cases had sprung its locks and was bound with a canvas strap. The cases were pale blue, a matching set unequal to its pretensions. They greeted Paul politely, but with no ready access of holiday cheer. Seigneurial serf, I relieved them of the cases.

I sat them in Souillac and went shopping for provisions. I had already returned, and proposed going home, before Jack thought of offering another round. When they visited us at The Wick, Catharine always brought a box of Old Gold, sufficient ticket for a day-trip. Now they gave us an already open bag of chocolate almonds, such as you buy at the junction of the Boulevard St Germain and the Boul'Mich. I once spoke to Beetle in Greek there, and the stall-keeper answered in the same tongue.

Well, we were not looking for a fancy present, and we certainly did not get one. They had been invited for a week, but seemed wary of promising to stay that long. Now they inspected the flat, took stock and announced, with flattering greed, that they would stay ten days, if that was all right.

They were amazed by the swimming pool. They had not realised we had our own. If childishly pleased by their amazement, I was quickly put in my place: they had no use for pools. Jack had not swum since leaving the navy; C. bulged in the wrong places and did not care to reveal them. They never came down to the pool together all the time they stayed.

Jack was grey and sagging. Things were not good at the office:

they were trying to get rid of him. Denis Hamilton had twice offered him the editorship of the *TLS*, a Greek gift: it is losing money. In any case, C. explained, Jack didn't want it: he's an Arts man, interested in opera and music and the theatre, no less than in books. I am not sure that he is interested in books at all; his knowledge of them is very limited.

C. glowed with confidence and ample femininity; she is never more up than when Jack is down. Although he depends on her (passing his work to her like a candidate to an examiner), he despises himself for his dependence. If she could cure him of his self-doubt, his first proof of health would be to dismiss her. If cowardice keeps him faithful, who am I to judge him? Dr Johnson was right: anyone who has not been for a soldier or a sailor can never have a good conscience in the presence of those who have.

Jack was at Tonbridge. The school means much to him. In the navy, he and an old schoolfellow refused to join the democracy of Christian-naming; under fire, they continued, with mock aloofness, to call each other by their surnames. Intimacy, for Jack, is a want of decorum; yet he casts furtive eyes in all directions, like a lighthouse that wishes it had legs.

He believes himself eclectic, but such a man has always lost the zest for excellence: his approval of things in general is a claim for general approval, a feature not of his likes but of his fear of being himself disliked. For J., social kudos, a place as of right in the cultural reserved seats, matters supremely; the notion of ideological commitment, any exclusive form of taste, will always unnerve him: privilege and open-mindedness go together, the latter being less the adjunct of the former than its season ticket. To like as much as possible is to be welcome in as many places as may be. The passive mind likes to keep busy, but is easily impressed. It asks only for the undemanding.

This is all as sarcastic as style dictates. There is a more humane reading: here is a man wrecked by the war, his mouth literally stopped by the hard bombast of battle. He returns to a woman who loves and heals him. He is comforted by the music of the arts, and strengthened by them. He recovers his fluency. He is almost capable once again of the endurance needed for the battle of life, but called to contend in the hard lists of editorial aspiration, he again loses his nerve. Having suffered the reality, and survived, he cannot go through the paper hell of a shadow play. Because Denis Hamilton did not want to forget his own glorious war, he did not forget Jack's; but Hamilton has now been promoted to comtemplative supremacy. The new generation does not honour old war records; they are signs of age, not of merit. J. is threatened by his own dated history. He becomes a stickler for yesterday's forms, and respects. Non-political man is always conservative. He is partial to well-made narrative because he fears he might miss what fails to declare itself. Erudition is a kind of cheating: it depends on qualities a decent chap does not always possess. His integrity – the insistence on seeing things with the whole personality – is a way of disqualifying the merely clever; it promotes the DSC and the CBE into intellectual credentials; he will put all of himself in the scales against mere talent, brains, wit, and so make himself the winner.

Yet, by God, he was low, and not from ponderous victories, when he reached Lagardelle: he was a beaten man. Paranoia flashed from his hooded eye, like the muzzled ill-humour, pugnacious and pallid, on the face of an old gangster, for whom years of protection have suddenly ended. He was even late with his regular monthly drama piece for the Arts Council magazine. ('He's bone idle,' Brian Glanville told me, afer the summer. 'Everyone at the *ST* knows you can never get Jack to do anything.') Starting as he did not, in the event, mean to go on, he borrowed my spare typewriter; he assumed me to have one. There was a discussion at tea-time on the first day about how their holiday should proceed. We suggested that we should all have supper together, but otherwise run separate establishments. I put it self-effacingly: we did not want them to suffer from a surfeit of Raphaels. Beetle guessed that they were dashed by having to fend for themselves in any way. They had certainly arranged to do as little fending as possible: without a car, they were immobilised and hence dependent on me. Said to be great walkers, they were greater sitters. The beauty of the house gratified and humiliated them: it confirmed J.'s apprehension that he was poor and about to be superannuated. Pensioned by inferiors, he wore his handsomeness like a suit that needed pressing: lustreless and baggy, vestiges of quality indicated that its owner had come down in the world.

For the first few days, while J. caught up with his work and with himself, and Catharine assured us how grateful they were for the healing pause, we had the complacent illusion that we were doing good; yes, and ourselves a little bit of it. I did imagine that there might be practical fruit in the form of, at the least, tactful placing for *April, June and November* in the literary pages of the autumn *ST*. My last three books had all had worse treatment there than anywhere; the last two had been submitted to the envious judgement of Julian Symons. If I was hoping to influence justice, I was also hoping to obtain it.

Jack hinted years ago at a conspiracy against me: I was deemed, as before, to be getting above myself. He had told me that it would take five years for me to purge my insolence. Five years were now up. Since the oracle had been right in predicting my degradation, I resorted to putting gold on its tongue in order to prime a golden recovery. I should not have invited Jack if I had disliked him, but I was perhaps straining to like him, in order to make his favour, should I be shown it, follow from the friendship, not the reverse.

We talked of many things, especially literature and the theatre. I sometimes feel deprived, because we do not live permanently in London, of the intelligent talk which all exiles regret, even when they have seceded voluntarily. Was it I who wished the tone on our dialogue, or Jack? It had a cursive lucidity, the sonorous tendency to quick agreement, suggestive less of the meeting of true minds than of the joinery of carpentered consensus. Our show of shared heresies issued more from the dread of unsociable dissent than from any deep sympathy. Any true relation includes a sense of separation. There was this wished-for 'seriousness', the straight-faced frivolity of those who dare not be frivolous. Had there been play between us, as between true friends, there would have been the risk of finding ourselves in dangerous dispute. Touring the horizon, we could almost ignore the uneven ground under our feet.

I had recently reviewed C.P. Snow's *The Malcontents*: whatever good could be said of it I said; of what it deserved, not a quarter. Snow is like a snail trying to imagine how it would be to be a greyhound. The aesthetic notion of the novel shared by J. and by C.P.S. was torpedoed by his example: it was not a matter of lifeless characters but of lifeless life, a language as false as what was said in it. The accusation is as obvious as a gargoyle. But Jack could not endorse it. Snow is a friend; he has given J. excellent advice: the advice J. wanted him to give. J. wants no exhortation to boldness or revolution, to fresh beginnings or abrupt endings: he has the mind of a civil servant and seeks counsel through the usual channels. In moments of political crisis, Snow advises studious inaction; when purges are in the air, be present, but silent. The inert are suspected of having already made a separate peace; their tenure looks already to have been confirmed. I gave B.G. similar nerveless advice when he was involved in an office war. The best of friends endorse prudent cowardice: how should a man be advised to be brave, or foolish? Jack's reverence for Snow does not inhibit bitchiness, itself a symptom of respect: we were told of Charles's repulsive appearance and of his habitual drunken incapacity: he has to be poured into his car.

On the melodrama of most modern fictions, I suggested that the need to invent a dramatic third act required exaggerations which give producer and audience the feeling that they had seen or read something worth their money. To illustrate the lumpy thesis, I improvised a drama from our present situation: a fantasist might see in our amiable summer gathering the seeds of hostilities and resentments which could spawn a tangle of poisonous possibilities. Despite friendly assumptions, we could believe that Jack and Catharine felt a strong antipathy to us: they might resent taking hospitality from those younger than themselves; they could be vexed by our good fortune and irritated by our children. Might they not also be displeased by the Jewish obsessions which I control less well than I imagine? They might feel captive or outnumbered, manipulated or patronised. It was possible (as well as false, I said) to believe that a great store of undetonated malice was buried under our pretty rendezvous.

When I look back on this fanciful fugue, it seems like the calculated arming of all the mines which could blow us apart. The accuracy of my predictions makes them seem almost like wishes. Of course, at the time we laughed away all these exemplary notes for a third act. I was made bold, however, by my own house, by the sense of qualified lordliness and by the confidence of finished work: the Ralegh script, the novel already in the press.

Before the Lamberts arrived, I chose a few books to put in their room: Beethoven's letters, Glyn Daniel's *Hungry Archaeologist*, *Bouquet de France*, and a few other shrewd (and flattering) choices. When they congratulated me on the selection, I said, 'Well, Beetle did say not to bother to try and educate them!' Unwise, but it was said in the flush of hospitable drinks, pleasure at their pleasure and to display how candour had displaced formality, a premature exit line delivered as we went in to supper the first evening.

They presented themselves punctually every night, clean and polished for Captain's inspection. We gave them supper; they dressed for dinner. Their formality smacked of appreciative reproach: they had taken trouble, we had not. My reckless fabrication of a third act seemed like humour, both wanton and wanting in probability, but it has a sour twist. I had been right to disparage melodrama, since nothing violent or furious occurred, but our disillusion grew from amusement to amazement. We waited for some vestige of generosity – *anything* unexpected – and when none came, it was too late for irony. Perhaps the wish to extract something positive from our (*my*) ill-judged invitation enforced our studied tolerance: we behaved *so* nicely that they might have guessed how sick we were of them, but then, if they *had* guessed, they would not have been the couple they were. They came every evening, bringing themselves freshly wrapped, like a gift for which we should be repeatedly grateful.

There was at least a term of ten days to their steady cropping of our green hospitality. Breaking point, in terms only of our private pretence that we were enjoying their presence, came when ten days turned out to mean Monday till Friday week. That extra day was a like a calculated provocation. We began the surreptitious retreat from generosity which is our only response to graceless guests: no more melons for supper; no less cheese, but less variety. We made do with wine from the farm. We still offered *cognac* after the meal, but sat down promptly to table: I still *offered* whisky, but not with the bottle in my hand.

What did they do wrong, the blameless charmers? They rarely (that is, hardly ever) spoke to our children. They once offered me tea (which we had supplied) down at the flat, but they could sit and talk to Beetle while they drank theirs, without offering her a cup. They had brought nothing for the children and never proposed a game or a walk. They ducked all communal proposals. We dined with them at the Scholly one early night, but I paid; a return was discussed, but no actual date proposed. Put the boots on the other feet and imagine: bloody Jews!

Beetle and I planned to go to Sarlat together on the Saturday: we had had little time alone. However Stee was not feeling well, and I decided to go with Paul. The Lamberts had expressed a wish to go to Sarlat 'sometime'; preferably Saturday. Since they had no transport, I had either to take them, or be available on another day. So Paul didn't come and I took them. We parted at the market: they would enjoy the town while I filled the larder. We met later for coffee. As usual, Jack was slow on the draw; I paid.

I had loaded the boot with my purchases before meeting them again. When we reached home, I took out the boxes of food and several bunches of flowers. They are cheap and beautiful in high summer and the fresh-faced stallholder always adds a free bunch to my selection, if it is fat enough. When Jack saw the flowers, he said to Beetle, 'That's lucky! We almost bought you some flowers.' She is very capable of responding 'Well, almost thank you!', but she did not. 'Just as well we didn't,' Jack said, as if I had rather slyly pre-empted a gesture he was actually about to make. The flowers were two francs a bunch. Wine at the farm is one franc a litre, but they never bought a drop.

After a few days, they went for some of those promised walks. One evening they came back, quietly, with a bunch of wild flowers. We happened to be outside in the courtyard. Catharine seemed to start when she saw us. Did a glance pass between them? She held out the flowers to Beetle. I am sure that she meant to take them down to the flat, had she not had the ill luck to bump into us.

Each morning now, Catharine went, in bra and pants, to swim in the pool. She had discovered its pleasures, but never conde-scended to make any social gesture when we were there. They stuck to their allotted territory like imprisoned warders. Jack was often in a sleeveless white vest, like a Devil's Island trusty, with a sad ciga-rette. He was a year behind on a study of Antonin Artaud for Frank Kermode's *Modern Masters* series. He worked with the French text and a dictionary. We had fun comparing the original with the offi-cial translation. The translator was an involuntary disciple of Pound. Jack wrote annotations in his usual handsome, invariable hand. What did he think of Artaud? 'Sad little man really.' He had perpetual headaches; nothing ever went right for him: 'No wonder he invented the Theatre of Cruelty!' Jack approached his task with a privileged wince. Presumably for prestige reasons, he could not refuse to take part in the series and had to make his target as preten-tious as those of other pundits. Linguistically taxed, he was weary of the task (or of its postponement). He soldiered on, he said, 'head sunk on breast'. He persevered under burdens with which he had schemed to be honoured. Never was a camel so ambitious for last straws.

His consolation was his family, and its affections. Yet C. confided to Beetle what a bad father he had been: jealous and impatient, he neither gave praise nor offered encouragement. He never read to or played with his children; he seldom proposed an outing or a treat. One of his daughters was determined never to have a child; his son was disappointed at being a disappointment. C. made allowances: he had had children too young and he was overworked. She had won the prize at her drama school and, she said, despite her legs (beauty always draws attention to a single, unimportant fault) everyone forecast a great career, which she abandoned, she says, because she wanted Jack more. Her creaseless face promises that she is untroubled by secret frowns; she has the open-eyed frankness of

someone who can bear, even invites, investigation. Her outspokenness makes J. anxious: he would prefer her to conceal her
naïvetés. Does she not notice his veiled apprehension? She is keen
enough to spot his gracelessness: when he came home to a special
dish for dinner, with a choice of vegetables, he greeted it with
'Hmm, no potatoes?'

He has rarely praised (never in print) anything that I have written.
At the Cape party last night, Fay Maschler told me that the editor
of *The Evening Standard* sent her a telegram of congratulations after
her first restaurant article. I cannot imagine being sent a telegram
by Jack or by Harry Evans if I had written the Sermon on the Mount.
Well, we lack the Beaverbrookian legacy of vulgarity, dear boy.
However J. did once tell me that he had had only three fiction
reviewers who made something distinct of the column: Charles
Snow, John Metcalfe and me. Of Snow he talks with patronising
deference; of Metcalfe, who has become rich in advertising, he is
more openly derisive: he and C. went to visit the M.s in their redec-
orated house and were astonished by the Moorish bedroom, a tented
boudoir complete with desert vistas to be seen through the swaying
veils of the canopy. What will they say of us?

Towards the end of their stay, when frankness could impersonate
friendship, Beetle or I referred sourly to Julian Symons. Jack said
that he kept him on because 'What can the poor fellow live on at
the age of sixty, if he doesn't get the *ST*'s thousand a year?' J. himself
made the air heavy with sighs; he wondered what they were going
to live on in ten years' time. He was treating Symons with prophy-
lactic generosity. Our abuse of Symons was supererogatory, he
assured us, since he never sent the same author to the same critic
three times running. I was safe from a third mauling.

Catharine told Jack that he should get Philip Oakes to do a piece
about me. Honesty compelled another sigh: he could try, but he
wouldn't succeed. I was everything Oakes would like to be, so why
should he give me space? I consoled myself with the hope of a solus
review and the certainty that I should not again be delivered to Julian
Symons. If scarcely full rent for their protracted stay, it was recom-
pense of a kind.

There was discussion about what they could take to their next
hosts by way of a little gift: they did not want to spend too much:
hardly the surprise of the season. We suggested a tin of walnut oil;
its purchase would surely leave them some change. They preferred
to work themselves into an attitude of contempt for their next hosts,
M. and Mme Meyer. Tony was 'a nice little man' who had been

cultural attaché at the French embassy. For several years he had 'pestered' them to come and visit Avignon. Jack had evaded accepting, but this year, after our invitation, he had 'refrained from polite refusal' and confounded the Frenchman by saying, 'Well, I think we might do that.' It was as if he had called a particularly tiresome bluff.

The 'little man' had retired since he first made the invitation. He renewed it on a return trip to London when, to Jack's amazed mortification, Meyer was given an elaborate luncheon at the Embassy. During his tour of duty, he had been nobody very much, but his retired presence brought out the ambassador's best china. It was on this occasion, of course, that Jack decided to accept an invitation rejected when Meyer was a mere *fonctionnaire*. I suspect that he was a rich man who became a dilettante diplomat. Once retired, he was entitled to the attention which his fortune deserved, but his grade had not. The prospect of his hospitality became instantly more luxurious.

The Lamberts approached their journey to Avignon as though it were a trek across the Gobi desert. Had they hired a car, as I had suggested, they could have ambled enjoyably across France's belly, but now they faced a train journey requiring an early start and promising late arrival.

After a due measure of days, we received the thank-you letter. It was long and affectionate, deeply grateful and deeply touched, amusing and vivacious. It was all the things which the actual visit, and our visitors, had never been. It promised a depth of sentiment entirely absent during the dull, demanding days of their presence. It amusingly disparaged their new hosts and the accommodation they were providing. It made Provence sound cold and windy, and the cultural activities which the Meyers had arranged both ludicrous and over-elaborate. The only gift of which they were capable, it was the acme of bread-and-butter art. We should be satisfied with it as with an artist's grateful canvas. Judging from the torrent of affection, we had put the Lamberts inestimably in our debt. Should I have known that those who can mint paper currency with the calligraphic efficiency of J.W.L. always imagine that, when they have uttered their numbered notes, they have discharged all of their obligations?

The weeks between their departure and the publication of *April, June and November* passed in sporadic speculation. To whom would Jack send my book? Might he enjoy it himself? Beetle thought he might send it to Charles Snow (he had hinted as much). A couple of weeks before publication day, John Whitley muttered to me, when I was in the *ST* office, how much he liked the book. A friendly leak? I was guilelessly unworried about what would be said in the paper. I had, God knows, worked at preparing a smooth birth. I was hardly the first man to do so: the Lamberts had gone to stay in Aldeburgh during the week before Laurens van der Post's latest (and now forgotten) book was published: he had received a genial solus.

Wishful thinking is rarely analytic. I should have reflected that Colonel van der P. is an established figure; a post to which one may safely hitch a lazy horse. Jack rang me a couple of weeks before publication (he had not contacted me in the three months since their visit) and offered a couple of books for review. Another nice omen? I took them with me to Florence, where we had a brown week; I have never liked the place. It was not until I went in to correct my proof that I discovered what Jack had done with *April, June and November*: he had sent it to Julian Symons.

Even now, although the news is hardly new, I gaze at the sentence I have just written and want to burst out laughing. It was perhaps what I deserved; it was certainly *exactly* what Jack would do. It may be a judgement on me, but it also displays, in its rightness, all the secretive, malicious, impotent, indecisive, lazy, forgetful, ungrateful, spiteful aspects of Jack's character: an act of justice by a judge without self-respect, shame or warmth, without independence or judgement. Jack faces so resolutely in all directions that he makes Janus a paragon of sincerity.

Full of rage, I concocted all manner of rough messages but prudence kept them in the realm of fantasy. The joke was irretrievably on me. I was stunned – the phrase was never more appropriate – as I read Symons' piece. As I sat there, pretending to correct my own proof, I presented a ludicrous figure: I was white with fury and shock. I should have guessed that something was up the moment I walked into the office. I had said that I would drop in, since there was a strike of messengers in Thomson House. When I arrived, the office was empty except for Jennifer Ward, the secretarial voice of them all. Jack could be seen in the cubby-hole between his desk and Leonard Russell's room. He had his glasses on and was writing with all the harrowed diligence of a heretic composing a recantation. He could not even lift his head. It was the first time I had seen him since the summer, but he was damned if he would see me.

When I read Symons' review, after catching sight of it hanging

on the proof hooks, I was so jolted with dismay that I reeled back
and sat down in Whitley's empty place. Distressed at my reaction,
Jennifer produced my piece and put it in front of me. John Peter
came in and was so disposed to be agreeable that he kept chuckling
at jokes I hadn't thought of yet. I made my 'marks' on the correct
proof (one tiny error) and rose to go, saying, 'If I meet him on the
stairs, he'd better be careful.' I met no one on the stairs: I took the
lift. I wondered later if Jack had heard my virile wailing, and imagined it might apply to him. As if I could dare to challenge the
Heligoland Hero in his own waters!

We left England on the Saturday before I was to be roasted and
drove all Sunday to Lagardelle. The garden has been newly land-
scaped; the shrubs are in place; it all looks so beautiful, even in the
dark, that I burst into shouts of laughter. They can't hurt me! Much.

30.11.72. The review which I wrote has still not appeared, but I
have been asked to do another one since. I appear to have been
forgiven for Jack's behaviour. If a benefactor consents to resume
sponging on you, it displays as much generosity as he is likely to
muster.

After the Lamberts' visit, I led Tom and Malou Wiseman to
Lagardelle like liberators: it was a school from which the boring
headmaster and his floral wife had departed. The Wisemans had
brought us – as if to demonstrate that it was possible to do the right
thing – a large cardboard box which we opened with grateful greed,
not for the present itself but for the wish to give us one. It proved
to be a pair of glass-hooded brass candle-holders, perfect for a place
where the electricity often fails. As we enthused, Boris and Stee
went to play. It was getting dark. When we called, they failed to
appear.

Tout d'un coup, c'était le drame! We shouted at the empty landscape. I was unworried: what was the danger? The boys were not
in the pool. Where else might they have fallen? Who could have
taken them? Tom was bitterly apprehensive; he pumped guilt and
menace into the stillness. He raged and threatened. There was no
response. Darkness came down thickly, like bad news. 'Where could
they have gone?'

Sarah was cleverer than the adults. She discovered the pair hiding
in the *cabine de service* of the swimming pool. They had gone to hide,
became alarmed at the shouting, and were waiting for it to calm
down. Tom was furious, probably with us, but he took it out on

Boris: slap, slap. We were embarrassed. Boris may have been misled by Stee; but if Tom expected us to punish him, he did not know us.

When I first worked in the movies, back in 1955, Tom was the youngest and most feared columnist in show-biz. He was barred from the set at Pinewood. Only Bernard Levin, in my time, excited equal animosity or enjoyed equal success. Levin, who satirised parliament in *The Spectator*, was a cleverer, if more narcissistic, writer: his sentences trailed like fuses and detonated in a flash mixture of dynamite and *feu d'artifice*. Wiseman did not play the intellectual, nor did *The Evening Standard* support a fancy prose style, but his indignation made a similar show. Tom's father died in a concentration camp. He stayed in Vienna, after his wife's and Tom's departure for England, and profited from the sale of exit permits and access to escape routes. Imagining himself immune from dangers which enabled him to exploit other Jews (Tom was blushingly proud of this romantic hard-headedness), he left his own escape too late. He was a chancer who had often arrived and disappeared during Tom's childhood. When he disappeared forever, it was painful but it was not a shock.

Tom and his mother were destitute. He was separated from her, although he had for a time been allowed to mix with the children of the family where she was employed. He was sent to a Jewish school where he was called Avrom (his original name, Alphonse, was unacceptably Gentile). He learnt quickly, lessons both orthodox and unorthodox. He rebelled against the closed society of the school when he was sixteen and became a journalist on the lowest rung of the shortest ladder: a suburban paper. If he chose to rewrite the releases and the manufactured pap which normally passed straight onto the page, that was his silly business, and his education. He became a prolific and inventive journalist. Rewriting trade press reviews of local films in his own observant and scornful prose, he grew to be a master of invective. He used his portmanteau position as film critic, reporter and editorial assistant to give himself a plethora of titles, which did not bother his idle boss but impressed those who did not know how easy it was to be 'Chief Reporter' in a reportorial staff of one. He wangled an official invitation to the Venice Film Festival, when he was eighteen, by asking for it in the name of *The (West) London Observer*.

He not only got his foot in the door, he knew what to do when he was inside. He sold a piece to *The Evening Standard* after achieving notoriety as a critic the film companies had excluded: they even threatened not to advertise in his boss's paper. Beaverbrook hated anyone who tried to push the Press around: he believed the Press should push people around. Tom was hired.

His technique was to allow celebrities to condemn themselves out of their own mouths. He had the questions; they were unwary enough to give revealing answers. The more the famous howled, the better Beaverbrook liked it. He believed in the value of praise: if you didn't get a pat on the back from the Features Editor, you were in trouble. The acme of praise was an invitation to go and see the Beaver; to be asked to stay to a meal was Ascension Day. One day Tom and Bob Edwards were asked to go and see B. together. He was standing at a table, writing. Tom and Edwards stood and waited. After a while, Tom said, 'Should we say we're here?' Edwards said, 'He knows. He doesn't like anyone to say anything. We wait.' Tom knew that Edwards would go a long way in the organisation. Tom also recognised that he himself lacked the required servility, though he continued to write a successful, cruel and scornful column. The desire for publicity was so great that candidates presented themselves for slaughter. In Hollywood at the age of twenty-three, he wanted to interview Sinatra, but S. had been bruised before and declined. Cary Grant, however, rang soon after Tom's arrival: he was free any time. A date was fixed; the interview took place, but T. never printed the piece. He figured that anyone who was that available must be on the skids. Wrong: C.G. had several great successes still ahead of him. Tom's sophistication was sharpened by a furtive innocence.

At length, he was invited to have a meal with Sinatra. Some fixer arranged it, and was present. S. was wary, but amiable, about giving an interview. He said that if Tom played ball, there wasn't anything he couldn't do or anyone he couldn't see 'in this town'. He punched Tom playfully under the jaw as he said this. 'I can open doors in this town. My friends can be your friends.' Tom made no promises, but he did want an interview. Sinatra said it would happen, but it didn't: stall, stall, stall. Finally, Tom said that unless he got his interview he would treat their meal, and all the bragging bullying that followed, as having been an interview. Which is what, eventually, he did. He seems to have had no fear, nor any desire for friends among the famous.

He interviewed Hardy Kruger when he came to take part in the Cambridge film which Leslie Bricusse and I, God help me, had written. Who could have guessed that an ex-member of the Hitler youth would find a central place in our mild, predictable comedy?

Pinewood, with its infinite capacity for absurdity, managed to find a piece of parochial fun the perfect vehicle for a humourless German actor. I cannot remember what Wiseman wrote, but he was furious. Kruger himself was charming enough. He had been conscripted at the age of fifteen and could hardly be accused of culpable wickedness, but his wife was 'a real Nazi'. At the end of the long interview, she escorted Tom to the door and said, 'Mr Wiseman, why don't we just agree that as far as the Jews and the Germans are concerned, there were mistakes on both sides?'

Tom was more than a columnist: he was a crusader. Having broken from orthodoxy, he was at once the guardian of morality and a renegade. The refugee is humiliated, like the pauper, by having to repay charity with conformity. When he recovers his social equilibrium, he reclaims his bias. In the special case of Jews being nice to Jews, there is always conflict between the new arrivals, tactless with grievances and manifest in their foreignness, and their hosts, who easily become censorious. They expect generosity to be met with deference; they can even imply that the refugees ought to have learnt their lesson and beware of making any more waves. Solidarity yields to fractiousness: it was the old New York Jews who first called the *ost-Juden* kikes. The new name forced on Tom was the symbol of his hosts' determination to impose their will. He later abandoned docility, but never his rancour: sexual aggressiveness, like his angry pen, paid back in unsociable style the debt which had been marked against him; it also stood for readiness to resume the battle. Having escaped from privileged asylum, where he was at once sheltered and victimised, he declared war against everything that had reduced him to his plaintive state. He had been certified as a weakling.

The defeat of Nazism did nothing to abate Tom's sense of loss, of the world and of the childhood from which he had been expelled. Peace proved that everything that is temporary is irreversible. The cruel wisdom of the deprived fomented ambition and excused deception. The undamaged had no idea of the depth of his fury. Tom's pieces were the fruit of systematic contempt. He imagined himself, I suspect, the lone incarnation of unforgetting unforgiveness. Journalism can punish, but it cannot judge. The use of a poisoned medium suited Tom. He lived with his prey, a Jungle Boy with a taste for meat. English society, in which he was now applauded but not welcome, had split him from his mother and denied him his father, and kept him alive. His pleasure was to repay his debt in society's own tainted currency: his journalism pushed up their noses what they were foolish enough to find savoury.

He had no political hopes; he had experience enough of ideology. He would leave the world as it was, but pick off exemplary targets. He lived like a private detective, exposing moral hoodlums to a public which relished what should have appalled them. Never doubting that the guilty would remain unpunished, Tom was the honest cop in a world in which the shameless or the well-connected always escaped what they deserved. To bring charges was as near as he could come to a conviction. Frustration vindicated what he did: if he had drawn real blood, he might have paused, but when the specious and the fraudulent continued, after he had exposed them, to be saluted as stars, he could be encouraged in his despair. Fortunately, everything was quite as bad as he dreamed and, dreaming, hoped: inability to change anything conferred impunity.

There is an element of camp in the adoption of a corrupt style (the journalistic mode): the dandy moves with elegant perversity in circles he disdains, and upon which he depends for his audience. Wits are always conscious of change, and hope that their *mots* will outlast the season. Camp makes fun of the very form it adopts: sincerity is its antithesis. It picks fights by flapping its wrist at the straight. Its put-downs demand to be put down; if it had any intention of winning, it would cease to be camp. There is no happy alternative to the world it derides. Camp longs for what it dreads, just as the homosexual, before Wolfenden at least, dreaded the day when he became unmistakably what he was. *Posing* as a sodomite was a sweet imposture: to be one was a sorry truth. Schlesinger still issues the rumour that he recently had a woman ('Not as good as the real thing' is the old joke that means what it says).

The columnist – always and only as good as his last piece, and always in search of his next – inhabits the same logic as the homosexual: his pleasure is in rocking the boat on which he cruises. He is a Jonah who finds fame in being thrown overboard. Only when everyone hates him does he feel that he has done the right thing.

The journalist, like the gigolo, must never consider his feelings: it will make him soft. The hardness of anger differs from the hardness of ambition. Ambition is a social desire: the snake needs his ladder. Anger, when appeased, grows weary with itself, and then nostalgic for what once excited it: what follows its dispersal is not the comfort of fame, but the anguish of futility. Wiseman, the adventurer, may have wanted to inflict pain, but not to be promoted for doing so. He lost interest in exposing the absurdities of the stars; he wearied even of twinkling himself. He ceased not only to be dangerous, but also to be entertaining. He became a novelist. I reviewed his first book, *Tzar*. Some time later, he said to me, 'I thought at the time that you had been very unkind. Now I realise that you were very kind.'

He had written an unoriginal book, but it sold well. He then wrote *The Quick and the Dead*. It had excellent reviews. I was no longer reviewing and started to read it only when Maschler sent me a copy. T.W. himself sent me the next book, *The Romantic Englishwoman*. I couldn't admire it; others did, but not enough of them. It sold badly. Tom lost faith in the novel of ideas, of which George Steiner encouraged him to believe it had been an example. Maschler proposed an essay about money: it would have wide appeal and command a lucrative commission. Tom has begun to collect material, but I detect the Casaubon syndrome: the collation of material as loss of nerve.

Conrad. He seemed angelic, if over-protected, a little Victorian child in a brown corduroy suit which he could scarcely be persuaded to unbutton until evening, when he was, it seemed, seduced by Stee's exuberance and started to jump from the pingpong table onto the sack chairs in the playroom. He was a demanding angel, spoiled not with goods but with his parents' obsessive supervision. His petulance was as understandable as it was maddening; it was unforgivable, but one forgave it, for he was pretty and misused, the image of pampered waifishness. He did not break things, or do anything irreparable, but he whined, a thin wailing whine, like some softly fettered animal whom one wished both to kick and to console. His puzzled, demanding face was handsome enough in its perplexed dolefulness to figure in a charity appeal. How could a child so persistently cossetted wear such an air of desolation? He was not used to playing; he did not know how to share. Happiness had been taken from him like a dangerous toy.

Summer visitors. They arrived on the Wednesday evening and we were glad to see them. On Friday, they announced that they would leave on the Monday, and we were horrified. How could we stand them for so long?

A casual visitor, the judge was very thin, as if he had been whittled from a single, hollow, tree. He wore a grey suit, of material as thin as himself, and a creamy open-necked shirt. One felt that holidays presented him an insoluble intellectual problem: leisure was his hardest test. His silent son went swimming with Paul and Sarah. His wife was huge-legged and walked fatly on sticks. She had the demanding hardness of those who are no burden to themselves but bear down heavily on others: she was so plumped with words that she was garrulous even in her reticence. Never trusting her allies in a conversation, she had to add her artillery to the war against silence. She always supplemented your speech with hers, a sergeant-major for whom no one else could ever utter audible commands. She had been a barrister; but although she had retired, it was not to become retiring.

If she never stopped talking, she did not give you the satisfaction of saying anything wicked or stupid. One waited for malice or absurdity like a close fielder, but she was not to be caught out. She constituted herself a court without appeal. When her husband spoke, she shouted him down with her help. She was, of course, an authority on the law. She asked me what I thought the greatest fault of the English legal system and I replied, 'Its language', to which her husband agreed. He recalled that Christmas Humphreys always believed in clear and direct English. In cases of rape, when the woman was in the box, he would say 'Did you bite him? Did you scratch him?' If she had done neither, he suggested, there can have been no rape. Curious that both biting and scratching are signs of passion.

I find it difficult to refuse friends, or acquaintances, when they suggest some joint project. Yet I rarely commit myself in the end. Last night (26.12.72) Jim Ferman told me that the theatrical producer whom he had solicited had decided not to proceed with the idea of an Intimate Revue which Jim had proposed to me. It was hard to keep the relief out of my disappointment: I have no desire whatever to work with Jim, though I had agreed to do so, out of vanity and generous greed (he needed my name). At the moment I am haunted by the difficulty of beginning the plays, *The Glittering Prizes*, which I am supposed to be writing for the BBC. The last four months of the year have been frittered away. I am a conscientious obsessive denied his only medicine: the sight of pages piling up. I need silence and simplicity, which I find only in France.

I have not been sufficiently searching or scathing; there is a want of loyalty in having shown so few signs of loathing. Pulling my punches, I hoped at once to stun and to caress; I have clapped my British audience too curtly for an admirer and too tactfully for a critic. I am at a knotty crossroad with my BBC plays. Can I make them new and powerful enough to constitute the TV novel which I have the opportunity to pioneer? Trapped in a velvet box of my own design, lockless and amiable, from which I can escape, alas, with great ease, what could be more difficult? The funny thing is, I have never had any large ambition. I regarded wealth as a joke I would never get; I am still inclined to laugh when offered big sums. What could I give that would be worth that much? I took money first for things I had no wish to do. Barry introduced me to the golden world. His vulgar ambition was so hairlessly naked that it had the grasping innocence of a helpless, help-myself baby. Such a man might be intrusive, but how could he be dangerous? When he asked me to do things with him, it seemed like an act of charity to agree to share his toys. His desires were disarmingly puerile: a desk with three phones and 'half a dozen buttons to press', a white 'drop-head', a room full of electric trains, *una ragazza ben dotata*. Because his private desires were all for public things, he was undividedly ambitious: the theatre or the movies were to him better places than his empty home. His generosity, like his courage, was public: he reserved nothing for privacy. His home was not a home but an investment: his place in Bel Air was, so people told us, like a warehouse of unsaleable furniture, but he could always rent it at fat rates.

Beetle hated him from the beginning. When he was a big-talking young man of no noticeable power, he already had fantasies of the big-time: a three-cities address book and whatever famous acquaintances he could find. With that unblinking certainty of hers, B. recognised him as a danger, even if he was petty and banal. Vanity led me to believe that one could give a part of oneself to the devil. B. knew that my illusion of superiority was exactly what gave the devil his lease: the mistake of intellectuals is to suppose that absurdity can be laughed out of countenance. In fact, the absurd banishes the serious, never vice versa. The victory of the Barries, our Snopses, is now so convincing that its march is cheered like progress.

If one thinks back to 1952, twenty whole years ago, the austerity is so unattractive that one flinches back to our present polluted pleasure-dome. Yet the possibility of a serious culture was much greater then: *Scrutiny* was still being published! The solemn legacy of the war was a belief that Justice had prevailed and that we owed a moral duty to the dead. In its chilly earnestness, Cambridge seemed to be the barracks to which the best minds had been conscripted. If it also embodied the solemn duplicity of English institutions, of the Establishment to which Henry Fairlie had yet to give its name, the preservation of its own privileges seemed a part of the national heritage. Yet within wartime patriotism was a furtive disenchantment with the rhetoric which had kept us buying our national savings stamps, and digging for victory. 1950s Cambridge fostered a critical hedonism. Enmity towards metaphysics lent grace to negation: many dull and difficult books were conveniently anathematised. Not reading Hegel or Heidegger was an achievement.

At the same time, the relationship between science and the state typified the dilemma of a no longer hermetic university. The prestige of the scholar began to be judged more and more by the public reputation gained by his discoveries: he was the New Elizabethan explorer, throwing his girdle around the world without leaving the lab.

If Cambridge was no longer the pure and good place of which one had dreamed, the dream continued to dress itself in the emperor's old clothes: Guy Fawkes' night licensed impunity, so did Boat-race Day, or Twickers, and anywhere tick was offered. Our vanity had its graduate counter-part in the privileges of Fellows: they had port; they walked across lawns we skirted; they had a permanent address where we had a short lease. The younger dons made no secret of their complacency: why reform a society which recognised their merits so handsomely? Their lectures and tutorials were a kind of theatre: they took trouble, but to be clever mattered more than to be radical. Renford had been an earnest candidate, but once elected, was he the most serious Fellow? Ambition turns easily into energetic conformity.

As for undergraduates, we were persuaded that Cambridge *had* to be maintained as it was. We *played* the fool, as much alienated by our idleness as the worker by his means of production. If we baited authority, we had no serious quarrel with it: how could we have any real dispute with what was designed to keep others in their place? Barry believed wholeheartedly in the myth. Lacking intellectual qualities, apart from the minimum required for entrance, he was a model 'undergrad': there was nothing he failed to get from Cambridge, apart from an education. One scarcely knew what subject he was reading. He taught us modern life by importing aspects of wartime Californian experience: he had more 'dates' with girls, though less desire for sex, than the rest of us. He favoured local girls who owned cars (which none of us did) and was adept at using Cambridge credentials to gain entrée into the wider world. In some respects, he was more honest than his critics. Between Scrutineers' affectations of maturity and Barry's Rodgers and Hartiness, there was a difference only of intent: the former hoped for applause, and Firsts, from Dr Leavis, Barry for royalties. Did either *believe* in the aesthetics they paraded and parodied? How much better a guide was D.H. Lawrence to sexual bliss than Cole Porter?

Barry was at once cynical and innocent. He was set apart at Cambridge by his determination to enjoy life and to take his chances; yet in this he was at one with John Sullivan: both came from backgrounds to which they had decided never to return. John set out on the path to scholarship; Barry to showbiz success. Though John soon deserted Mother Church, it supplied him with a language larger than a docker's son might be expected to speak. He was as much an old boy of Catholicism as I of Charterhouse: nothing would have got either of us back, but we were formed by what we had rejected. Barry had neither scholarly nor class allegiance, but he was franked with the American dream. While I drilled in the JTC, he was learning about cars (and drove his first 'wagon' into a sand-bank) and kissed girls, if only goodnight. He had been spared both the bombs (not unenjoyable if they missed) and the grey piety of rationing and patriotism. The new era of the Conservative govern-ment found an apt ally in him: he was the type of apolitical, militantly peace-loving careerist for which it catered. He had seen and lived in an unscarred continent where peace had been unbroken since the Civil War. The 1930s had ended, in Europe, in 1939; in San Diego, California, they were still going on. What is more eter-nally youthful than an anachronism?

Barry was not handsome, but he was clean; he was not experi-enced, but he had know-how. In the aftermath of Belsen and Buchenwald, he was your good old optimist: at once dated and pris-tine, there was not a mark on him. If he had never had a woman, he had had many dates. The desire for success was his night-school. His U-certificate dreams were more focused than our reality; the girls whom he imagined on his arm (rather than in his bed) always had nineteen-inch waists and shaved armpits. He wanted everyone to be beautiful, or at least pretty. He would always wince at those who reminded him of reality, which was so unreal to him. It began with sex: the urgent itch was alien to him. It did not visit him as it did others, at all sorts of hours, rigid, impersonal, insistent. He could *decide* what he desired; there was no inner world of compulsive lusts. Only dirty girls could be disappointed with him, as he was with them. How could he have known that Nadine, who seemed so pretty and so decorous, so decorative (in those sweet veiled hats of hers) and so virginal, was such a vampire? He loved females purely, as ornaments and companions and kissing cousins. Female desire was repugnant to him: when a pretty girl climbed into his college at night and slid naked into his bed, he told a friend, 'I reckon if I'd played my cards right, I could've had her.' The same girl later said to me, 'When's your fiancée leaving? Because I rather fancy you.' I was as prim as a curate touched up by a bishop.

Leslie Bricusse. He had neither prejudices nor snobbishness: there was no one of whom he disdained to make use. Those who jibbed at his approach could always walk away. He went up to Cambridge with a reputation as a sprinter, but before he arrived he had 'done his ankle' and never ran even in a trial. When he appeared in the Footlights, it was with genuine reluctance: he preferred being behind the scenes. On stage he might be corny, but he was never inept: even his worst jokes got laughs. He recognised the basic ordinariness of Cambridge audiences. He always wanted to be rich more than he cared to be admired. That desire drove him into the big world. He read acclaim even in the most scathing reviews: they might, after all, have been worse.

He lived out a scenario that called for heartache and disappointment, tears and laughter, followed by final triumph. How else could his life warrant the biopic which he never doubted would be made of it? Unmoved by trends or fashions, he did not affect a bold philosophy or radical ideas: he clung to the eternal falsities. He sought the good opinions of his elders: his first appeal was always to the mums. He called my mother mum, and he called Beetle mum, and he called Norma mum. The middle-aged liked him: he was clean, he was polite and he seemed to share their values. His Noel Cowardly rhyme-schemes bridged the gap between pre-war and post-war audiences; never on the side of hairy youth, never aggressive nor resentful, he found the commonplace congenial: there was always a moon in his June.

Immune to sarcasm, he had no time for nuance. When opposed, his face grew pink and his eyes narrowed: he drew on reserves of pursed self-confidence which were positively officer-like. He surfed every wave of hostility until it fractured into harmless foam. I remember, with little pride, how he persuaded me that the cast of the 1954 Footlights was too large. The first part of the discussion was abstract: a matter not of whom to drop but whether, in an ideal world, the cast should not be smaller. Having agreed that it had to be better if weaker members of the cast were cast off, I was helpless when the name of my friend Tony B. was among the proposed redundancies. Tony and I had written several numbers for the show together, and the three of us others yet; he had also collaborated with Leslie on the Cambridge Diary column in *Varsity*.

Here, I suppose, was a moment of conscience. Did Leslie know, consciously or instinctively, that he was offering me the pleasure of betraying a friend? I had known Tony B. since my first day at Cambridge. We shared a 'bedder' in our first year in Third Court; we were recruited to philosophy together; Tony stayed with me at Christmas (his parents were still in India). How could Leslie hope to supplant him in my friendship? Well, he had already recruited me to the Footlights and flattered me into writing a musical comedy, *Lady at the Wheel*, which gave me my first experience of the thrill of laughter and applause (how the *Granta* people hated it!). All of this was frivolous, however, and I was a serious person. Every moment with Leslie was enervated and uneasy. If he held the key to seductive doors, I never talked to him about anything that concerned me deeply. Why then was I often with him? Because I thought that I could do things in a fraction of the time they might take anyone else; hence I could lead five lives and retain my integrity.

At the same time, I was weary of the laundered neutrality of Cambridge moral scientists and their determination never to apply their methods to any specific or practical topic. It sorted ill with Wittgenstein's assertion that philosophy had no specific subject matter that all our discussions were so deliberately vacuous. Why not apply the method to more vexed matters?*

Did Leslie have any conscious plan to separate me from my fellow-Johnian philosopher? If he was jealous, it was in a very cool way. He recognised my ambition, and Tony's, and that they were different. Tony would not give up his hopes of a First in order to raise Leslie's Footlights show to professional standard. I would try to hit both targets, out of vanity and appetite. Tony knew that he had to work. He was somewhat guilty of that less-than-whole-heartedness which L.C.B. said that we could not afford. Tony might

---

* I recall a tutorial in which I embarrassed both Renford Bambrough and Tony Becher by reading out an essay on 'Persuasive Definitions' in which I took anti-Semitism, very timidly, as a *locus classicus* in which the definition of Jew entails the history of persecution which followed it. I cited Macaulay and I declared my own interest in a manner chaste enough to pass for impartiality. Nevertheless there was a tincture of anger, and disdain, in my affectations of detachment: I had been too serious for a serious occasion.

resent the sudden eviction, but he could not declare it entirely
unwarranted. If he hated Bricusse for it, it resolved certain anxieties:
he could go on unimpeded to get his First. I was a more willing ally
of Leslie's than I cared to appear. He had not only recruited me as
a kind of Kamenev, he had also given me my first taste of the pleasures of disloyalty. To see a friend cast to the wolves and to ride on
safely oneself is an exquisite stimulant. The sense of destiny being
on one's side is never more finely felt than when one accedes to the
condemnation of others. I can see and feel the sunlight on our faces
as Leslie and I paced round and round the Caius courtyard on that
summer afternoon, preparing the proscription. It was an enlight-
ening, even a spiritual moment: the flesh seemed to dissolve in the
closeness of our conspiracy. We were as light as angels, transub-
stantiated by diligent malice. I wished Tony no harm; I merely
acquiesced in his amputation. Did I guess that he might get a First
and revenge myself by preventing his having any part in our planned
triumph? I don't think that it occurred to me that he might be so
honoured: usually, no one in Moral Sciences got a First. We had
been told that a 2.1 was sufficient qualification for Research.

Tony worked. I did not, not hard enough. Perhaps he did his
share at Montague Road (he was a great humper of empty Express
Dairy yoghurt jars in order to get the deposit on them), but he was
resolutely anti-social. His room did not have to be locked to keep
us out: it stank of overworked socks. He shut himself in with glum,
malodorous purpose. My joy was not, I think, in hurting Tony but
in being among those who passed judgement. I had had enough of
him and now came the chance to put him down. His diligence in
philosophy seemed selfish: he would never share his ideas. It was
absurd and also somewhat true: we went together to supervisions
with Renford and Tony was always reluctant to divulge anything
which I might use. I, however, was as garrulous then as now: it is
not in my nature to save things for more appropriate occasions.

By way of mitigation, I could claim that Tony had struck the first
sly blow: at the end of our first year, he and John Sullivan had agreed
covertly to share digs in our second year. I felt rejected. How docile
I can be: on J.P.S.'s recommendation, I accepted Colin K., another
classical scholar, as my room-mate in my third year. Colin wore a
tie-slide, round glasses, sports jackets and grey flannels, used Silvikrin
and had spots. He was as boring as Valerius Flaccus.

My introduction (by Tony) to Leslie liberated me from the
banality of college life. I had never auditioned for the ADC; I never
dared to speak at the Union; I did not appear in *Granta* until after I

had gone down. If Leslie was the vessel of corruption he was the cleanest and most presentable vessel from which one could ever hope to enjoy it. Optimistic, good-humoured and generous (there were always Penguins with the coffee), he was never bitchy, often funny, and gave himself no airs. He liked, and easily procured, the company of females, provided that they did not have designs on him. Neither in the dressing room for the Footlights nor after tennis did I ever see him naked.

The last time I saw Leslie was when we were living in East Bergholt. It was in Vivian Cox's *garçonnière* in Curzon Street. Vivian had sent me a script about the Tichbourne claimant. *The Limits of Love* had been published, and was, if briefly, a best-seller. Leslie was with Anthony Newley. As they left, Newley offered his hand and said, 'Good luck in whatever you choose to do in life.'

The agnostic Jew sees his qualities rejected because of what he is said to be, yet does not feel himself to be, except in the eyes of others. Cursed by a past which he longs to lose, and has never inhabited, he may denounce the society that excludes him, but his opposition – however passionate – is unstable. Let society's embargo on him be lifted and his hostility abates. He has no followers to hold him to his rage. The outsiders whom he previously championed are as ignorant of his pity as the powerful were of his merits. The latter may be corrupt, but they are not stupid: they have opened their door to him. He relishes their company because he need have no conscience about them: he punishes them with his honesty; his ridicule makes them laugh. With the uneducated, however, he is at ease only when they are rogues. Genuine simplicity, because artless, embarrasses him. Byron consorted easily with boxers, jockeys and prostitutes: he led them in rout through the courts of Cambridge and brandished them in the face of authority, but he would have been ill-at-ease in a humble home, unless a toff were present in front of whom he could prove his geniality. Byron lived a critical life: everything he did was done *to* someone, yet nothing was his fault: the fault was in what had been done to him.

My Jew lives in a city of which he is the only citizen. He cannot have Justice, Plato (or Eliot) would tell him, because he can never associate with others in a natural community. He 'belongs' only dramatically: his performance demonstrates to others their unworthiness or ingratitude. What can be 'natural' to such a man? He lives; he dramatises; he acts. If Byron was homosexual, he was not 'queer':

he ranged too widely, was more divinely (and vulgarly, and nobly) frivolous than any aesthete. He had – and here the Jew returns – a gift of mimicry which went beyond doing 'impressions': it was his method of conveying sympathy, and of experiencing it. The egotist understands other people most keenly when they become aspects of himself. He then has a sensation of liberty: by becoming another, he is free of self and displays a tenderness which sweetens malice with maudlin regret. The accuracy of his scorn becomes a kind of flattery: his keenest fellow-feeling is for those whom others think contemptible. He is amazed, and hurt, when the subject of his satire takes offence. I wrote recently to Renford Bambrough, who had sent me the review of *The Limits* he wrote twelve years ago, 'The barb seems to have lost some of its penetration with so long a gap between the twang of the bow and the plunk of its arrival. *One must, in the circumstances, take what offence one can.*' Yet I had sent him *April, June and November* by way of apology for Thornton Ashworth.

The young egotist imagines that the future will supply escape, but he cannot leave the past. He is forever washing his hands of the things he is holding on to. He lives many lives, has many houses, inhabits many worlds. He is a polyglot but not a linguist. He displays true solidarity with those whose company he cannot wait to leave. In constant flight, he is always taking stands.

1973

Lunch with Michael and Elisabeth Ayrton. When I agreed to review his *Fabrications*, Jack Lambert said it would be rather a service: 'No one much likes him.' I liked the book, more than somewhat, and wrote to him, since I had discovered from internal evidence that he lived in North Essex, in the same telephone area as The Wick. I asked him to tea; they asked us to lunch. Beyond Sudbury, we might have been in a different country. Unsheltered fields under unrelenting drizzle wallowed on either side of a twisting road. The huge milk lorry in front of us greased our windscreen. What would the food be like? Would there be other guests?

Eventually, we were under straddling pylons (M.A. had described them as 'Lynn Chadwicks') in a long valley made dramatic by their grey grids. We turned down a clayey drive, over a small stream on a humped ochre bridge, and headed for the lit house. It was double-gabled, with an empty lattice against the side wall, a charmingly obtuse place, with no strict right-angles, set on a domed plateau of rain-punished grass. We parked in a gravel yard behind a white barn. A red Volvo estate was up by the kitchen door, which soon opened. Ayrton leaned out while we twisted for our presents from the back: wine and Perigordine walnuts. Protruding but not actually venturing from his beautiful house, M.A. was tentatively welcoming. It was one o'clock, but there was no sign of other guests.

The kitchen was narrow, with a long window over the yard and signs of palatable preparations. Drinks were offered; we had sherry, like adolescents, or at least like the adolescents of our adolescence. There were antiquities in a glass window which penetrated the sitting room wall, and made them visible from both sides. Nothing very special, I thought: probably Cretan.

M. and E. had the confident timidity of those who are on home ground. I was not very well, flushed and cold with the usual January thing. The sitting room sported a log fire, with ammunition piled on both sides for a long winter siege. The low beams had been painted white, the asymmetrical woodwork of the furniture showily polished. Michael's work was sentinel everywhere. Warmth opened us like oysters. Beetle said that, for the first time in England, we had seen a house more beautiful than ours. Elisabeth said, 'I'm sure you have a beautiful house too.' It sounded more patronising than had been intended: one immediately doubted that our house was beautiful at all.

The table was laid at the far end of the square room, under the garden windows. I had not counted the places. Soon, however, there was loud and enthusiastic noise at the kitchen door: George and Zara had arrived, old friends! But who were George and Zara? Steiner. He came glittering in, like a lump of precious coal dislodged from a passing truck. He punched away his social doubts with a sort of academic doubling-on-the-spot, as if he had to generate some extra energy before he could begin to shine. He did so very soon, dark eyes baleful with furious bonhomie, a sabbath basilisk. He and Zara had motored from Cambridge. It was as if they had come from above the snow-line and had brought a couple of snow-balls which they were anxious to throw before they melted. Names began to drop like rose petals. Yet I was glad to see Steiner. Would I have been happier with some mundane neighbours of the Ayrtons, a solicitor and his wife, a nurseryman? The arrival of the famous is flattering, and reassuring: you do not need to feel your way with them, there are no awkward silences. Steiner plumped beside me like some worldly cleric, sincere with rumours: he had heard – was it true? – that I was involved with the screenplay of John Caute's *The Decline of the West*. 'John?' I said. 'I thought he was David.' 'He's called John in private; David is a *nom de plume*, possibly *de guerre*.' But was it true? Caute had been staying with G.S. and desperately needed the money: he was a freelance (the word had a terrible ring for Steiner, like unemployment, but less glamorous) and he had school fees to pay and '*no income whatsoever*'.

Steiner likes to dispense favours; it is the measure of his power. He had arrived with a letter to M. from Penguin's: *The Mazemaker* was to be a Modern Classic. 'That's what I'd like to do for *Lindmann*,' he said, 'a marvellous book.' He began to rehearse his enthusiasm, an actor in the wings of an audition. A judge in the last Booker prize, he had been responsible for G. winning: 'The others hadn't even read it.'

April, June and November he had not liked: it did not contain 'more than a particle' of my intelligence. The novel was, in any case, dead. Biography and sociology contained infinitely more interesting material. Elisabeth Ayrton, with her bold, wrinkle-guarded eyes, a headmaster's wife in glad retirement, was also, we were told, a novelist. Steiner was a shiningly candid mortician in a gathering of the moribund. He counted himself, *of course*, among the doomed. He had written a novel, he told us, about 'the final war' between China and Israel, the only two countries with a continuous linguistic tradition going back thousands of years. And who won? I wanted to know. Ah, that was a secret. Not, I failed to say, a very interesting one. The idea that such a story could be a 'novel' reveals the desperation of the generaliser. Adrift on a shoreless sea of regrets, S.'s only raft is a crate of texts.

Caute, he reminded us, had been the youngest Prize Fellow in the history of All Souls. He had discovered that the college had immense unspent funds and suggested, with brilliant naïveté, that research grants should be established from them. Warden Sparrow affected sympathy: Caute and another stormy petrel (you can bet they were called that) were asked to draft a scheme. When the scheme was shelved, Caute threatened to resign. No one challenged his right to do so, but there were resignations and resignations: if he went quietly, All Souls would make sure that he got other appointments. He went noisily. Since that day he has never been shortlisted for any English academic appointment. He has been a lecturer at Brunel; *ecco tutto*. Steiner was keen to help him, but keener to gloat and keenest of all to parade the many academic bookings to which he himself is committed: Japan and UCLA had already made their reservations. Steiner knew the ruthlessness of the English but he also knew – so those gleaming, proud, intimidated eyes kept promising – how to sup with the devil, and at High Table too.

G.S. filled in his own background like a man in the early stages of one of those novels he believes to be dead. He won a scholarship to Yale, but then heard that they were very anti-Semitic there: all avenues to advancement would be heavily patrolled, if not barred. He elected to go to Chicago, where students were still sleeping in Nissen huts. He was paired with an ex-paratroop Captain tough enough to honour the stereotype. To demonstrate his agility, he crouched down and jumped, without trouble, into the top bunk. He then asked Steiner, 'Are you smart?' ('"Smart" meaning clever,' S. glossed helpfully.) 'Yes,' replied the seventeen-year-old, 'very'. S. snapped out that 'very' with the decisiveness of the refugee face to face with the main chance. 'In that case,' said the paratroop Captain, 'will you see me through my classes?' In return, the Captain escorted him through the minefields of college life. 'I was the pilot fish,' he said, 'moving unimpeded through the most dangerous waters. Always with my paratrooper behind me.' He spoke as if his private Batman might yet sail through the window to look after him: he had acquired protection. The famous Captain now runs 'one of the biggest filling stations outside of Akron, Ohio'. They correspond occasionally. It may well be the great romance of Steiner's life, but I'll bet the Captain never gets sent any of little George's books.

L.B.J. died yesterday, 22.1.73. Steiner will hardly mourn him, but Johnson was, in a way, G.S.'s paratrooper grown old. For years, the US government intimidated the world into giving American brains a smooth passage. The marines and the military, under the benign command of the President, ensured that no one made trouble for the high-flyers. In return, the star thinkers enabled the brutes to pass their grades, to appear to be the guardians of culture and civilisation. The thinkers improved the weapons and the tactics and strengthened the hands of their protectors with their venal intelligence. The intellectuals' contempt for L.B.J. was less to do with his morals than with his failure. His fatal flaw was to make *them* look foolish by failing – even when armed with their smart ideas – to look clever in the eyes of an examining world.

Until Vietnam, the minders who promised American academia a quiet life did so with a measure of discretion, but when the war offended the scruples of the protected, the scholars became like those 'clean' officials who, having profited from gangsters with the assumption that they could remain unpolluted, realised that there might be a price to pay for having been paid their price. Professor Faust had always imagined that the devil was the one whose soul was in hock.

L.B.J.'s good intentions (The Great Society) did nothing for the mandarins. The contempt of the kids for the government and for their professors was only partly about foreign policy; it was also about compromises which were already scandalous *before* Vietnam. Steiner's apprehension of the notion of being a freelance exemplifies his generation's faith that intellectual honour was compatible with lolling on institutional cushions. The gullibility of accepting CIA funds for *Encounter* was a mild aspect of a general belief in the propriety of passing the hat as long it belonged to a big enough head. When applying for money becomes a way of making a living, success in doing so can be taken for a symptom of merit: 'all grants are deserved' is a truism of academic morality. The irony of Nobel and his explosive prizes is so delectable, and so straightfacedly disregarded, that smaller comedies cannot be expected to get many laughs.

I mentioned at lunch with the Ayrtons that the arrival of James I (VI of Scotland) marked the entry of the perverse into English life and literature. Steiner's eyes glittered like reassured creditors. 'Now there's a subject for you – the arrival of perversity in English writing.' One could see him buying in order to re-sell, the intellectual broker *dans ses oeuvres*. He has the mind and will of a worldwide Director of Studies. After I outlined the typology of a range of public schoolmen, he had a new subject for me: The Anatomy of Britain. True, Sampson had done something of the sort, but I could do it better, and it would give me a better chance to display my qualities than the boring old novel.

Dr Jonathan Miller came, inevitable as Christmas, into our conversation. Steiner was inclined to reverence. I suppose that he is keen for a long life and no one who wants to survive ever denigrates a doctor. Jonathan, he said, had 'destroyed McLuhan'. At the same time, he quoted gleefully one thing which 'only McLuhan could have said' in a recent *Listener*: 'As Zeus said to Narcissus, "watch yourself"!'

Zara sat next to me while we ate an excellent *quiche*, with pastry so short it was close to wit. Elisabeth is bringing out a cookbook and here, I suppose, was the preface. Zara is a fellow of New Hall. She does not affect G.S.'s exalted style: she confessed to having been impressed by Maugham's *Of Human Bondage*. Like me, she had read it before any other novel. But when I suggested that W.S.M. deserved to rank as a Modern Master (the Fontana series seems to have very long arms), S. shuddered and said, 'Why not Coward?' Such commonplace talents were of no interest to a man whose son had recently shaken Borges by the hand. The son is fourteen; I did not catch why it was so impressive that he had shaken the old, blind man by the hand, except that the hand was a famous one.

Zara is George's human book end: she sets her weight against the avalanche which might otherwise so voluminously overwhelm the unwary. Was Canetti's *Auto-da-Fé* a prevision of Steiner? Irony cannot tell it all: he has a smiling and attractive villainy. A *coureur* of ideas, forever tweaking their bottoms and pinching their cheeks, an intellectual lecher who lives for the chase and whose consummate pleasure is to go bed with a good book, or two, he is American in his impatience with any restraint on his gregarious opportunism and an exile in his feverish industry and captious charm. Agility has taken the place of any interest in society: the cultivation of the famous is his alternative to a passport, acquaintance with the powerful is all his politics. Knowing that he cannot defend himself against the many, he has committed himself, without moral illusions, to the company of the prized, prize-winning few.

The main course was a rehash of turkey and ham *en casserole*, with mashed potato. It was tasty but hard; the ham resembled a *ragoût* of boiled bottle-tops. There was also cold pheasant; what we did not want, the cats finished; or had already begun. The wine was a decent '66 Burgundy.

They were all disgusted with the Amises for their venal obituaries of Cecil Day-Lewis. The couple had hurtled into print with quasi-clinical accounts of the poet's last days. If Kingsley's was bad, Jane's was worse. And had we seen Amis's short story (article?) about their stay in a pub which had exactly resembled The Green Man in his novel? We had not. '*Well*, it was all about how Amis and Jane had stayed in this pub and in the middle of the night they woke to feel this presence outside the window. Amis got up and went to investigate. And when he got back into bed, Jane said, waking, "I'm glad you decided not to go out." He said, "What do you mean?" She said, "Well, you just had sex with me."' He said he never, and the next morning, as I understand it, he took her to their doctor – name and address supplied – and had him take a swab to see whether there was any semen in her vagina. Why was everyone so outraged? The story suggested a desperation about material so cannibalistic that one could imagine the Amises driven to eat their own children out of the dull need for something more economical than beef. But so what? Any stick was good enough to whack Amis who, to prove the almost miraculous badness of a film, once said that both he and George Steiner had walked out of it. (George will cite anyone who mentions his name.)

Amis will always be forgiven his boorish, boozy gaffes because his broad bum fits a broad British bench. Steiner (and I) will always have to run to stay where we are, if we ever got there; Amis is where he is because he never had to run, and never means to. He may shock; he will never offend. If he is insulting, no one will ask him to leave: they will refill his glass. All the labile energies of Steiner, racing to make rings round Amis's parochial complacency, prove only how much of an outsider he is. George has the surging electricity of a man who has to rely for power on his own generator.

Zara, being a mother, is less stridently exceptional: she does not deny common impulses, nor having got an extra-curricular charge out of Maugham. One of her colleagues at New Hall is Miss Anscombe, who brings her children into lunch, although she has no right to do so. Zara always calls them 'Anscombe' and is reproved: 'Their name is Geach.' Anscombe's husband, Peter Geach, was a research fellow when I was up. He never wore socks.

When someone mentioned Koestler, Steiner was prompt with personal reminiscence. They had been in Austria together and were in conversation with a Hungarian. Nostalgic for his youth, K. said he would like to visit Budapest. The Hungarians, he was told, would be proud to have him, but could not guarantee his safety: he was one of a very few, a very *select* few, who had done the Russian case such harm that, given a chance to grab him, they might find it irresistible. What would Steiner have given to be on that shortlist?

What would the Russians actually do to Koestler if they nabbed him? If they wanted to kill him, they could manage that without his visiting Hungary. Would they lock him up and savour the thunderous impotence of the West as it hammered on their gate? Steiner declared that Koestler had written two modern classics, two *essential texts* (one sensed him gearing himself up for a commissioned preface): *A Dialogue with Death* and *Darkness at Noon*. The former seethes with the frisson of being in imminent danger of that ultimate full stop, the firing squad. Evidence under such a threat carried *oracular conviction*: in such circumstances, *why lie*? Why not, I wondered.

I have no strong memory of the book, though I do remember thinking that it proved that, before falling into the hands of potential executioners, it would be as well to belong to the union of international celebrities. As for *Darkness at Noon*, I accused it of being sentimental. S. denied it, *ex cathedra*, but Zara took my point. George would not, because he shares K.'s fault of believing that wickedness needs to employ reason to subvert humanity. Rubashov is *persuaded*, not to say flattered, never mind how ruthlessly, into committing perjury, as if it were an intellectual accomplishment. The lesson that neither G.S. nor K. wants to learn is that *force* is the master of society: no strengthening of our arguments will alter the behaviour of those who cannot endure the mildest objection. The primacy of the intellectual is an illusion G. and K. cannot relinquish; nor yet could Marx: his reprieve of the brain-worker from the general anathema on the bourgeoisie gave intellectuals a metic's place at least in the workers' world. It also tempted them into clerkly treason.

S. and K. cannot bear the idea of a mindless society, in which having an opinion of any kind is a dangerous luxury. That is why the drama of Rubashov is so crucial for them. The Russian answer to *Darkness at Noon* is not merely to ban the book (it sells well on the Prague black market) but to plan the physical intimidation, or elimination, of its author. They don't care what he says, but will fight to the death for the right to prevent him saying it. Steiner listened only to himself. His solemn pilgrimage is a search for the deeply buried Excalibur which will enable him to swagger past the guards into a neglected Eden or at least to join the (Swiss?) angels at the gate and share their rations from the Tree of Knowledge. He cannot endure any dislocation of the central myth. The idea of the banality of evil is more disagreeable to him than the actual consequences of iniquity. He must find deep reasons for deep wickedness: if shallowness was what led to the Holocaust, no amount of research can defend us against its recurrence. He wants, therefore, to *refute* violence, as K. did to show how reason could turn the world upside down.

Neither can endure the vile possibility that reason is the phlogiston of social physics. The question is not whether we reason but whether Reason is determinant. Steiner had to have it that criticism was *action*. He wants K. to have done something significant, not merely to have offended those who expected flattery. 'Steiner,' Tom Maschler said, 'likes pretentiousness'; yes, and especially his own. Of course, simultaneous with S.'s championship of K. was a willingness to concede that he could be intellectually specious. However, he thought well of *The Midwife Toad* and granted K. a masterly clarity of exposition; his vanity was suspect but it was the only authority for his detective skill, and persistence.

Cass was one of Michael Ayrton's earliest girls. He told Beetle about her. He discovered her to be very kinky: she liked to be tied up and stuff like that. One could imagine the wince of a man who imagined himself loved for his genius and who found himself playing the hired hand. Ken Tynan brought Cass to a party we gave in Chelsea, fifteen years ago. She was dark and very beautiful then, bright with the ardent chill of the witch James MacGibbon is sure she is. She seems to specialise in famous artists. With her specific requirements, she leaves a man all the free time which a well-run prison affords its executioner. She asks no favours of love; she does not need to be wooed into amorous complicity. Her appetite may be for servitude, but it is no less peremptory for that. Her defined desires now spice the routine randiness of a once anxious husband: he is not obliged to be limited to the licensed routines which, as in his art, make him a paragon of Englishness. Her precision allows him to handle her without prelude or apology. He does her as he did National Service: with conscripted snap. Sex may once have been something he got away with; now it is demanded of him. He wallows in forbidden territory: the Rubicon, once crossed, proves quite shallow. Wedded to a witch, he has a 'wife' to whose pain he is expected to cater: previously tempted to cruelty, he has become its commissioned provider. Cass's callousness (for which she required punishment) twisted Michael out of true: he was young enough to be dismayed. Her new husband was already ugly, pasty-faced, beer-bellied before he discovered the liberties available to the conscienceless. For all that, Cass strikes me as a frightened person: her loftiness has the dignity of despair.

M.A. continues to write because his father wanted him to be a scholar. I recalled that he had done the jacket for Peter Green's *Achilles, His Armour*. They are no longer friends; M. fell out with the Greens and the Goldings over the Colonels. Steiner mouthed some rococo platitude about Peter having come home at last to a calm harbourage after many stormy years, 'A *professorship*,' he said. '*Professor* Green.' He might have been a toast-master.

The dislike which Peter once so thoroughly aroused was, I remember Simon Raven telling me, because he had refused to become an officer in the RAF: he got below himself. Ayrton says that he cannot stand Peter; he is surprised but resolute: he has never had such splits, for such reasons, before. He will never return to Greece until the Colonels are evicted, nor to Franco's Spain.*

The Ayrtons lead a withdrawn life. They know no one in the vicinity. They have owned Bradfields for twenty years. They bought it for three thousand pounds, with seven acres, three years before the 'Lynn Chadwicks' were put up. The village had asked them to a few sherry parties, but they never returned the invitations. M. knew the house as a child. When the owner died, the son contacted him. A Dean of the Church of England had made an offer, but the son so hated clergymen that he let M. have it for less. Now it is worth a lot. M. cannot conceal his wry pleasure in its accelerating value. His main expense is casting his bronzes. He had something like two thousand pounds worth of stuff in the place which he had to shift. One of his Minotaurs, hunched and muscular, cost sixty quid for the bronze alone.

James Cameron was much discussed. I was rash enough to doubt

---

* Peter Green once told me that he would never go to Spain, but that was because he was convinced that if he did, he would die there. He had had a dream about it.

his claim to journalistic importance, but M. was vigorous in his defence: he was brave and dedicated. Steiner, of course, knew him too: Cameron had told him that Bangladesh was worse than Belsen. He had been one of the first into the camp and had written *devastatingly* about it (I wondered what Steiner would have to say to Beetle's hairdresser, Xavier, who had had to organise the clearing up of Belsen). In Bangladesh the starving reached from horizon to horizon. There was nothing to be done. Cameron drove on; and when the next horizon had been passed, the starving could be seen to stretch to the next. His jeep hit a landmine. He woke with three dead men around him and started to drag himself along the road with four broken ribs and a broken pelvis. Eventually he was taken to Calcutta and managed to pulls strings to be put on a plane. Coccooned in plaster in Fulham hospital, he remembered that he had a deadline to meet. He wrote his piece, in a sedated stupor, and then passed out. It took him three months to recover. Why can I not warm to the man, whom I have never met? They interview him in El Vino's and he talks precise platitudes between sips. Having worked for years for the Beaver, he has the hobbled honesty of those who work honourably for dishonourable men. However, it must be conceded, and humbly, that Cameron takes the risks and earns the rewards. (I suppose Nick Tomalin is in the same tradition.)★

Jack Lambert was mentioned once at lunch, not by me. No one said a word against him and no one said a word for him. (Michael remarked only, 'One's fond of the old thing'). In his absence at least, Steiner spoke of Jack as an amiable weakling, the endearingly corrupt chief of the literary police, an Anglo-Saxon Claud Rains in *Casablanca*, dexterously vacillating and postponing decision, like my Mr Andreadis in *A Wild Surmise*, until the last possible moment.

Z. was anxious to get back to Cambridge: they had left their thirteen-year-old daughter alone in the house with some boys. The daughter of the same age of a friend of theirs had recently got pregnant, and had the child (no one explained why). Steiner donned – what else? – his ankle-length tweed coat while Z. gave enthusiastic cold kisses to her hosts.

We were left in tranquillity with M.A., and his work, which we began to inspect. Abruptly we became strangers, stranded between

★ This parenthesis was written at the beginning of the year in the autumn of which Nick Tomalin was killed by a heat-seeking rocket, on the Golan Heights, during the Yom Kippur war. Three fellow reporters had got out to pee. Nick's sound bladder killed him.

the cold homage one pays to what is offered for sale and the geniality of guests. The Steiners had paid no attention to the work at all: it had never been on a short list. M. has been experimenting with rotating, multi-faceted pieces, and also with reflection: slabs of polished bronze or coated perspex slice sections through classical forms and rupture them into new perspectives. Yet there is nothing outrageous: no leap in the dark. The daring is of conscious deviation from a standard once classical and now, in the shift of time, made personal. M. still seems old-fashioned: the carefully correct work reflects the formal propriety of his decision not to visit Greece, or Spain. He seemed weakest in the large heads. One of them had three faces, but the modelling, which owed something to the Picasso of the neo-classical period, was uneasy in bronze: one was left with a sense of the dominance of the scheme.

Steiner claimed to have won the Booker Prize for John Berger by his advocacy of G., which none of the other judges were said to have read. He had not met B. before the award ceremony and was quick to scorn this 'unbelievably female creature' who had accepted the money with such malicious ingratitude. On the other hand, *'four thousand copies'* (Steiner talks in italics) had been sold since the announcement. G.S. might have pushed some shares he had bought at the bottom.

Another meeting with Norman Jewison. It was like shaking hands with fog. He wore brown slacks and a turtle-necked sweater. His big leather belt had a big JC buckle. He smoked successful cigars, and did not fail to offer me one, once. He did nothing disagreeable. The character of 'The Mercenary', a guy who says 'You're all full of shit', recurred in his conversation. I was filled with the sense of acid apprehension I felt years ago when Norman Panama kept saying, 'What makes Tommy run?' We oscillated between using 'the book' (David Caute's flagellating novel) and breaking right away. I never believed that we would break far enough. He asked for a one-page outline which would crystallise what we were telling. I sent him three pages on the Tuesday before our Thursday meeting. I had had the idea of beginning at an army surplus auction somewhere like Saigon: the Mercenary was also an arms dealer. The trouble was, he had no face, unless it was that of McQueen/ Newman.

When we met, my pages were on the glass table in Bob Shapiro's office. Norman thanked me for being 'a good professional'. *Le mercé-*

naire, c'était moi. He thought the characters too 'Belgravia'. He had said of my novel that he had 'never met people like that'. I was not offended. It confirmed my sense of being ill-matched. Yet our conference continued. He was reasonable and undemanding: when it came to the plot, he was pleased to leave it to me, but what he was leaving was how to please him. The sense of being a masseur, a Greek to this prancing Crassus, filled with me shame, and disdain. I said, with cobbled sincerity, that there was a limit to what I could do in discussion. I needed to get out and see the ground. He said he would put in to UA for my ticket. I saw that a certain timidity went with that big JC buckle. He gave me a lift in his red Jaguar, with his cute, elderly, jauntily-capped driver, as far as Berkeley Square, where I had left my car. 'I'm excited,' he said, as we parted, and I thought, 'Oh Christ, I wish I was!'

Almost immediately I decided to resign. Beetle's instant endorsement of my decision was so promptly joyful that it seemed almost to be hers.

They showed us some slides of their children in earlier days. How sad they always looked, and how separate! The shadow that fell across the youngest at Oxford seemed, in retrospect, always to have been there, blanched by the sunlight, but over her like a bridle.

14.2.73. Three teachers from Langham School came to see me about the PTA meeting due next week. They were not happy: they felt dragooned. They were hostile to this idea of a forum, though not clear what it was. I was keen only to create the climate for a dialogue between parents and teachers. My motives were dangerously pure and led me to a certain loftiness in my remarks to the three young persons (I have been reading Edel's *Henry James*) who trooped into the drawing room with the self-important humility of their profession. They feared that people – '*certain* people' – would ask provocative questions and lure them into contradictory frankness. Teachers, they thought, should present a common front. Why? Well, because of their Union and because things had a way of getting back to Park Parade, the seat of the County Education Authority. Things might be entered on your record. I was shocked: the indifference to honesty as an absolute demand on their pride was as puzzling to me as it was 'natural' to them. I told them the story of Alain teaching at the *Lycée* in Rouen, on the subject of Duties Towards Prostitutes, when the Inspector of Schools and the *Recteur* came in. Alain continued his lecture, which recommended to the young men that they always remember their manners with the girls, whatever their social status. The teachers could not see the relevance of my story. Embarrassed by the mention of brothels, they could not be excited into anything except suspicious resentment. Returning to the charge, I suggested the need to educate and recruit the parents. A PTA, I said, depended on the teachers. What did they think? *Could* they think?

Mrs S. is a slim, blonde almost beautiful girl, with high cheekbones and dulled blue eyes. She was supposed to leave at Christmas, 'to start a family' as they say. The family was not started: she is still there. Anxiety has drained her enthusiasm. The look of sullen dissent, of principled obtuseness so common among the young could well be taught in her class, so could truculence and a sort of sneering evasiveness in that of her colleague Ralph G. He has the pitiless deference of Uriah Heep crossed with Robespierre. He affects opinionated purposefulness but has neither opinions nor purpose. He doesn't approve of the Eleven-Plus and he denies the importance of handwriting: scarcely a programme to take to the people.

Mrs Leaf is more genial, and more supple. Yet I had explained to her everything that I now said again and had asked her to relay it to the others. They showed no sign of having heard it. If want of grace was a sign of integrity, they did not lack it. Their unrelenting attitude qualified them more as bailiffs than as educators. They faced the smallest challenge or hint of innovation with morose narrow-mindedness. I wanted at once to plead with them and to send them to the salt-mines. Neither moved nor shamed, they had come to protest against a 'Forum' and that was that. They meant no harm; they failed to mean even that much: they were employees who had come to prevent something. I suggested that teachers must teach not only the answers but also the questions: so what questions from parents would they *like* to be asked? They did not understand. They wanted a committee. They wanted to avoid complaints.

It was decided that *all* the parents should be encouraged to attend (as if our earlier meeting had been a cabal). I was asked to write a letter setting out why everyone should come. I drafted all of two paragraphs and took it to them. They approved it solemnly. Ralph G., who made Quasimodo look like a fine upstanding lad, could not bring himself to look at me at all. It was hard to believe that he had not entered the room on all fours.

The main, unstated problem is Mr Sanford, the new headmaster. Hot from East Africa, he is hurrying progress with the unconscious

authoritarianism of a District Officer. He is small and unprepos-
sessing, with a rumpled nose (he has had an operation for sinusitis)
and tobacco breath. He is friendly and, as Derek G. puts it, 'inclined
to be presumptive'; like an heir, I suppose. He arrived from Africa
last summer, in a beige many-pocketed bush jacket, to replace Miss
H. who had been at the school for forty years. I should not have
recognised her if I saw her, though Sarah was at the school under
her. Sarah's form mistress was Miss Baisting, an old woman so indifferent to parents as to be literally deaf to their questions. She used
methods now obsolete in reformatories: she made the infants put
their heads down in their hands and remain silent for a period of
minutes. She spoke of 'the slipper' and may have administered it.

When Sanford arrived, there was no modern equipment, no playground climbing frame or slide, no balls, nothing. Of all the pupils
of James and Paul Digings' year, only they passed the Eleven-Plus,
a derisive proportion in the light of the national average. None of
these things incensed or even touched the parents. The village
accepted its contemned status without comment. Before Sanford's
arrival, I doubt if the school even claimed its full financial entitle-
ment. At the moment, it is three hundred pounds for all
expenditure, for over a hundred pupils. How all the new material
has been delivered so quickly, and how significant it is for the children, no one has seemed to notice. No one complained before, but
they murmur now: Mr Sanford has worked modest miracles, but he
has made few friends. The masters at the 'Naughty Boys' School' –
as the village calls the Borstalian institution on the Straight Road (a
witty siting, I suppose) – will have nothing to do with him: he made
assumptions about their availability and willingness to do *pro bono*
work. Yet Sanford is tireless: he spends his free time on 'clubs' and
on organising activities. Yesterday he put up a puppet theatre which
he had built himself. But he is not liked, even by people such as
ever-happy Hazel at the garage, who has never met him.

While a Chief Inspector of Schools in Africa, after independence,
he must have displayed plenty of self-effacing tact, but he has not
repeated the trick in the old country. Unaware, it seems, of his lack
of support, he grasps the nettle of English country life as if it were
an outstretched hand.

The 'Naughty Boys'' school (for psychologically damaged boys) is
housed in a mansion allegedly built by Edward VII for one of his
mistresses. Eddie Wingate, a teacher, invited me to Christmas lunch
there and I have been playing weekly football with him and the

boys. Ill-used by parents or by fortune, they are clumsy, but not violent or malicious. One day, some boys were standing and talking in the goalmouth as Eddie came out with the ball. He turned and kicked it very hard towards the goal. It flew straight at a boy who was unaware of its coming. It hit him smack on the forehead and he went back like a felled sapling. He lay in the mud with a faint grey smile on his face. We ran up and immediately, hopefully, took the smile to mean that he was faking. We lifted him much too promptly to his feet. He was out. He came round slowly and Eddie pumped air into him in the accepted hearty manner and sent him indoors to the matron. I was struck by E.'s amiable callousness. He did not blame himself, nor did he apologise. Later he allowed the boy to rejoin the game without wondering whether he had been concussed.

I first met E.W. because he wanted money for the 'club' the boys were building in the basement. I gave them a fiver. Eddie called to thank me, and then explained how much more they needed. I suggested the Variety Club of Great Britain and they came through, quite handsomely. A year or so later, Eddie approached me again. He had got the lads interested in cutting up old cars for scrap. They toted the stuff to dealers on a small trailer, but now needed a bigger one. I volunteered to write again to the Variety Club. This time I received a testy answer: they had already given money for a trailer. They had even sent a Variety Club plaque to screw onto it. The organiser seemed more piqued by the possibility of a plaqueless trailer than by outright embezzlement. He said he would 'come down' (in a fiery chariot perhaps) and 'have a word with E.W.'

No new trailer was provided. The headmaster had, in any case, had enough of junked cars. People were delivering them unsolicited. The school yard was clogged with bangers. It was time to junk the junk. E.W. never alluded to the matter again. He has taken to making jewellery. He and a bearded Canadian and their wives have 'gone into the business'. E.W. himself looks like an understudy for Jesus: he has the thick brown beard and the thick brown look, compassion without the passion. He speaks in a manly voice which is kept menacingly under control. His mildness is mined with reservations and frank with evasiveness. He does a hard job and I imagined him ill-paid. In fact, he is on the usual scale and is no shorter of cash than any other schoolmaster in the jewellery business. Eddie is always right; he has that kind of implacable courtesy. His children are as correct as a grammar.

He will have nothing more to do with Mr Sanford. Why? S. rang him about a climbing frame which was advertised in the *Essex County Standard*. Under pressure, Eddie and the Canadian volunteered to get it, with the trailer. On the way home, they stopped in Coggeshall for a beer and then, as they came along a straight road out of the town, a car turned across their bows from the centre of the road, and they hit it. Eddie said that, according to the garage, his Standard was a write-off, though they had come to dinner with us in it. The other car, with a man and his family in it, was superficially damaged. When the crash happened, Eddie leapt out and the Canadian yelled, 'Steady, Eddie!' E.W. insists that he was in a hurry only because he had seen children in the other car, but the Canadian's shout suggests that I am not alone in sensing unexploded rage in E.W.'s egregious self-control.

When telephoned by Sanford, wanting to know how they had got on, Eddie said, 'It's going to be a rather expensive bill.' Sanford was bemused (understandably) until E.W. explained that his car was a write-off. Sanford muttered about making a contribution, but has never spoken to E.W. again.* He has, however, continued to send welding jobs down to the school 'with a boy' and expects Eddie to do them. E. is grim with resentment, though it might be said (but not by me) that the welding equipment was bought with the county's money and it is no great scandal to put it to use.

3.73. While we are away, the electricians are rewiring The Wick. There has been a smell of fish for too long. They must have alarmed the burglar alarm, which went off one night at one a.m. and did not stop till seven in the morning, after Jack Smith came over to work. How do we know it went off at one? The neighbours heard it, but no one, of course, called the police. Such is the community spirit of Langham. Our nearest neighbours have been sending their children 'over ours' to play with P. and S. for the last ten years.

Mr D. senior, whose house is next to The Wick, used to run a shop at Severalls, the big mental hospital. He is a superficially jolly man who calls Mr Spooner, the morose farmer in the cottage down our lane, 'neighbour' and mutters, a few seconds later, about what an old fool he is. When we first came to Wick Road, there was a row of sagging clapboard cottages opposite old D.'s house. The

---

* I am still puzzled by E.W.'s apparent belief that Sanford owed him something, even 'morally', for damage which he never caused and which E.W.'s insurance policy should have covered.

owner promised old D. first refusal, but didn't keep his word: he sold the property to 'some Jewboy from the Lea Bridge Road'. The subsequent row of spec houses has dispelled our rural illusions. Now old D. intends to make a few bob by building a spec house himself, on the patch of land between his house and his son's. A year ago, his wife was struck by lightning while cooking in her kitchen. She was not seriously injured, but very frightened: age hit her like an accident. Short ly afterwards, her little white poodle was seized through the hedge by an Alsatian, and killed.

P.G. was a clever boy in a school of fools. He was so badly beaten that he says that he is now indifferent to what people say: he fears only what they do. He hides behind a beard and glasses which might have come from a disguise kit. He has had many jobs. You know when he has started a new one because he has a new car. His wife says 'For some reason, he can't seem to settle.'

I had an autobiography of Dennis M., a journalist, to review and asked J.D. about him. He told me a few things and later telephoned me because he had recalled that 'the paper' had had the bright idea of 'exhuming Tommy Farr' to cover the Cassius Clay–Henry Cooper fight. Dennis was going to be Farr's ghost. He and J.D. went over in the afternoon in a taxi to Harringay. D.M. kept saying, 'I want to get laid, I must get laid.' 'Who says a thing like that?' J.D. asked me. Eventually, Dennis M. said that he was going to ring up 'a little photographer called Sally', and he did. She came over, 'But it wasn't Dennis that got laid,' J.D. said. Point of story.

They told us of the suburban medium through whom dead composers are said to transmit their work. Beethoven and Schubert and Schumann allegedly lined up to dictate to her. Various author-ities had sat in judgement on what she claimed to have transcribed and, even at its worst, deemed it very plausible pastiche. The pundits were more aggrieved than sceptical: what they could not under-stand was how great men chose *her* as a confidante.

7.3.73. At the beginning of February, the Israeli air force shot down a Libyan 727 over the Sinai desert. It had lost its way from Tripoli to Cairo. About one hundred people were killed. The Israelis were formally sad, but fell short of unfeigned apology. They claimed that there had been threats to send a civil aircraft crammed with explosives to crash on an Israeli city. The pilot of the crashed plane was French; neither he nor the Libyan co-pilot recognised the Star of David on the fighters which were seeking to make them land (there was thick cloud), and presumed themselves over Egyptian territory. They never made radio contact with their pursuers. The Israelis claimed not to know that it was a passenger aircraft and that they would not have opened fire if they had. They also maintained that they flew within five yards of the 727 and exchanged hand signals with the crew. Did no passenger put his face to the window during all this? It seems unlikely. *The Times* was vigorously condemnatory: what would the reaction be of 'Jews in this country'? Gerald Scarfe, in the *ST* saw Dayan as consuming the last crumbs of comfort left for Israel. A leading article accused Israel of shameless double standards.

A few days later, the Black September guerillas kidnapped five diplomats in Khartum and shot two Americans and a Belgian before surrendering without conditions and without liberating their imprisoned comrades. The coldbloodedness of the killings appalled the Powers. Those who died in the Sinai were a collection of Arabs, though there were a couple of celebrities (a children's TV announcer and her producer) among the crated remains. The assassination of diplomats, on the other hand, no longer promised immunity from the common lot. As a result, little more was heard about the Libyan plane. Madame Meir has been to Washington and has obtained the 'advanced weaponry' she was after. She was the guest of honour at a three thousand plate dinner, where she hoped to raise $300m. Before they had reached the Caesar Salad, $135m. had already been subscribed. The murders of the diplomats could not have come at a better time for her.

A cynic could believe that the Egyptians had been behind the crash of the 727 and the Israelis behind the machine-gunning of the diplomats. The acts of both sides serve their enemies better than themselves. The gentleman advocates of the Arabs (Mayhew, Nutting, Adams) wrote a proper letter to *The Times* denouncing the murders at Khartum. Some supporters of Israel sincerely regretted the downing of the Boeing: Goodman, Sieff, and others deplored the intransigence of the Israeli government and hoped that both sides would seek a decent settlement. The Egyptian ambassador welcomed this, and asked the dignitaries to use their influence on the Israelis. A leading article yesterday urged 'Arab leaders' to make a declaration of their attitude to Khartum.

La question se pose: what difference will it make what anyone says?

The Arab leaders may condemn Black September, but will continue to sympathise with it: it does their dirty work. If Arab governments repressed terrorists with due vigour, they would face even stronger pressure to resume the battle with Israel on a national scale. It is as futile to reproach the Arabs for their feelings, however disagreeable, as to hope that Israel will defer to amiable criticism. The condemnation of means insists on the merits of the end. Mayhew and his colleagues do not withdraw their support of 'the Arab cause' any more than embarrassed Tories voted Labour after Profumo was known to have bedded Christine Keeler.

To hope that the supporters of the other side will be alienated by excesses committed in its name leads to a cruel paradox: one begins to look forward to brutalities against the innocent. The more 'unforgivable' the damage done to one's own side, the livelier the hope of sympathy from 'the world community'. What happened over Sinai seems part of a terrible scenario in which the Egyptians sacrificed their own people as a symbolic gesture of humiliation at being unable to hurt the Jews. The Carthaginians resorted to human sacrifice (of their own children) when things went badly. Jews slaughtered themselves, at Masada and at York, rather than be taken. There was surely a triumphal element in this: their own deaths stood in for those of their irresistible oppressors.

Philip Guedalla: History does not repeat itself. Historians do.

Before he became an officer, he had been to a concert in Liverpool and was on his way back to the ship when, in the blackout, he met a lower deck messmate, a practised lecher. He had a woman with him and they went along together until they came to a lamp. Albert suddenly called out, 'Jack, what time do we have to be back on board? Eleven, isn't it?' Jack was about to say no, twelve, when a heavy nudge reminded him of his duty as a mate. 'Um, er,' he said. 'Thought so. We'd better run,' Albert said, ditching the woman with brief regrets. When they were out of her sight, Albert said, 'No need to run.' 'What was up, Albert?' 'Didn't you see?' Albert said. 'When we got under that lamp? She'd got no teef.'

8.3.73. Terrorism has long been the key weapon in the Muslim world. The Assassins were the ultimate menace: 'the bomber will always get through' had its equivalent in their determination to hit unsuspecting targets. If warlike Arab tribes have been 'awakened' from time to time in the last six hundred years, they have usually been primed with sovereigns. Terrorism of the kind we have seen since 1967 is their traditional style. The Arab states were not effective in 1948 nor in 1967: organised warfare against organised enemies is not in their character. What then is the source of the martial enthusiasm of the new Jews, after centuries of sufferance? During the Diaspora, argument has been their only weapon. They were forced to become the reasonable people *par excellence*. The Enlightenment encouraged them to take a part in the world's argument. Was their vigorous participation, which led them to excite first the admiration and then the odium of Europe, the result merely of release from the Ghetto? The standard view, on the liberal side, has always been that Jews were ideally placed to benefit from the age of trade and secularisation, since they were often polyglot, in-the-middle men inhibited neither by old ideas nor by national/ linguistic parochialism. But they were not *quite* the mere individuals which Liberalism made of other citizens: a certain Hegelian *geist* continued to give them something in common, of which democracy was depriving its other citizens. Whatever the competition between them, the Jews had lines of mutual understanding, and even of purpose, which made them, in some sense, 'reasonable' scapegoats. It would be absurd to claim that Gentiles lacked a social structure on which they, more than the Jews, might rely, but the unemployed and the new urban proletariat might well believe that the Jews – the only new element in a society which both seemed similar and had changed irretrievably – were those responsible for draining their energies: the Jews as bloodsuckers was a plausible metaphor which had been taken literally, for centuries, in the Blood Libel, which Reason never quite refuted.

Zionism is often attributed to a defensive reflex on the part of Herzl and his friends, who as if for the first time saw the incurable vulnerability of Jews in western society. The Dreyfus Affair has been taken as the clinching evidence of the untrustworthiness of the West (with Russia included). Could it not also be argued that the *pro*-Jewish excitement manifested by Dreyfusards signalled that the moment had come to realise the old hope 'Next Year in Jerusalem'? Herzl's Big Idea was always implicit in the despair of Ghetto Jews. The Jews had now come into the open as members, however marginal, of liberal society. They saw each other for the first time as active agents, not pliant victims and passive fossils (Arnold Toynbee's term). In the Age of Imperialism, Zionism was no less parodic of Gentile ambitions than other forms of assimilated Jewish gentility. What were they planning that the European Powers had not already done? To carve off a slice of the Ottoman empire was hardly an act of anomalous or intemperate aggression when Africa had already been jointed.

The Balfour Declaration was no symptom of British affection for Jews, or their rights. It was based, in part, on a misreading of Jewish economic clout and cohesion: the British feared that the Jews would put their money on the Germans unless they had good reason to do the opposite. The Foreign Office also saw the need for a balancing force against the Arabs, even though it favoured them. It is an old rule of diplomacy to take prudent measures against one's allies. The Arab 'nationalism' which the British had primed with persuasive gold was, for the moment, under their control, but should it become *genuinely* nationalistic, under some new Mad Mullah, the Jews might have a use.

The misfortune of Israel is that the western powers lacked the will or the nerve to assert themselves when the Arabs did indeed turn stroppy. 1956 was the climacteric of European imperialism. Eden was an appropriate Prime Minister for the time: he personified the contradictions which reputation, charm, wealth and gallantry had concealed in the British style until Suez.

The cohesion of the British collapsed at the very time that Israel's was fused. 1956 not only signalled the end of Britain's capacity to have a common national policy (which had given foreigners the impression that she would always fight ruthlessly in her own interests), it was also the moment when Israel acquired all the stock in Jewishness and hence became, like it or not, the definitive locus of world Jewry. That this localisation had taken place was not obvious for another eleven years, when failure to see that sufferance was not an element in Israel's character led to Nasser's fatal hubris. He acted as though the *Der Stürmer* image were still valid: the Egyptians of 1956 had been defeated by a stab in the back, like the good old Germans in 1918. In 1967, the Israelis were able to rely on the world's inactive sympathy because it was generally believed, if not openly hoped, that the 'warlike' Arabs were certain to crush the cornered Jews this time. The Arabs suffered from having been sentimentalised; the Jews profited from their own vilification.*

---

* Attitudes to Israel are incurably affected by a 'double-bind' in western minds. Israel would not have existed, in its present form, had it not been for the Holocaust (few would contest this), and therefore the Holocaust was a Bad Thing. But Israel is a disappointment: it has failed to prove what piety would like, that being persecuted gives you moral superiority and that the Jews can

After 1967, it was said – notably by General de Gaulle – that the Jews were clever, ruthless, unyielding and sure of themselves. Are these not the very qualities of which anti-Semites always accused them? Their cohesion may be attributed to ancient virtues or to ancient vices, but it is resented and suspect in either case. Whether they have changed (into pugnacious and conscienceless Israelis) or not (as squeamish Diasporites suggest), they are still all the same.

How 'modern' is Freud's theory that, roughly speaking, there is no such thing as an accident? Isn't it present in Homer? One might even claim that the sexual origin/motivation of the typical Freudian error is the archaic *ate* internalised. Freud put scientific clothing on mythic bones. What proof is there that 'everything has a cause'? Such an axiom is essentially religious. *Ate* explained the conduct of Greeks when it was contrary to rational procedures or interests: e.g., when Glaucus exchanged his gold armour for bronze. Could a Freudian account of the same event do better in explaining Glaucus's unprofitable bargain? The acceptance of the accidental as 'inexplicable' endangers the idea of a rational world, full of caused effects. Hence it might seem to admit the demonic, the numinous, the spiritual, but it would also imply a world without *necessary* order, a genuinely modern world in which the search for meanings would cease to be a covert form of prospecting for ultimate truths.

Consciously or not, Freud tried to exonerate us from guilt by returning us, in E.R. Dodds's sense, to shame. *Ate* as the daughter of Zeus is his personal attribute (and hence presages monotheism and the centralisation of power). Nilsson claims that Homeric man believed in psychic intervention because he was 'impulsive'. Dodds prefers 'he gives way to impulses because he is socially conditioned

---

rise above what Gentiles do to them. The conduct of Israel is criticised like that of no other state. Now comes the unadmitted, manifest conclusion: if the Jews can't behave better than everyone else, they are a nuisance. Therefore it would have been better, if the Holocaust had to take place (and how can it now be reversed?), if it had succeeded more thoroughly. The Jews are more irritating since Hitler than they were before him. It is *all their fault* now, which is a relief, since it lifts the guilt from Europe back onto the Christ-killers, who tradition-ally deserved it. So, granted that Hitler was a monstrous murderer, he should have finished the job once he started it, although we must never say so. This does not, of course, take away from or deny the genius of some Jews; it is a matter of candid political analysis. Israel and the Palestinians provide the centre of attention of the last ideologues: no longer able to legislate about Capital and Labour, they can rule Israel off the map by pure intellectual moralising. Self-destruction is the only Israeli policy which the pure-in-heart will ever applaud.

to believe in psychic intervention'. As a result of Freud's 'discovery' of the fundamental ubiquity of libidinal motivation (*le bon* Charcot's *toujours la chose génitale*) men feel themselves made powerless (and hence empowered) by the 'logic' of sexual primacy: *id* trumps *ego*. They then become 'sexier', just as Homeric heroes – pressed by the desire for glory – became ruthless or capricious. *Kleos oblige*. Men will inhabit any theory which absolves them of personal responsibility. Here is the attraction of Nazism. As long as the system provides rewards and excuses violence, no one *within it* finds it either implausible or disgusting. Once its power/logic/language collapses, only maniacs defend it. A public licence will trigger orgies of righteousness, fucking, or human sacrifice: moral and immoral become the same thing until, with the revocation of the licence, the Bacchants return – embarrassed, bewildered, and sometimes hung over – to life as before.

Harrison, old man! A story set in Kenya during the 'Emergency'. Geoffrey Harrison, a National Service officer, discovers that Gareth Morgan, the head of one of the white families which his platoon is deployed to protect, has dismissed Joseph, an African employee, whose daughter has been killed in an accident when a party, including the white family's daughter, Lucy, was on its way home from a piss-up. The African has disappeared from his home and gone into the bush. Harrison is in love with Lucy. When Joseph is captured by Geoffrey's platoon in a sweep against 'terrorists', Geoffrey intervenes to prevent his torture. He also arranges for him to be 'compensated' for the death of his daughter. Joseph returns to his village and a new job, in the militia of 'loyal Africans'.

One night the Morgan farm is attacked and Gareth's wife, Mary, is killed. Morgan himself is paralysed by a machete wound. Harrison leads the hunt for the attackers and shoots Joseph as he comes out of the bush with his hands up. Harrison is commended and promoted for the successful mission. He asks Lucy to marry him and 'get away from all this'. How can she? She has to look after her now invalid father. Harrison goes to a black prostitute in the nearby town and then walks into the bush.

The play between the 'neutral' *erinys* – an external, initiating motive – and the vengeful *Erinyes* helps to articulate the analogy between sex and original sin: the reference back to Adam and Eve lifts the individual burden of guilt at the cost of making it inescapable, *the* fact of life. The inevitable thus becomes the one thing we can avoid:

we need feel no *personal* responsibility for what *cannot* be our fault. Modern man has eliminated 'awe' (the mythical) by a 'logic' which confuses 'has a cause' with 'is scientifically explicable'. He imagines that he has discovered the truth about the universe when he has merely decided on the style of truth he will accept. We march in lock-step with Marx and Freud: privately, all motivation is believed to be sexual; publicly it is all economic. Hedonism is reconciled with determinism. All inexplicable behaviour can, in principle, be explained. There is nothing to be done about it. On we go.

A writer's wife must resign herself, no matter how successful he may become, to living above the shop.

25.3.73. Last Tuesday was Beetle's birthday. We went to see a new play at Colchester: David Turner's *The Prodigal Daughter*. On the way home we were lamenting that there were never any new good movies. 'As a matter of fact,' I said, 'there's one on there.' The Cameo was showing *The Last Picture Show*. When we got home, someone had telephoned from Hollywood: Peter Bogdanovich. Isabel was anxious lest she had got the number and name wrong. P.B. and I talked for over an hour, with the eager assumption of intimacy that precedes partnership. There were three films he wanted to discuss: we have agreed *Daisy Miller* and a new musical, based on the songs of Cole Porter.*

25.3.73. B.M. told me about an old Communist Party member who was also a millionaire. He owned a printing business. When it went public, he made half a million pounds. He could have lived modestly on his capital for the rest of his life. He invested the money in a new plant: modern and highly efficient, the factory of his dreams. There was no dirty work; it was a plant of which an enlightened boss could be proud. Many of his old clients were impressed; they promised him contracts. But when it came to it, they remained loyal to the firm he had left. New customers were hard to find. The shining modern plant ran at a fraction of capacity. The boss guaranteed it

---

*   I did indeed write the screenplay for *Daisy Miller*, but the film was not a success. Somewhat to my relief, Bogdanovich elected to write the musical himself. It was called *At Long Last Love*. It was a turkey, and then some. When Francis Ford Coppola announced that he was going to make *The Godfather II*, someone remarked to Billy Wilder, 'That's courage!' Billy said, 'No, no, making *Godfather II* isn't courage. Courage is *At Long Last Love II*.'

with his private fortune, down to the last of the pictures on his walls. When the firm went bankrupt, he went with it. During his successful years, he had lent money to his mother, on his accountant's advice. The receivers required him to declare all his assets. No one would ever have known any different if he said that the money he gave to his mother was a gift (the only reason it had been said to be a loan was to avoid having to pay death duties on his own cash when she died). To the fury of his family, he declared everything: he did not conceal a single canvas or a single shilling. He considered it his duty to hide nothing. He now drives a Mini and represents a big printing company. He rang B.M. hoping for some business.

Naïveté for a writer is not a matter of how he looks at the world but of how he looks at writing.

An opened book made a circumflex over the arm of the chair.

Wittgenstein the Silentiary.

1.4.73. Roger and Katie came for the day. We telephoned them out of sociability, wanting some variety for the children, not from any strong desire to see them. We learned, with some vexation (*amused* vexation) that they had had T. and Anne to lunch. The two couples had met while Roger and Katie were staying with us in the summer. R. and K. have come often to our house and stayed at Lagardelle several times. What do *we* have to do to be asked to, say, tea? Have them for a month?

The day was, however, a pleasure. I quizzed Roger about being an executive. He confirmed the unreality of a job concerned only with management in the abstract. He has the vulnerability of an overseer in paradise. We seldom find new subjects to discuss: we talk about Cambridge, schools, how things are going. We act agreeable parts. There is no progression. Friendship *chez les Anglais* is marking time on the spot.

After they had gone, Paul and I played 'football tennis', which he had invented. It worked well. We played until dark.

Flaubert: 'I look for new scents, larger flowers, untried pleasures.' Could one restore Symbolism's shock of novelty with a book which depicted our 'reality' in terms of fantasy, with Flaubertian clarity and morbidity? The myth of the twentieth century is, after all, the myth of actuality. Suppose that one '*criticised*' the news as if it were a work

of art, a wilful collage, *for such it is*. A page of *The Times* as artefact;
TV news as montage.

A book cocked open on the desk, ready to fire both barrels of
quotation.

Madame Scholly. During the war, she told us, the French called the
Germans '*Fridolins*'. In Mulhouse, the main street had always been
L'Avenue du Sauvage. The Germans renamed it *Avenue Adolf Hitler*.
The Mulhousians immediately made a habit of a slip of the tongue,
which was then instantly corrected: '*Avenue du Sauvage... Adolf
Hitler.*'

Mai Zetterling. An old and close friend of hers died in Sweden. Mai
was genuinely fond of her and duly dismayed by the news. At the
same time, she thought, 'Now I shall never get back the $800 I lent
her.'

2.4.73. Paul cooked us an excellent pizza pie. After lunch he and I
were about to play some more football tennis when Charlie began
to bark and there was a ring at the front door. It was the second
coming of Kennedy Thom. He wore a smart, silky black suit, over
a smock front topped by a dog-collar on an elastic band. He still has
a heavy black beard and many teeth. He entered our house with the
confidence of a habitual visitor. The authority of his cloth armed
him with a spiritual search-warrant.

K.T. was already well established in the Footlights when Leslie
Bricusse introduced me. I did not get a warm welcome, but K.T.
had a certain official benevolence. He was Vice-President. Both he
and Peter Firth, the then President, are now clergymen. Kennedy
was remarkable for his diction: he topped and tailed his consonants
like beans. In a generation of people who imitated Noel Coward,
he was among the best. In the 1953 May Week show, *Cabbages and
Kings*, he performed 'There is not a man/On my Ottoman/And
there hasn't been one for weeks...' When *Out of the Blue* went to
London a year later, Dermot Hoare made it, as they say, his own.

On leaving Cambridge, Kennedy joined Shell. As a performer,
he belonged to the amateur tradition whose last fling had been the
diffused production of *Cabbages and Kings*, ill-matched pearls
unevenly strung on the thin theme of 'Alice on the Moon'. The
chaos of the dress rehearsal was such that I believed that the show
would be cancelled or that we should be pelted with contempt. We

opened in triumph. I had written a parody of the weekly Bob
Boothy–Michael Foot discussion programme, *Free Speech*. I gave
myself the line, 'We in the Labour Party will do anything in our
power to get everything in our power.' I conceived it as a laugh; it
received an ovation. I realised for the first time, sitting up there on
the Arts stage, that the majority of the audience was not simply
amused but was ready, like a well-heeled mob, to institute the
Counter-Revolution.*

   At the end of the Revue, there were elections for Footlights officials for the coming year. Only committeemen had the vote. I was
now well established in the side, but very much as a Bricusse man.
He proposed me for Press Secretary, hardly a cabinet post. He
assured me that I was a shoo-in. The decisive meeting was held
backstage. Leslie came to me white-faced: my election had been
obstructed by two people who did not think there should a Jew on
the committee. I had had almost no experience of anti-Semitism at
Cambridge. Intellectual arrogance and social naïveté led to me
believe that where the mind was king there could be no malice. At
pains to adapt to the colour of the place, I was only secretly preoccupied with awareness of the Holocaust (as it was not yet called)
and maintained, at least in Footlights company, an appropriate
levity. I imagined that the six million dead would remain so shameful
a burden on the world's conscience that one would have only to
allude to it in order to draw on almost unlimited credits of good-
will, and apology. I was a fool.

   I had one uneasy moment in my second year. I appeared in a
C.U. Mummers' production of *Musical Chairs* so miserably ill-
conceived that it was a tribute to Cambridge philistinism that the
modest audiences did not crown us with derision. I played an
American businessman and had just one good scene. After the first
night, audiences were small. We hammed it up, and I more than
most. One of my lines began 'Well...' I did it in a Jimmy Stewart
drawl which brough the (limited) house down. I wore a seersucker
suit and a straw hat and too much 5 and 9. One evening, I was going
round backstage when I met a small man called Harry, a hanger-on
of Cambridge theatricals. His father owned amusement arcades. He
said, 'Congratulations, you're the most convincing Jew I ever saw.'
There was shy malice on his sailor-boy face. His compliment was a

* The Tories had, of course, been in government, under the revenant Churchill,
  for three years, but I had not yet spoken to anyone of my own age who confessed
  to being a Conservative.

challenge. I could easily have crushed him physically. I thanked him and pushed past. I was amazed by Cambridge's failure to be that great and good place, open to the talents, which my father had promised. Its final fall from grace was Beetle's discovery of the systematic anti-Semitism at the University Appointments Board. Jack Lambert was to refer years later (last summer to be precise, while our guest) to Beetle's 'disloyalty'.*

I think it was during *Cabbages and Kings* that Leslie went out of the theatre alone to confront a Spaniard who was threatening to come in with a knife. There was certainly an occasion when a petrified cast was besieged by some angry dago whom L.C.B. went out to pacify.

Leslie let the embargo on me stand until the following year, when he was President, and then he co-opted me onto the committee (and I went).

Kennedy had been to lunch at Langham Hall, where the owners were 'very devout Romans'. He knew one of the family when he was out in Buenos Aires with Shell. K.'s brother used to farm up by Langham aerodrome, where the new road is coming. He has sold out at seven hundred pounds an acre. His father paid seven, in 1931. K. has been chaplain at Essex University since February. Before that, he spent eighteen months in a monastery near Oxford. He speaks clearly, with articulate diffidence about the fullness of a life devoted to study and prayer. He met a contemporary in the monastery, a Double First who abandoned the Foreign Service for a Buddhist monastery and has slowly worked his way back to Christianity. K. was impressed wth the man's intellectual span and by the generosity of his faith: he could not accept an exclusive idea of salvation. One felt that he had told God to go away and think again.

K. had been offered the chaplaincy of Churchill College (where a scientist once resigned his fellowship because they had decided to build a chapel), but he declined it because, he said, there were too many clergymen in Cambridge. 'A small Barsetshire?' He agreed, and remembered Colin Pearson who wrote a trim Footlights number about Anthony Trollope ('You've hit the jackpot one hell

---

* She had the courage to take copies of the personal files of Jews who had been interviewed and secretly anathematised and allowed Bernard Levin to publish them, in 1959, in *The Spectator*.

of a wallop'). One cannot but admire K.'s refusal to go to Cambridge: what nicer place for a lonely man? The job at Essex is unofficial: K. doesn't belong to the faculty. The previous incumbent was given a hard time. K. will be on the fringe of a community which can scarcely be termed Christian. Without church or colleagues, he will live alone at Wivenhoe.

I alluded, politely I thought, to the paradox of the modern cleric: he is the successor of generations of bigots, anathematisers and inquisitors, yet today he is one of the few people willing to speak unashamedly of moral obligation: he denounces the hatred and prejudice which religion has established and endorsed. He deplores unreason in the light of the irrational. His licence comes from a metaphysical 'reality'. Either God had ideas of His own or He is merely a good idea of man's.

Beetle said that I had been patronising. I thought I had been tactful in announcing my scepticism in a philosophical way. K. left for Tiptree where he is to address a local society on the meaning of The Christ.

K. told us that, during his selection board for Shell, one of the panel turned out to be connected with Cambridge House. He approached K. afterwards and asked if there was a chance of the proceeds of the Footlights Midnight Matinee going to his charity. K. promised to consider it (he was still Vice-President). 'My letter offering him a third of the proceeds crossed with his offering me a job.'

3.4.73. I played our new game with Paul and was as uncoordinated as a landed fish. I felt heavy and foolish. Judy phoned in the morning to say that the deal on *Daisy Miller* was all but set. I affected relief, but was not relieved. I spent the day in clumsy study; in the evening I resumed my wrestling with Wittgenstein and Russell. We had tea outside in the sun. I threw a black tennis ball for the dogs. They failed to see the line of its flight, scampered to the tennis court and succeeded, during their manic search, in bringing down the tennis net and actually breaking the post, inevitably the one with the winding apparatus. I had to have a bath to restore my equanimity.

Dinner with Piers Garland, an architect, and Vickie, his allegedly Cordon Bleu wife. She wore a long red woollen skirt and a black sweater. Her hair was elaborately piled. Piers has expanded his practice, but laments his luck: he is not unhappy, he says, but he is certainly disappointed: 'The ball hasn't bounced right, you know?

There's no reason why it shouldn't just as well have gone into the six as into the two.' Dinner was egg and shrimp mayonnaise, casserole of chicken, cheesecake. During dinner, there was a telephone call. We heard Piers agree to go to some village production of *Salad Days*. 'Poor Piers,' I said. Vickie said, 'It's not the show, it's the girl.'

Piers had had some early success in civic architecture and received an Award, which emboldened him to propose a conference of local architects to discuss the development of the town centre. When he was ignored, he wrote to the local paper, which then featured his criticism of the Council. At the Award ceremony, one of the local potentates came up to him and said, 'Young man, if you want to get on in this town, you'd better learn to keep your mouth shut.'

5.4.73. I worked all morning on W. and Russell. Beetle asked, 'Who are you doing it for?' She has been reading where Vita reproaches Harold Nicolson for the 'dispersal' of his talents.

In the post came a letter from Mr Tong, the Sixth Form master at the Comprehensive where I gave a talk ten days ago. The Sixth want 'another chance': they think I carried away a poor impression of their intelligence. I'll say. Should I go again? Is this 'dispersal' or duty? As for W. and R., it does have a certain aimlessness. There is unlikely to be a market for such a piece. I may well be making a fool of myself. It is certainly hard work to understand the psychodrama of two men engaged in passionate intellectual antagonism.

9.4.73. I waited all week, in an adolescent sweat, for some verdict on my play* for the BBC. I had decided by Friday that Mark Shivas disliked it and was too embarrassed, or too serpentine, to declare it. I spoke to Judy in the late afternoon and she was amazed, she said, that Mark had not called: he thought the play was brilliant, etc. Beetle was busy planning the lunch to give the Ayrtons on Sunday. Paul and I played squash, on a perfect spring evening, at Essex University, where Roger and I used to play. P. started well, but his concentration yielded to ambition and he lost his poise. I felt great and undiluted affection for him. Was it simply that he repeats my temperamental excesses? I find him much nicer than I was: his ill-humour has humour in it; mine was simply rage and has served me very badly. He cannot learn from me any more than I could from C.M.R.; I go through the motions of instruction, but make no

* The first episode of *The Glittering Prizes*.

impression. Paul has a sweetness I lack: he is more at peace with himself than I am, or was. He is a great enthusiast, above all for football: he plans ahead diligently, hoping always to ensnare one in his schemes. There is a game tomorrow – a Texaco Cup semi-final – which I have managed to evade with the utmost difficulty.

On Sunday we woke early and worked hard all morning at the Ayrton lunch. The pea soup was as good as Lapérouse's Parmentier. The *filet en croûte* would not have disgraced M. Thuillier. I made an avocado and cabbage salad as good as Maudie's (our cook in Jamaica). The apple amber was impeccable. They ate nothing. Lumps of meat remained on the plates. *Ca coûte!* Yet they arrived promptly and were extremely friendly. They noticed – and were interested in – our eclectic treasures, though not in the icons. Beetle thought it was because they are badly hung; I think it's because Michael knew nothing about them. He knows plenty about everything else: he recognised our (unsigned) Derain drawing at once and remembered him, drunk and enormous, designing a production at Covent Garden. He believed in adjournment and always relied on something coming along in due course. It always did.

Michael claims to have picked up all his knowledge in pubs. His father reviewed fiction for *The Observer* regularly from the 1920s. He was extremely intelligent and astute about all literature except masterpieces. He got them all wrong: Joyce, Eliot, Wyndham Lewis. Michael discovered a cache of his review copies, annotated in pencil. On Forster's *A Passage to India*, he had written 'Good, but not very good.'* I was reminded of the senile Leavis, as reported by a pretty (but not *very* pretty) teacher at the Colchester Comprehensive, saying that if he saw Morgan Forster in the streets of Cambridge, he would like to 'fill him with bullets'.

Ayrton's father was an alcoholic, like any number of his friends. He likes drink better than food, that's clear. Before we went into lunch he declared that he didn't like soup. Beetle opened a Scholly *pâté* for him.

I did not clearly remember Elisabeth's daughter, Michael's stepdaughter, Prue, although she was at Cambridge with me. A gaunt, blonde girl with Monica Ferman's voice, she has fine haunted eyes. John Hopkins (her ex-husband) is the ghost in her life. She was soon talking about him. He had been commissioned by Zeffirelli to write

---

* How wrong was he there?

a film of *La Dame aux Camélias*. He said that he wanted to go back to the book, and Z. agreed, eagerly. The first scene took place in a cemetery. Prue imagined Z.'s ignorant dismay at a funereal opening. He had promised to call Hopkins the day after receiving the script. He never called at all. Perhaps it was not the glum opening but the deadly writing which appalled him. Hopkins has all the levity of a deep-sea diver's boots. Now Prue sneers at Z.'s pappy pictures, but what if he had liked the script?

They had brought a black poodle with them in their orange Volvo. He came into the kitchen and peed under the Miró. I suggested that Justine (Prue's twelve-year-old daughter) put him out. On the way back, Justine, in brown slacks and a white shirt, misjudged the kitchen step and fell, with a cry. She was not badly hurt (none of her family moved to help her) but she emitted a series of confused cries, as if searching for a suitable register for lamentation. She hobbled to her place, red and reproachful and sat holding her hurt ankle. The family began to speak of 'having you put down': 'We shall have to take you to the vet. It would probably be the kindest thing. He'll probably give you an injection or a pill. It would probably be quite painless.' The joke seemed to me morbidly protracted. The girl was joshed into repressing her pain, but the incident failed to ease her shyness. Nor did it stimulate her appetite: she ate only a little mashed potato.

In spite of their disappointingly meagre appetites, the Ayrtons – or at least Michael – seemed to like us. They want to make a huge detour (from Aix-en-Provence) to visit us at Lagardelle in June. Beetle says that M. asked three times whether we would come to Africa with them at Christmas. M. claims to know more about Mycenaean Greece (and Crete) than anyone, though he has no formal scholarship and little Greek. He believes in osmotic assimilation. I liked him: he has no wish to reduce us. They spent some time disparaging the Steiners, whom they greeted so keenly when we went to Bradfields for lunch.

Daisy Miller. For all the admiration one feels for H.J., he is a hard man to admire: he is so frightened. He cannot bear the nakedness of the human animal. He dresses it with scruples as children dress dolls. He sees Daisy as clean and fresh and more honest than the Europeans who mortify her, but he insists on her innocence: she must be void of desire as of experience. He is determined that she be a victim with no motor of her own, except tactless enthusiasm. He kills her because he cannot bear her to be alive in flesh and blood and appetite. He gives her looks which she 'cannot help', like the talent of which schoolmasters forbade one to be proud, since it was a gift not an achievement. Obsession with her face gives Daisy the bonelessness of an academy portrait. H.J. sees the face as an asset, as a fortune-hunter does. The idea of Daisy as a *deep* person, with uneasy depths, would appal him and unbalance his tale. No less than Winterbourne, H.J. is a Puritan: it is not sin that he hates but its attractiveness. He sides not with sophistication, not even with Values, but with frigidity. If you want to understand what a writer really fears, or hopes for, you need only look and see whom he condemns to death. *Daisy Miller* is a virgin *witch*.

11.4.73. I drove up to London in the afternoon to join B. for dinner with the Deutsches. The huge spring sky was scorched with aircraft trails, a Dame Laura Knight sky, sunny and transparent. But a cold wind was blowing. A man in a painter's coat thumbed for a lift outside Chelmsford. I stopped reluctantly. He ran up the road to me, eagerly, almost incredulously, but slowly. The wind fought him. He climbed in awkwardly, kicking the tapes in their tailored box. Pale, dirty and unemployed, he came originally from Birmingham but had been living in Clacton. His wife's father was in 'property'. They had been given the use of a bungalow in trust for his wife but managed by Trustees. He and his father-in-law didn't get on. His wife was in hospital: she had an abortion last week. They already had a two-year-old son: he showed me a photograph of a blond boy standing against the wall of a new house. There was no work in Clacton, especially out of season. The last job he had was as a mechanic in a fairground: seventeen and a half hours a day, seven days a week, nineteen quid. Now he was on his way to Tottenham: he'd been offered a job as a market-porter. He had not eaten since Sunday (at dinner, someone would say, 'It's only Tuesday today,' as if that made it a poor hard-luck story). He coughed steadily. I opened the window to evict the germs.

When we reached Gant's Hill, he had to go right. I gave him a pound to get some food. I was relieved to give it before he asked for it, though his tone and despair already had. He took out his social security card and showed it to me. I thought: either it's stolen or he isn't going to attack me. I made a mental note of the address (119, Stanley Road) and he said, 'Here, you can have this, if you want.' 'What for?' 'It's no use to me,' he said, 'I've had hundreds of them.' He tore it in pieces and posted them through the slot above his window.

I resolved not to mention the incident to Beetle because I felt that I had been either insufficiently generous or too easily gulled, but after we had met (in the foyer of the Hilton) and had some coffee, like two fugitives from domestic bondage, she told me how her hairdresser, Xavier, had been approached by a woman whom he had not seen for fifteen years (and not known well) and asked for a fiver. He gave her the money but said, as firmly as kindly, that that was the lot: she was not to come back for more. She was back within two days; she leaves notes for him all the time. This is the genuine version of *L'Amour l'Après-Midi*: the girl is not an autonomous seducer but a parasite, on whom the tree comes to depend, not for sex, not for pleasure, but simply in order to have a secret, and a drama. After Beetle told me this story, I told her mine.

Jocelyn Rickards was at the dinner. She lived for several years with Freddy Ayer and then with Osborne. She likes to talk about sex, but I do not find her in the least exciting. Barbara Ferris had been very touched because Noel Coward came to the modest preview of a play she had done at the Court. She remarked whimsically that the opening would be more like a birthday party than a première. On the first night, flowers arrived from The Master, inscribed 'Happy Birthday'. Wasn't that lovely of him? Someone at dinner said that Noel's private secretary had become so adept at forging his signature, and was so thorough a tabulator of important (and unimportant) dates that he was in methodical charge of all Noel's spontaneous gestures. Probably Coward never even knew the flowers had been sent.

A friend of Jocelyn's had been a model for Balenciaga and Givenchy. When her marriage broke up, she went to New York and took a male whore as a lover. She was entirely satisfied. She decided that she too would become a prostitute. It would give her a comfortable living. In the event, she was unable to stick it. 'I was very, very surprised,' Jocelyn said. She gives the impression of soft restlessness, like the sea: strong but unmuscled. Exophthalmic eyes give her an air of curiosity, even of intrusion: they reach out like round limbs. For all her knowingness, she seems constantly surprised and turns her slow monosyllables on you like beams from a pencil torch. 'Do they?' she says. 'Yes? I see. Oh! Yes.' She turns your ideas over in front of you, like a Frenchwoman marketing.

She has the rumpled commodiousness of a bed in an old Paris hotel.

You will not get much sleep, but you will wallow comfortably, even if the sheets have been used before.

Two days reading Larry Durrell's *The Black Book*. I still haven't finished. How odd it is to read for sustained periods! How little of the body is employed! The legs are remote and soon bored. They shuffle and regroup, like children in a museum. The stomach sags and has interests of its own. The nose itches. The tongue goes shopping between the teeth. The eyes, resenting their sentry duty, frown and march with reluctant punctuality. The brain reacts to the text as it did to Greek Unseens, scouting anxiously for a thread of meaning in the dense print. Durrell mints fine phrases, but what use is the currency? He shares with exiles the stopped clock of nostalgia. Systole and diastole? Enough already.

23.4.73. Two weeks of nameless illness seem to have come from my meeting with the desperate man from Clacton. I finished my Durrell piece, commissioned by Der-der-der-went May for *The Listener*. The novel was forced, juvenile and tedious. Philip Toynbee covered it with dull, Sunday praise in *The Observer*. I was due to have my first meeting with Peter Bogdanovich on the Tuesday. I had to be better; I decided to be better; I felt awful. I went by train, headachy, too bleary even to read. I presented myself, briefcased and grey-suited, *en bon bourgeois*, at the Connaught and was shown to the suite. A blonde girl in a blue robe opened the door: Sybille? No, Cybill Shepherd, the girl. She might have been a Californian tennis player: high cheekbones, blue eyes, young skin.

Bogdanovich came into the sitting room blind from the shower, a greyish-skinned man in a white robe, eyes coming to terms with the rectangular gold-rimmed glasses he was applying to them. He seemed cold and shy, with none of the intimate tone that had seemed so attractive on the line from California. I had expected, or hoped, that we would be instant old friends. I was ill, though he couldn't tell, since he had no idea of what I was normally like. He imagined that he was meeting me; I that I was meeting him. But if I was sick, he was dislocated by the flight. Both of us might have been awakened in the middle of the night for an unfriendly interrogation.

B. is the most successful current director. His films have made enormous profits. He has enabled Hollywood to recover its confidence. Since he has made his bosses feel good again, they will pay him anything if he will prolong their euphoria. Immodesty gives him a certain boyish candour. He doesn't worry about himself as

Schlesinger does, nor take himself too seriously; he expects other people to do that. He refers to himself in a tone of well-deserved awe: a name-dropper who drops his own name.

He was nervous, or more nervous than I expected, about any kind of cinematic innovation. He dislikes fantasy and he dislikes 'bittiness': he prefers the old cursive continuity. He started as a critic, but only of Hollywood. He is indifferent to European cinema and he has never seen an Andy Warhol. With no foreign gods and no uncommercial ambitions, he is almost aggressively 'overground'. He worships only Orson Welles. Our working schedule was postulated on Orson's arrival on Friday: we had to be finished in time for them to have lunch.

When we met on Wednesday, he had spoken to Orson, who approved my opening idea, though he made one suggestion: we should have several shots of corridors full of shoes before we came to the scene where Randolph changed them all around.*

Cybill, a buxom girl, flitted in and out from shopping. She bought him sweaters and shirts. He criticised the way she looked: 'You look funny today. The right side of your face is OK, but something's happened to the other side.' 'The left,' I said. 'That's right,' he said, 'can you see that?' 'No,' I said.

She bore it patiently. She is an ambitious girl. Anger competed with caution in her eyes and caution won, just. We ate in the room. The Connaught is supposed to be the best hotel in London. The service was sullen, the food mediocre. P.B.'s father was a painter: he died during the shooting of *The Last Picture Show*. P.'s marriage broke up at the same time. He has two children, five and two-and-a-half. He feels 'some guilt'. The first thing his wife did after the divorce was go out and buy herself a Mercedes. He didn't know why. He told me this in the Rolls Royce showroom in Berkeley Square where we had gone for a walk. He said he didn't care about cars. He has two Fords which Ford gave him in the hope that he would use their cars in his movies. He agreed, but has not yet made a modern movie: *Paper Moon* is set in the 1930s in Kansas. Paramount expect great things of it. If it grosses over $17m. they have promised him a Rolls, which he declared to be 'the only car'. I remarked that if it grossed only $16m. he might still be able to buy himself one.

---

* My opening image was a declared *hommage* to Max Beerbohm's cartoon of Henry James in a hotel corridor sniffing the shoes left out for cleaning in order to try and divine what was happening behind the closed doors of the bedrooms. I doubt if P.B. had ever heard of Max Beerbohm, but he bought the idea.

He did not smile: he is not used to being generous, even to himself. He looked balefully at Cybill when she helped herself to cash. He prefers putting things on the bill. I wanted (and want) to like him, but he is less charming that he assumes. I am ill-advised to ignore his treatment of others merely because, at the moment, he does not treat me as he does, or did, them. Why had he called me in the first place? Because Orson suggested an English writer and Mark Shivas suggested me. P. used to write for *Movie* when Mark was an assistant editor.

P.'s 'English' friend Bill Cameron had a girlfriend called Jill. When he broke up with her, she went to work in California. P. had never met her, but Bill wrote asking P. to look out for her. She called and they met. 'She was just about the most horrible girl I ever met in my whole life. *Ugly*. Tooth missing. Terrible voice.' She kept calling, but he never called back. They met again at a party. 'I think you've gorn orf me,' she said.

Peter is an excellent, and addicted, mimic, especially of the old stars (Cary Grant a speciality). He has a young unknown Californian in mind for Winterbourne, an actor who wrote him a letter recommending himself for the part. It was long and stilted and rather frigid. P. was made very uncomfortable until he realised that it was written *à la façon de* Winterbourne.

On Wednesday at lunchtime, we finished talking about the 'first act', set in the *Trois Couronnes* at Vevey, and had to decide how to change gear. Though still taking aspirin, I had begun to feel better: I made clear my anxiety about dullness and stuffiness. Thereafter things moved well. When Shivas came to dinner on Thursday night, we had worked our way right through and could celebrate with champagne and Scrabble. We had had no disagreements, no sarcasm, no tension: professionals at work.

Cybill made me uneasy until she advertised her age as twenty-three or so (she saw *Two For The Road* when she was eighteen) and I realised how anxious *she* was. We had shaken hands the first day; but we kissed keenly at midnight on the third, when their limousine swept me – Scrabble victor and old buddy – back to Langham. P. saw Cybill first on the cover of *Glamour* and said to his secretary, consciously imitating The Great Days, 'Find me that girl.' She has never acted: she was a model, and is now taking singing and tap-dancing lessons. She leaves the acting to the director. While we were working, she went into the bathroom to practice tap. She was asked to read for Daisy in *Gatsby*. Everyone else had been obliged to *test*, as well as read, but she still refused. David Merrick was furious. Peter was scathing about Jack Clayton, whose academic style he does *not* admire. I was about to defend Our British Director when I realised that P.'s accusations of his being two-faced were amply confirmed by my own experience. Clayton never called me again after our meeting. Peter had read the Capote script, at which, he told me, Truman had worked diligently. Bob Evans was, however, very embarrassed when he called him. 'Truman,' he said, 'it's just like the book!'

Orson (O. God/Godot) never did materialise. P. told me that *Citizen Kane* was not really a commercial failure. It did big business in major cities, but was not shown at all by the large chains. Even movie houses which had booked it were so intimidated by the Hearst press that they chose to pay the basic fee and then not run the movie. It appeared to be a failure when it was simply not given a proper showing. Tuxed Welles met tuxed Hearst, by chance, in the elevator of a hotel on the opening night in San Francisco. They went down, side by side. 'Are you coming to the opening, Mr Hearst?' Welles asked as they hit the lobby. Hearst strode out of the elevator without a word. 'Charles Foster Kane woulda come,' Welles bellowed after him.

Bedales. Several girls were already in Sarah's dorm. They were noticeably unwelcoming. Perhaps it was the entry of two large adults, but Sarah was dismayed by the *froideur*. She had been so apprehensive that the atmosphere quite unnerved her, despite it being her twelfth term. Later B. took her up to the dorm again and the malevolent 'Fats' was not there. Things were slightly better, but we left with the sourest fears. Our impotence seemed to warrant the unnaturalness of boarding schools.

As we backed away, I saw a lumpy, reddish man, perhaps the Area Manager of an insurance company, with the rolling walk of someone who takes a long time to get nowhere, heavy and jaunty all at once. He was fussing around a grey and black Citroen DS. Something in the undistinguished face held my attention. As we said goodbye to Sarah, I said, 'Is there an Olivier in your group?' 'Yes,' she said, 'he's the ugliest boy I've ever seen.' The Area Manager was Lord Olivier.

We drove in the dark from quiet Geneva. We must have taken the wrong road after Lausanne and found ourselves on narrow wet roads in the heights about Lake Leman. Vevey was big and dull. The *Trois Couronnes* may once have had a garden to the shore, as H.J. described, but it now has a terrace to the road's edge. It is paved with composition flagstones, wide and grey and improved by pots of vivid pansies; borders gaudy with the same flowers are stabbed here and there with blood-red tulips. The high cliff of the hotel rises above the terrace where four huge plane trees, pollarded horizontal, are beginning to bud. One of the heavy boughs leans on a metal crutch. From the others hang lanterns of *fer forgé*.

The façade facing inland is grey, and very tall. There are balconies with dusty gold shutters. No doorman greeted us, but the longitudinal lobby – the hotel is quite narrow in cross-section – was politely staffed. The rooms with their raspberry velvet settees and chairs, their antique bureaux and not-for-sex single beds, had the opulence in which one glories only when not paying one's own bill. The most pleasant feature is the long galleries which serve each floor. Light comes from a well at the top of the building and the galleries are bridged at four points and supported by white wooden pillars, like a sumptuous jail. The inlaid wooden floor creaks like a seasoned ship. The light is vaguely citrous as it filters down four floors.

Chillon. Byron's name, shamelessly incised on a pillar of Bonnivard's prison, is under glass for your admiration. How nice for a vandal to be framed! One could imagine H.J. and Byron nodding anachronistically from separate walkways of the well-furnished castle. Who would choose to live in Bonnivard's day? The suffering of a man who endured agony and death for the sake of a religious principle is as absurd as it is moving. His endurance is more obstinate than noble: to spend four years in a vault for the sake of a schismatic prejudice smacks less of doctrinal conviction than of pigheadedness. *Logique de Collabo*.

Switzerland is the utopia of impotence, a gelded Germany reduced to the humane efficiency which the French might admire, and Nietzsche dreaded and denounced. The proudest possession of the Swiss is their currency: they stand in front of Exchanges admiring its strength. They handle it with the appreciation Spanish women lavish on the cheeks of their grandchildren. Their '*septante*' and '*huitante*' are coined endearments: 'We are Swiss,' they say, 'and we count more than anyone else.' In the shops of Montreux there are boxes for the children of 'The Third World'. One *franc Suisse* will give them a meal. It could not buy a Swiss a slice of ham, but the children of the Third World do not have to eat in Switzerland.

In a watch and clock shop, a Scotsman was buying a silver minia-ture cow-bell. Slim, dark, blue-suited and wearing tinted glasses, he had a name plaque on his lapel. His 'firm' had flown him out, along with a whole party: three days at the Montreux Palace, all expenses paid. He had a shifty pride in belonging to a company, 'Golden Products', rich enough to fund it. There was nice humour in these jaunty folk lodging in the same hotel as Vladimir Nabokov. I toyed with calling him, or of writing him a note, but would he remember who I was, and what did it matter? I neither called nor left a note, but still felt demeaned.

Evian. We lunched a couple of times at *La Bourgogne*, a pretty little restaurant like a tea-shop in an Edwardian resort: big plate glass windows with gilt frames and lettering, waitresses not waiters. The menus were in large script, with a small choice, but the *quenelles* were excellent (like Saulieu in the old days) and the steaks tender. The place had the pinkness of early lingerie. The first time we were there, the only other customers were a couple with a baby. The bespectacled mother fell off her chair. She sat on the ground like a non-swimmer in the deep end, waiting to be rescued.

A lighter was anchored off the promenade. A tractor paraded on deck, dropping hunks of grey stone onto the foreshore to make a breakwater. A young man was operating the claw while his father ate his lunch. He dug for big rocks and worked to raise them. Still eating, his father wagged a finger at one which threatened to over-balance the tractor.

Rain fell, grey out-of-season rain, as if nature were delivering the dullest and most depressing of her products. Through it, with the doomed gaiety of a POUM battalion heading for the Front, marched a detachment of Spaniards, in caps and berets, playing on simple instruments and simple emotions. I read Nietzsche. I never finished *Zarathustra* in 1950: I left my Everyman on the tube. How appropriate that he wrote much of the book in Switzerland where, in his image, they 'put planks over the stream'! The combination of melodramatic landscape and provincial primness was just the thing to stoke a rhetorical boiler. The alternations of sun and cloud, of happy skies and glum ceilings were the perfect projections (systole and diastole, Durrell would be bound to say) of the Nietzschean style.

At Cambridge no one mentioned the influence of N. on Wittgenstein, though the mantic style was common to both. N. was the dottier, perhaps because he was less dedicated to the monastic and ascetic life: he was a hermit who craved company and who, at least once, hoped to marry.

3.5.73. Barry Norman has become the resident presenter of *Film 73*. The new supremo of the department is called Malcolm. Young and dull, always in a suit, he has the unstable charm of someone whose smiles come from Montague Burton and whose frowns from those above him: ambition is the most pliable of all qualities. He embraces the standards and ideas of the generation before last. 'Get your hair cut,' is all his philosophy. His tight lips announce that the Sixties are at an end.

Malcolm said hullo to Barry, but not to me. One could not have a face-to-face meeting with him because he has no face. He comes up beside you; he doesn't approach, he drifts in; he joins you as a spectator. I was promised that he had said that even Barry's hair was too long. They asked me to review the script of *O Lucky Man*, Lindsay Anderson's new film. I read the first couple of pages and then said, 'I pass.'* They laughed and all of them confessed how much they had disliked the film. 'Go on,' I said to Barry Norman, 'sell out: tell them what you really thought.' Someone said it was a story about Everyman. 'Fuck Everyman frankly,' I said, and thought of them. They had told Mickey Medwin I might do a piece. 'That doesn't sound like very good blood-grouping to me,' he said. Golfer.

WANTED. A man has absconded to the continent from his dull job, with a lot of money. Another is deputed to follow and find him. The latter is dutiful and law-abiding. Obsessed with the pursuit, he is, it seems to us, and to him, incorruptibly determined to bring the man back. It never occurs to him, until it does, that he too might escape from the mundane.

---

* Although, for a brief time, I reviewed films and film books irregularly on TV, I had no ambition to become a resident anchor-man.

Sunderland won the Cup. Tears in the eyes as we watched eleven paid bruisers from one unvisited place managing to beat eleven others. How can such an event have leverage on the emotions?

24.5.73. *Daisy Miller* is finished. The question always arises with a script of this kind, commissioned as a professional assignment, however you dress it up: have I done enough? How does one 'earn' all that money by writing a hundred and fifty pages? The cant answer is that fees bear no relation to the services rendered. The fact is, I have earned a top executive's salary in just over a month of strenuous, but never exacting, labour which has interrupted neither my social life nor my pleasures.

29.5.73. Paul is a croquet player. How does a child become suddenly competent at a game he never practised, and which seems quite specialised and complicated? He came along while we were playing with Roger and Katie and gave grand instructions. He then gave an excellent display of knowing what he was talking about. He is now half an inch taller than Beetle, slim, cool and handsome. He has spent most of half-term tape-recording the many records he has borrowed from school-friends.

Roger and Katie came to Sunday lunch and stayed till tea on Monday. We greeted them with enthusiasm and said goodbye with relief. They are nice people; their children play delightfully with Stee and Sarah; but they are takers. Roger now works for a big drinks company, but he 'forgot' the bottle he meant to bring us. His thank-you for the weekend took the form of a request for them to spend a weekend at Lagardelle at the end of June. What better response to one free weekend than to book another?

Do we want friends or not? And how far do Beetle and I have the same wants? She fears above all being taken for granted, and then being taken advantage of. The two men she has disliked most are, I think, Leslie and Tom: both wanted me, for their own purposes, and both longed to trespass on our privacy. I remember Leslie knocking on our door at the *Deux Continents*, thumpingly urgent for attention. Yet these eager, perhaps venal, suitors are at least in part the impersonations of my own ambitions. I confess to a certain greed for their greed, a wish to be had, to be wanted for things I should not do.

29.5.73. The night before we left for France, Peter B. called from

California. I had taken Paul and Sarah to Waterloo after half-term. I returned exhausted with guilt and regret. I returned the call with anxious calm. 'Freddie,' he said, 'it's terrific.' I bathed in the radiance of his praise. The movies, at that moment, were the greatest. He and Cybill, who had read and loved the script (well she might) were coming to Europe on the 25th of June. He had much to arrange but 'The script, as they used to say in Hollywood, is licked.' I said, 'Do me a favour. Make the fucking thing.' 'We will, we will.'

11.6.73. Bedales to see Paul's teachers. The first half hour of the two allotted to Paul's group was taken up by Tim Slack appealing for money. Only twelve out of forty-six sets of parents had responded to the brochure. They had probably been contacted by Mr Bassett, who telephoned one Monday morning, after I had already offered my mite, and announced his huckstering vocation. After Slack – in whom the Civil Service lost a natural permanent under-secretary at the Ministry of Pensions – we were treated to Stephanie Gedge, a buck-toothed lady of the type with whom you pray not to be drawn in the club Mixed Doubles.

Shirley and Jolyon Kay (Old Carthusian, old Johnian, scholar of both) arrived as the appeal spiel was ending; Jolyon is no fool. At Christmas, we took them and their son, Tim, out to dinner and to see Peter Cook and Dudley Moore in *Behind The Fridge*. Jolyon arrived from the FO (and later departed, in order to re-meet his family at Paddington) on a motor tricycle. They failed to send us a word of thanks for our uncalled for munificence. Nor have we heard from them since.*

Paul's form master is Mr K. McLeish. He is a classicist, a translator of Sophocles and, I later discovered, a scholar of Worcester College. He was volubly forthright. Might we not be well-advised to send Paul to Millfield? He is in his middle thirties, soapy-skinned, bespectacled, his face purged of youth but shining with excited ambition, with the forearms of a charwoman. He seemed rather to gloat in his Sibylline bookishness and soon disclosed that he was actually leaving the school, deeply disillusioned after a mere three years. Paul later said that McL. was 'disturbed, perhaps hysterical' and reduced everything to personal terms.

* Nor ever again.

Mr Cregan. One of those semi-polished, blue-eyed men whose candour is limited to his false teeth. Tufts of gilded hair exploded either side of the beige dome of his baldness. He said, 'Your son can't punctuate': probably one of the dullest opening gambits in the history of banality. Paul's relations with Mrs Evans, a remedial teacher supposedly improving his punctuation, had dwindled to the point where they sat in the room and smiled at each other. I said, 'From which I infer that Paul has taught her to smile and she has taught him nothing.' The man boiled with self-control; he burst with restraint. I asked what models of critical prose he had recommended to his class. Like whom were they supposed to write? He replied that if they asked him what they should read, he would tell them.

I did not know how much of a fool the man was until I saw a piece of fiction which Paul had written for him. It was imaginative and succinct; if it was indifferently spelt, it was more legible and more literate than one could have hoped a year ago. The comments were disdainful and unintelligent. Mr Cregan found it incomprehensible and gave it a beta double-minus. He noticed that haemorrhage was misspelt, but offered no correction. Punctuation is god; and this is a progressive school. What tactics did Cregan propose to adopt? 'In another school,' he said, 'there would be detention and lines.' Did he favour those methods? 'I wouldn't be here if I did.' Then why mention them?

After lunch, McLeish and I sat by the cricket pitch where a series of lamentable strokes was on offer. McLeish had been very bored at the school, so much so that he had written eight books in three years. 'I don't know whether to congratulate you or kick you,' I said. We enjoyed a prickly intimacy. He had some resemblance to Peter Green, whose historical novels he deplored but whose scholarship he enjoyed. I felt that quick sympathy that a stranger can excite (and often does not merit) when he has a fortuitous similarity to an old friend. McLeish dislikes Tim Slack: 'Did you notice how he backed away whenever he mentioned a difficulty?' He considers Cregan 'third-rate' ('Flatterer,' I said) and has little respect for the other staff: 'The place is full of effeminate men and masculine women.' Mr M., he said, was a latent homosexual. 'We're all latent homosexuals, aren't we?' I said. 'I thought that was one of the things one learned from a classical education.' 'We're not living in classical times,' he said.

We proposed, with unlikely speed so far as I was concerned, that we be friends. 'Despite the fact that I'm leaving?' he said. 'Think carefully.' I paraded classical credentials, as if applying for a post. I told him about my Catullus novel, especially the *donnée* concerning slavery. 'You *are* a clever bastard,' he said. He felt my cleverness like a bruise. If the friendship comes about, it will be awkward. He asked if I didn't think that Catullus' poems were 'masturbatory'. He added that, of course, there was nothing *wrong* with masturbation. I said, no, it was an accepted element of the Roman erotic repertoire: the comfortable class could call on their slaves to toss them off whenever they felt the desire. He asked for textual authority.* 'The Pompeian wall paintings,' I said. He had been to Pompeii, but not to Ostia antica, but he had not broached the *arcana*: the obscenities remained literally closed to him. He went to Greece for the first time last Easter, with a school party. His most sublime moment was watching dawn over Delphi. He was shy of personal revelation. Scholarship is often a lace dress of motifs designed to cover embarrassed nakedness. (George Steiner, on the way to the beach, looked down at his plastic sandals and silly shorts and said, 'Is there anything more ridiculous than the idea of a Jew going to the beach?' Is there anything more ridiculous, he meant to say, than the idea of *George Steiner* docked of his doctorate, a Pharisee *en tenue de plage*?)

McLeish is going to teach in a Comprehensive in Lincoln, but means to retire in a few years' time in order to write. He thought we lived in Eaton Square and had heard that we had a 'villa' in Greece, a term I have never applied to our shack on Ios. I said we would lend it to him, but he would have to leave it exactly as he found it: we had, I said, and he did not smile, not so much a catalogue of ships as a catalogue of chips.

McL. thought that Paul would have the last laugh: it was reasonable to imagine him a TV journalist or commentator. He had been struck by P.'s unprompted vision of *The Odyssey* as a spiritual no less than a spatial journey. Such insight was remarkable (isn't it?) in a boy of, then, fourteen.

Jack Skerball is one of the two producers of the Vincente Minnelli movie I am supposed to write. In his late sixties, he is said to be one of the richest men in America. He studied philosophy and is a patron of universities. He told me a story which may be old, but which I had not heard: An outgoing President of a College tells his successor, 'I'm leaving you three letters in case you get into any

* '*Vous avez un texte, monsieur?*' would become one of our catch-phrases.

serious difficulties.' After a few months, there is a crisis with the students. He opens the first letter, acts on its contents and all is settled. A year later comes a crisis with the Regents. The second letter saves the day. Two years later, a third crisis, with the State authorities. The President opens the third letter. It says, 'Start writing three letters.'

Daisy Miller starts shooting on 13 August, in Rome, less than five months since my first conversation with P.B. He has behaved with enjoyable enthusiasm, tact and urgency: a man to treasure. Liza Minnelli has committed to her father's picture, so it will probably be made. Bob Shapiro told me that my deal was 'Better than Terence Rattigan's.' 'I should bloody well hope so,' I said.

15.6.73. Dinner at the Wisemans, an intellectual gathering with Al Alvarez as the prime intelligence. Money was not far from their minds. Alvarez' book on Suicide had terrific notices and sold very well in the States. I sat on my Hollywood cushions and denied any great desire for sales: to be published is enough for me. Alvarez said that when he took Schools in 1952, he believed nothing to be more valuable than to be a literary critic. He has now given up criticism. Having become a world authority on Suicide, it could fairly be said that self-destruction has been the making of him.

Index

INDEX 213

Stamp, Terence 126
Stanwyck, Barbara 72
Steiner, George 6, 92–3, 94, 96, 153, 164–70, 172–3, 194, 207
Steiner, Zara 164, 167, 169, 173, 194
Stern, Daniel 118
Stewart, James 190
Stewart, Max 121
Sullivan, John 157, 160
Summerskill, John 22
Summerskill, John-Paul 22
Sutton, Dr 44
Swanson, Maureen 104
Symons, Julian 141, 145, 147, 148

Tanen, Ned 66–7
Tanner, Gordon 8–9, 10–12
Taylor, Jeremy 77
Taylor, John Russell 64
Thom, Kennedy 188, 190–1
Tomalin, Nicholas 172
Toynbee, Arnold 182
Toynbee, Philip 197
Treves, Frederick 59–60
Trollope, Anthony 190
Trotsky, Leon 35, 42
Turner, David 186
Tynan, Kenneth 92–3, 94, 137, 170

Updike, John 35

van der Post, Laurens 147
van Dijk, Rein 109
Van Eyssen, David 37

Van Eyssen, John 34, 36, 37, 52, 64–5
Van Gogh, Vincent 117
Vassilikos, Vassili 118

Walbrook, Anton 17
Walden, George x
Ward, Jennifer 147–8
Wasserman, Lew 67
Waugh, Auberon 64
Waugh, Evelyn 80
Welles, Orson 198, 199, 200
Wesker, Arnold 16–17, 94
Whitehorn, Katharine 47
Whitley, John 94, 147
Wild, Frank 115
Wilde, Oscar 20, 67
Wilder, Billy 186
Wilson, Edmund 34, 35, 129
Wingate, Eddie 177–8
Wisdom, John 48
Wiseman, Boris 148–9
Wiseman, Malou 127, 148, 208
Wiseman, Tom 16–17, 85, 87–8, 127, 130, 149–53, 208
Wittgenstein, Ludwig 48, 95, 106, 115, 134, 159, 187, 191, 192, 203
Workman, Skete 59
Wright, Tony 104

Zanuck, Darryl 51
Zanuck, Richard 51, 66, 137
Zeffirelli, Franco 193–4
Zetterling, Mai 188